The Challenges of School Reform

Implementation, Impact, and Sustainability

a volume in
The Milken Family Foundation Series on Education Policy

The Milken Family Foundation Series on Education Policy

Improving Student Achievement: Reforms that Work (2005)
Lewis C. Solmon, Kimberly Firetag Agam,
and Tamara W. Schiff, editors

*Talented Teachers: The Essential Force for Improving
Student Achievement* (2004)
Lewis C. Solmon and Tamara W. Schiff, editors

The Challenges of School Reform

Implementation, Impact, and Sustainability

Edited by

Lewis C. Solmon
Kimberly Firetag Agam
Citadelle Priagula

Greenwich, Connecticut • www.infoagepub.com

Library of Congress Cataloging-in-Publication Data

Milken National Education Conference (2005 : Washington, D.C.)
  The challenge of school reform : implementation, impact, and
sustainability / edited by Lewis C. Solmon, Kimberly Firetag Agam,
Citadelle Priagula.
       p. cm. — (The Milken Family Foundation series on education policy)
    Includes bibliographical references.
    ISBN 1-59311-519-9 (pbk.) — ISBN 1-59311-520-2 (hardcover)
    1. School improvement programs—United States—Congresses. 2.
Educational change—United States—Congresses. 3. Educational planning—
United States—Congresses. I. Solmon, Lewis C. II. Agam, Kimberly Firetag. III.
Priagula, Citadelle. IV. Title. V. Series.
    LB2822.82.M535 2005
    379.73—dc22

                                                                      2006010576

ISBN 13: 978-1-59311-519-7 (pbk.)
             978-1-59311-520-3 (hardcover)
ISBN 10: 1-59311-519-9 (pbk.)
             1-59311-520-2 (hardcover)

Cover Photo:

*English comes alive in 2005 Milken Educator James Darden's 8th grade class at
Thomas Jefferson Middle School in Teaneck, NJ.*

Printed in the United States of America

MILKEN FAMILY FOUNDATION
Leading Advances in Education and Medical Research

The Milken Family Foundation (MFF) was established by brothers Lowell and Michael Milken in 1982 with the mission to discover and advance inventive and effective ways of helping people help themselves and those around them lead productive and satisfying lives. MFF advances this mission principally through the various programs it initiates and carries out in the areas of education and medical research.

Guided by a belief that "the future belongs to the educated," Lowell Milken created one of MFF's signature initiatives—the Milken National Educator Awards—in 1985 as a means to attract, develop, and motivate high caliber individuals to teaching. The program has evolved from spotlighting a dozen California educators to becoming the nation's largest and most visible teacher recognition program, now in 48 states and the District of Columbia, annually honoring outstanding teachers, principals, and specialists with individual, unrestricted $25,000 prizes. They join a national network of more than 2,100 Milken Educators committed to excellence in the teaching profession, and in demand as expert resources for local, state, and national education policymakers.

The nation's students benefit from the commitment of many capable teachers. Yet experiences with Milken Educators and thousands more teachers in classrooms across America made it increasingly apparent that if every child is to have access to quality teachers every year, far greater numbers of talented people are needed to teach. Thus in 1999, Lowell Milken introduced the Teacher Advancement Program (TAP) as a complementary initiative to the Milken Educator Awards. TAP is a research-based, comprehensive school improvement model to attract, develop, motivate, and retain the best talent for the teaching profession. The program is built on four interrelated elements: *multiple career paths, ongoing applied professional growth, instructionally focused accountability,* and *performance-based compensation.* In just a few short years, the Teacher Advancement Program has been implemented in over 100 schools across the nation with more in the planning stages, and preliminary research findings confirm the value of this comprehensive education reform strategy to students and teachers alike. TAP's huge growth spurred the creation of the Teacher Advancement Program Foundation in May 2005. The TAP Foundation is an independent public charity that operates TAP and responds to the urgency and scope of teacher quality reform by establishing public/private partnerships among educators, policymakers, corporations, governments, foundations, and individuals to ensure a quality educational opportunity for all students.

Others initiatives of the Milken Family Foundation include the Milken Scholars Program, the Milken Archive of American Jewish Music, and the Milken Festival for Youth. In the realm of medical research, Foundation efforts include the Milken Family Foundation Epilepsy Research Awards Program, as well as programs that have gone on to become independent organizations, including the Prostate Cancer Foundation, created by Michael Milken in 1993 and today the world's largest philanthropic organization dedicated to better treatments and a cure for prostate cancer.

For additional information concerning Milken Family Foundation initiatives in education and medical research, visit *www.mff.org*. Additional information regarding the Teacher Advancement Program Foundation can be found at *www.tapschools.org*.

CONTENTS

PART III
TEACHER QUALITY

PART IV
FRAMING THE FUTURE: PRE-K THROUGH HIGHER EDUCATION

Panel Contributions

ACKNOWLEDGMENTS

We had the pleasure of working with many talented people whose hard work and dedication made the process of working on this book significantly easier and the final product itself one of high quality. First and foremost we appreciate the efforts of Maggie Bava, Sara Erickson, Daren Reifsneider, Starr Smith, Donna Tikosky, Diana Wardell, and Jennie Weiner, who helped with the editing process. Much appreciation to Larry Lesser and the Milken Family Foundation Creative Services Department for their technical talents in videoing the conference sessions and then providing us with transcripts of each session. Thank you also to the Milken Family Foundation Communications Department under the leadership of Bonnie Somers for providing input and editorial guidance. Much gratitude is due to the Milken Educator Awards Program Staff and their leader Jane Foley for putting on the Milken Family Foundation's 2005 National Education Conference.

Thank you to all of the contributors to this publication who participated in the conference and helped to bring to fruition the important ideas laid out in this volume. We would also like to thank Information Age Publishing Inc. for their continued involvement with this project and for investing time, energy, and support for such a worthy cause. Finally, special gratitude goes to Lowell Milken, chairman and cofounder of the Milken Family Foundation for his continued support and contributions to the goal of improving the educational experience for all children.

INTRODUCTION

Lewis C. Solmon, Kimberly Firetag Agam, and Citadelle Priagula

As a nation, we have spent the past four decades in various attempts to reform our K-12 educational system. From the implementation of innovative policies to the introduction of countless reforms and spending billions of dollars on programs designed to raise student achievement, these efforts amount to little change, as evidenced by students' scores on the National Assessment of Educational Progress (NAEP). Even in comparing the United States to other countries' performance on international tests from the Programme for International Student Assessment (PISA) and the Trends in International Mathematics and Science Study (TIMSS), we have fallen short.

Now, more than ever, a quality education is essential to the livelihood of our nation. We live in an increasingly competitive global economy, where today's students vie for jobs not only available to their geographical peers, but to candidates in other countries as well.

Although our nation's efforts have not produced satisfactory gains, it is evident that the focus of our nation on accountability, narrowing the achievement gap, and improving teacher quality speaks to an unyielding and unprecedented commitment to actualize change. This book, *The Challenges of School Reform: Impact, Implementation, and Sustainability,* explores why reforms to-date have failed to live up to expectations, and it discusses promising practices and strategies for sustaining increased student achievement.

The Challenges of School Reform: Impact, Implementation, and Sustainability is a compilation of the proceedings from the 2005 Milken Family Foundation National Education Conference (NEC) held in Washington, D.C., in April 2005. The NEC is an annual event attended by practitioners, policymakers, and private sector representatives that focuses on critical issues in education. This work expands on the ideas and themes discussed in the first two volumes in this series on education policy: The first book—*Talented Teachers: The Essential Force for Improving Student Achievement*—examines the importance of teacher quality. Years of research have repeatedly confirmed what we inferred to be true—outside of the home environment, the quality of a student's teacher has the strongest impact on learning. After talented teachers were found to be a powerful component for bettering education, the second book—*Improving Student Achievement: Reforms that Work*—introduces reform ideas and programs that positively impact both teacher quality and student work.

Now, *The Challenges of School Reform: Implementation, Impact, and Sustainability* deepens these discussions by exploring the answers to questions regarding ensuring the longevity and sustained success of effective school reform.

Just as this work serves as the next step in this discussion's progression, an initiative developed by the Milken Family Foundation—the Teacher Advancement Program (TAP)—mirrors a similar trajectory of growth. Since its inception in 1999, TAP has worked to redefine teaching as a collaborative professional effort focused on student needs and directly impacting student achievement by attracting, developing, motivating, and retaining high quality teachers. TAP accomplishes this through its four key elements: multiple career paths, ongoing applied professional growth, instructionally focused accountability, and performance-based compensation.

The combination of strong political and school-based support along with remarkable results in current TAP schools led to plans to create the Teacher Advancement Program Foundation. These plans were publicly announced at the 2005 NEC; soon after the Foundation was created in May 2005 to operate TAP and take other steps to enhance teacher quality. As arguably the most visible performance-based program in the nation, the growth of TAP from a Milken Family Foundation initiative to its current status as its own foundation is reflected on many levels.

For example, TAP has experienced national visibility and the support of leaders at all levels, including U.S. Secretary of Education Margaret Spellings, former U.S. Secretary of Education Rod Paige, many state education chiefs, U.S. Senators and Congressmen, governors, local leaders, and many others. Perhaps partly due to such high-profile support, the program continues to grow, with many schools slated to begin implementation in existing TAP states, and new states expressing strong interest in joining the program. In a successful effort to ensure quality program implementation, the first TAP Summer Institute reached approximately 160 master and mentor teachers and principals in July 2005.

Additionally, the state of South Carolina has included TAP as a technical assistance program option for schools in need of improvement. The state of Minnesota modeled its Q Comp, a nation-leading compensation reform package, largely on TAP. Finally, the Algiers Charter Association in New Orleans committed to reopening as TAP schools, the first five schools in Orleans Parish to open since Hurricane Katrina, and an additional eight schools will soon follow.

As TAP and the TAP Foundation continue to grow and to sustain the successful gains made thus far, they will also continue to face similar challenges to those presented throughout this book. Each part of this book includes speeches made by government leaders at the NEC, panelist discussions from the conference, and companion articles. In an effort to preserve the ideas presented in May 2005, we have printed the original thoughts that were shared. Although education reform is generally a slow process, in some cases the information herein may not be the most up-to-date. Further, several of the conference participants have changed employment positions since the completion of this publication; titles reflect the positions those individuals held at the time of the NEC.

PART I: THE CHALLENGES OF SCHOOL REFORM

In the "Challenges of School Reform: Implementation, Impact and Sustainability," Lowell Milken, chairman and cofounder of the Milken Family Foundation, sets the stage with his discussion of the enormous problems in K-12 education today and the difficulties inherent in implementing comprehensive school reform. Panelists provide an overview of the educational reform landscape, beginning with former New Orleans Superintendent Anthony Amato, who discusses the roadblocks to sustaining successful reform. U.S. Congressman Chaka Fattah stresses the need to allocate resources evenly between low-achieving students and schools and their high-achieving counterparts, including access to high quality teachers. Jennifer Marshall, director of domestic policy studies for the Heritage Foundation, advocates focusing on the art of teaching, while Boston Public Schools Superintendent Thomas Payzant echoes her sentiment and promotes the importance of strong leadership in conjunction with highly qualified teachers. United States Deputy Secretary of Education, Ray Simon praises No Child Left Behind for focusing on teachers. Paul Vallas, Philadelphia Public Schools superintendent, applauds the support of high academic standards, effective curriculum instructional models, and professional development, pointing out the problems of sustaining such effective reforms at the level of finance and operations. The panel proceedings are followed by remarks by U.S. Congressman Ralph Regula who underscores the importance of a quality education for all students, as well as the role of talented teachers to deliver it.

PART II: NO CHILD LEFT BEHIND (NCLB)

In a plenary session, U.S. Secretary of Education Margaret Spellings frames the discussion on "Meeting the Requirements of No Child Left Behind." She praises teachers for their integral part in moving all children toward success. The next panel examines the current situation in implementing NCLB and speculations as to where the law will lead us. Panelists include David Driscoll, the commissioner of education for Massachusetts, and Andrew Rotherham, director of the 21st Century Schools Project at the Progressive Policy Institute. Mr. Rotherham concludes that questioning the law's effectiveness is premature. Antonia Cortese, executive vice president of the American Federation of Teachers (AFT), stresses the need for a solution to accelerate learning by the poorest performing students. Assistant Deputy Secretary for Innovation and Improvement Nina Rees claims that while NCLB is making progress, there may be a need to offer some flexibility to states that are working hard to make the necessary progress toward closing achievement gaps. However, the momentum and spirit of the law are key pieces in the future implementation of No Child Left Behind.

PART III: TEACHER QUALITY

Performance pay has been catapulted into many conversations concerning school reform. The Teacher Incentive Fund (TIF), recently passed by Congress and signed into law by President Bush, adds further momentum to the performance pay movement. TIF is a program designed to reward effective teachers and offer incentives to attract highly qualified teachers to teach in high-need schools. However, performance pay alone is not enough to sustain lasting change. Tamara Schiff, vice president of education and associate director of the Teacher Advancement Program Foundation, provides an overview of TAP, highlighting major elements of the program, including performance pay and professional development. Dr. Schiff defines the link between high quality teachers and success in any reform model. This is followed by Louisiana Senator Mary Landrieu's address, praising Milken Educators and all talented teachers for stepping up to the challenge of educating our nation's children. Senator Landrieu paves the way for a panel examining the "Intersection of Performance Pay and Professional Development." T. Kenneth James, Cecil Picard, and Alice Seagren, superintendents of instruction in Arkansas, Louisiana, and Minnesota, respectively, comment on their efforts to enhance teacher professionalism, effective practices and programs in professional development, as well as the impact of TAP in their states. Representatives from the TAP Foundation—including President Lewis Solmon and National Director of Training Todd White—describe the elements of TAP in the context of a comprehensive system to debunk concerns about traditional merit pay systems.

PART IV: FRAMING THE FUTURE: PRE-K THROUGH HIGHER EDUCATION

Education is an unending process, and this section imparts insights from leaders working in each stage of the formal education spectrum: Pre-K, K-12, and higher education. The first panel, "Early Childhood: The Proper Path for the Future," underscores the importance of quality Pre-K teachers and examines the challenges of accountability, funding and access that are encountered when providing high quality early childhood education. Libby Doggett, executive director of Pre-K Now, emphasizes the need for universal Pre-K education, while Sharon Lynn Kagan, associate dean for policy at Teachers College, cautions that in making Pre-K accessible to more children, providers must exact the same standards of quality. Ron Haskins, a senior fellow at the Brookings Institution, points out that early childcare is also necessary in allowing low-income mothers the opportunity to work. Elanna Yalow, Knowledge Learning Corporation's president and chief operating officer, reminds early childhood educators of the obligation to prepare children for success in school. Dennis Vicars, executive director and CEO of the Professional Association for Childhood Education Alternative Payment Program, links private sector efforts to the early childhood movement.

Next, Minnesota Governor Tim Pawlenty discusses the importance of both teachers and parents in shaping their children's futures. He continues with a discussion on TAP's role in ensuring high quality teachers and professional staff development in K-12 education.

Panelists then discuss the "Reauthorization of the Higher Education Act" and the importance of innovative partnerships linking K-12 education with higher education. Moderator Ted Sanders, former president of the Education Commission of the States, opens the conversation with an overview of facts pertaining to teacher supply, demand, and quality. Sally Stroup, assistant secretary at the U.S. Department of Education's Office of Postsecondary Education, talks about the power that both partnerships and partnership grants have in teacher preparation and recruitment. Ohio State Superintendent Susan Tave Zelman speaks about her experiences with partnership grants in her state. Guilbert Hentschke, professor at the Rossier School of Education at the University of Southern California, emphasizes the importance of communication in forging partnerships between K-12 and higher education. Last, Ben Wildavsky, education editor at *U.S. News and World Report*, provides a journalist's viewpoint of the accountability piece in reauthorizing the Higher Education Act.

IN SUM

Education reform at any level remains an arduous process, with constant challenges to confront. In today's competitive global society, it is more important than ever to use the wisdom gleaned from past efforts to overcome these obstacles. As we have learned through our work with the Teacher Advancement Program, successful implementation of a program with lasting and positive impact on student achievement growth is possible and sustainable. We hope this volume serves as an engaging and effective guide to overcoming the challenges of school reform.

PART I

THE CHALLENGES OF SCHOOL REFORM

CHAPTER 1

THE CHALLENGES OF SCHOOL REFORM

Implementation, Impact, and Sustainability

Lowell Milken, Anthony Amato, Congressman Chaka Fattah, Jennifer A. Marshall, Thomas W. Payzant, Ray Simon, and Paul G. Vallas

Lowell Milken

Reforming K-12 education to ensure that every child has access to a high quality education has been, and continues to be, a key focus of our work at the Milken Family Foundation. For over 30 years, our nation's K-12 system has tried, with little success, to significantly improve student academic achievement—especially the academic performance of as many as nine million students who attend schools in inner cities and poor rural areas.

No Child Left Behind requires that all students reach a standard of proficiency by 2013-2014. Thus, educating at-risk children has become not only the biggest challenge for our schools, but arguably *the* Civil Rights issue facing our nation today. What are the precise school reform strategies and solutions that need to be put in place, and once implemented, how do we ensure that these strategies and solutions have the impact and the sustainability to enable all students to reach a level of proficiency? The stakes are extraordinarily high, for most of these young people whose families are poor, there is a window of opportunity while they're in school to develop the intellectual and moral character that, if achieved, will yield them a bright future.

This morning we are fortunate to have six knowledgeable, experienced, and opinionated voices in education reform on this panel. They will advise us on school reform strategies and programs that can result in sustained student achievement growth. Later in the session, you will have the opportunity to ask them questions. Let's move forward and meet our distinguished panel.

In the corporate world, there are chief executives known for taking on turnaround situations. In the education world, we have leaders like Anthony Amato taking on some of the nation's most challenging school districts. When Tony took over New York's District 6 in 1987, it was dead last among the city's 32 districts. Although the district ranked at the top of the charts in crime, overcrowding, and non-English-speaking students, by the time he left in '99, it had risen to the middle third in language arts and the upper third in math.

Facing the same demographics in Hartford, Connecticut, a district that ranked dead last in the state, Tony realized significant changes within six months. He is currently the superintendent of New Orleans' public schools and will serve at this post until the end of June 2006. Tony has initiated reforms, including district-wide reading programs and an innovative system of mandatory parent meetings. Tony is currently pursuing his doctorate at Columbia University Teachers College.

I had the pleasure of meeting U.S. Congressman Chaka Fattah at a Milken Educator Award notification in Philadelphia. Congressman Fattah is highly committed to increasing educational opportunities for low-income youth. Now in his sixth term and representing the Pennsylvania district that includes parts of Philly, Congressman Fattah is a leader in education. One of his many accomplishments is his work in the creation of GEAR UP, a nationally funded program, which stands for Gaining Early Awareness and Readiness for Undergraduate Programs, one of the largest precollege awareness programs in the nation. When I was with the Congressman at the notification, I saw first hand his deep commitment to educational opportunities and his ability to capture the attention of the students with his inspiring remarks. It's a great pleasure to have you join us today.

Next is Jennifer Marshall, the director of domestic policy studies for the Heritage Foundation, a well-known research and educational think tank. Jennifer oversees the Foundation's research in education, welfare, marriage and the family, and religion and civil society. As an advocate of school choice, Jennifer has coauthored work characterizing charter schools as "America's greatest experiment in school choice today." Before joining the Heritage Foundation in 2003, Jennifer worked with former U.S. Secretary of Education Bill Bennett on cultural policy issues at Empower America.

Our native Bostonian, Dr. Thomas Payzant, was appointed superintendent of Boston Public Schools in 1995. Before this, the road home first took him to superintendent positions in Eugene, Oregon; Oklahoma City; and San Diego; with a stop in Washington, D.C., to serve as U.S. assistant secretary for elementary and secondary education under President Clinton. Since his return to Boston, Tom has created a wide-ranging plan for educational reform known as Focus on Children and has increased the business community's support for public education, raising over $30 million to support professional development in every Boston school. He was also the recipient of the Council of Great City Schools' 2004 Richard R. Greene Award for Excellence in Urban Education.

Now, April 15th means tax day for most of us, but in the case of Ray Simon, the date brought good news. President Bush nominated Ray as the next U.S. deputy secretary of education, second in command to Secretary Margaret Spellings. Ray came to Washington about two years ago from his home state of Arkansas to assume the post of U.S. assistant secretary for elementary and secondary education. We had the good fortune to work with Ray when he was state chief in Arkansas, and we saw firsthand how effective he was in moving forward education reform in his state. Prior to serving as state chief, Ray served as director of the Arkansas Department of Education, district superintendent, and university professor, with his roots in the classroom as an outstanding high school math teacher. As a former math major, I know how important it is to have highly qualified math teachers.

I first met Paul Vallas in 1995, when he was the chief executive officer of Chicago Public Schools. He joined me to notify the 1,000th Milken National Educator Award recipient, and it turned out that we were live on *Oprah Winfrey* that day. It was a very exciting day, and Paul joined me once again just last fall as CEO of Philadelphia schools to surprise third-grade teacher Jennifer Wong.

Of course, the parallels between Paul's work and the two big city districts are strong. In Philadelphia, he is implementing district-wide reforms, including initiatives to create better trained teachers and a unified curriculum. These efforts reflect his leadership of Chicago's public schools from 1995 to 2001, when he implemented a broad series of educational reforms to reverse the system's persistent failure. Paul is credited

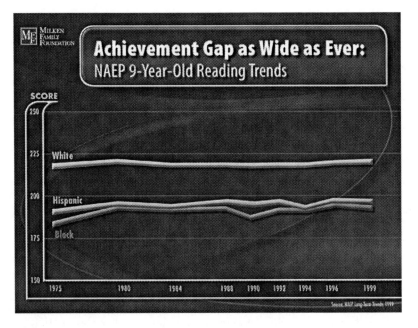

Chart 1.1.

Chart 1.2.

with restoring financial stability to the system while ending social promotion, reorganizing Chicago's high schools, and establishing the nation's largest after-school and summer reading programs. All of this work paid off with six consecutive years of improved elementary reading scores. Paul, your leadership and work is exemplary and we are very pleased you have joined us today.

Before I begin with questions for our panel, let's take a brief look at the enormity of the challenges facing K-12 education today.

Over the past 30 years, there has been virtually no progress in closing the achievement gap. (Chart 1.1) You are familiar with statistics showing that only a minority of our students overall—whether in fourth, eighth, or 12th grade—reach proficiency as measured by the U.S. Department of Education's National Assessment of Education Progress (NAEP).

Most students score at or below the basic level (Chart 1.2). A basic level is defined as a student who understands only the literal meaning of what they read. There is an extraordinarily high percentage of fourth-grade students in urban districts who do not meet a basic standard (Chart 1.3).

Every student is not only going to have to know how to read, but be able to possess the skills and knowledge of a level of proficiency, in order to obtain gainful employment in the twenty-first century. (Chart 1.4)

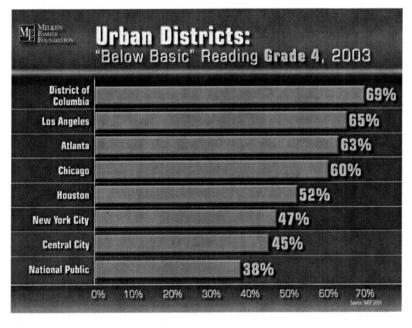

Chart 1.3.

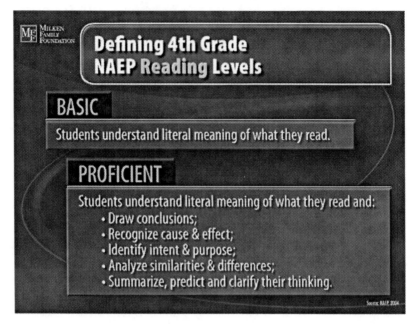

Chart 1.4.

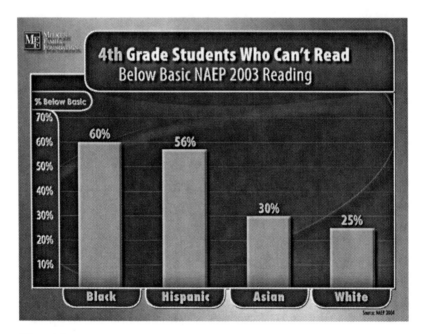

Chart 1.5.

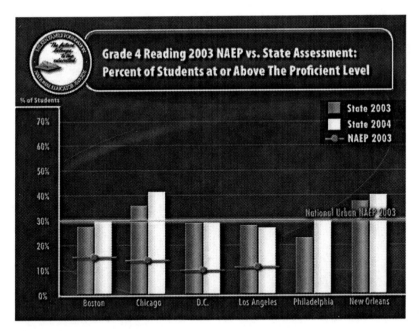

Chart 1.6.

Thus, it is quite disturbing that we have so many students in large urban districts who score below basic. These tragic results are further confirmed by the fact that 60% of all African-American children and 56% of all Latino children in fourth grade score at below basic (Chart 1.5).

Let's spend a moment to look at state assessments in reading (Chart 1.6). This chart shows the state reading assessment scores of six districts as compared to their NAEP reading assessment scores. As you can see under either assessment measure there is a significant amount of ground to cover to get students to the proficiency level.

We have all seen the reports which show that American students do not perform well on mathematics and science exams when compared to their peers in other developed countries (Chart 1.7). There are a lot of reasons put forth as to why this occurs. Some people argue that U.S. students do not take these international exams seriously because there are no consequences to students. Others argue that because our curriculum is a mile long and only an inch deep, we don't fare as well as other developed countries. Whatever your particular point of view is about international comparisons, the fact is that the longer our students spend in school, the poorer their comparative performance on these international exams (Chart 1.8).

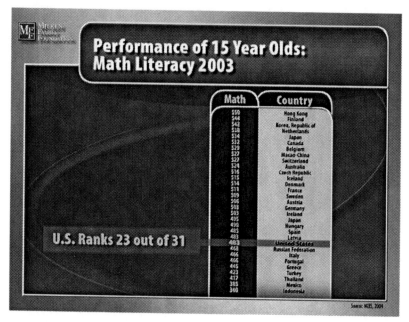

Chart 1.7.

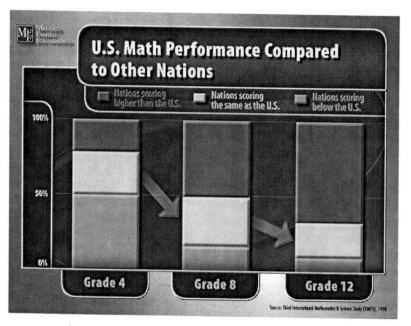

Chart 1.8.

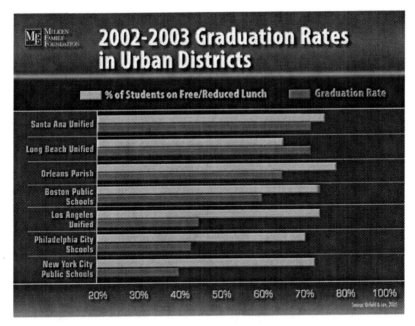

Chart 1.9.

When it comes to graduation rates (Chart 1.9), we also have a lot of work to do. This is especially so in the case among students in poverty. Look at the results of a recent study of the graduation rates in California's five largest districts (Chart 1.10). Looking at the Los Angeles Unified School District with approximately 740,000 students, the graduation rate is approximately 45%. Today, the Los Angeles Unified School District is approximately 72.5% Hispanic with graduation rates among Latino students of only 39%. This is in stark contrast to a district like Santa Ana when 92% of Santa Ana Unified is Hispanic with a 73% graduation rate.

Research confirms that aside from home and family, the single most important element driving student achievement is the quality of the teacher in the classroom. But in our nation today, students who need the most help have teachers that are the least trained in terms of subject matter and pedagogy; and out-of-field teaching is high generally but especially so in high-poverty areas (Chart 1.11). This is a tragic state of affairs when we know that effective teachers have a substantial impact on raising the academic performance of low-achieving students and student performance on high-stakes exams (Chart 1.12 and 1.13).

I could go on and on, but it is clear that for all too many students in our country, the system has not been performing well. One might be able

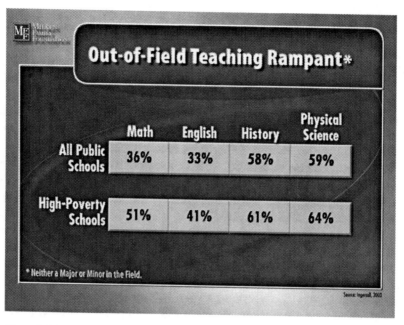

Chart 1.10.

Chart 1.11.

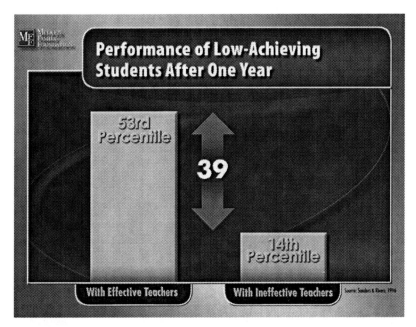

Chart 1.12.

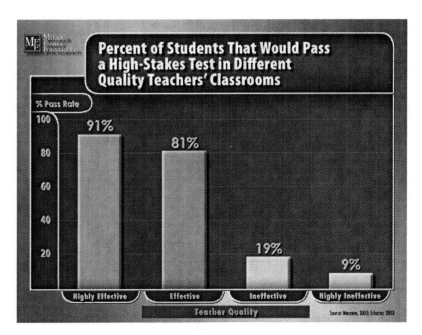

Chart 1.13.

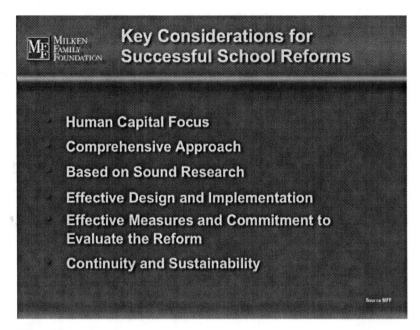

Chart 1.14.

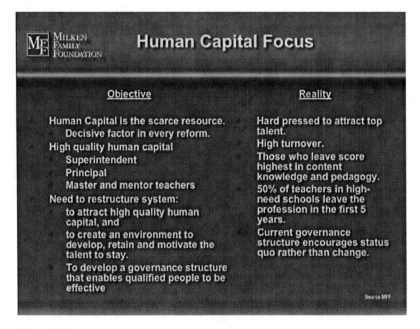

Chart 1.15.

to understand this state of affairs if little effort had been made to try to reform the system. However, over the past three decades, the lack of progress in terms of outcomes has not been the result of a lack of attempted reforms. At the Foundation, we have studied more than 300 school reforms, ranging from federal reforms to those based in distinct educational philosophies, to those focused on specific subject matter, to others based on instructional tools, and still others respecting the structure and management of schools.

Our work in analyzing school reform also has confirmed that there are certain key considerations that must be addressed if a reform is likely to succeed. These six elements are presented in Chart 1.14.

The first is a human capital focus (Chart 1.15). In business, we know human capital plays a decisive role in forming value and fueling growth. The success of any enterprise is determined by the skills, knowledge, and commitment of the people involved. In education, the same principle applies.

The second is comprehensive approach (Chart 1.16). How many times have we seen a reform take hold to address a problem only to cause another? Class size reduction is an example. In California, class size reduction was legislated for grades K-3 to require no more than 20 stu-

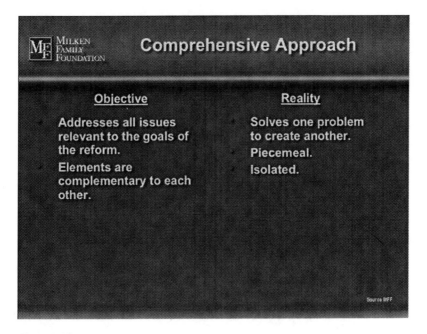

Chart 1.16.

Chart 1.17.

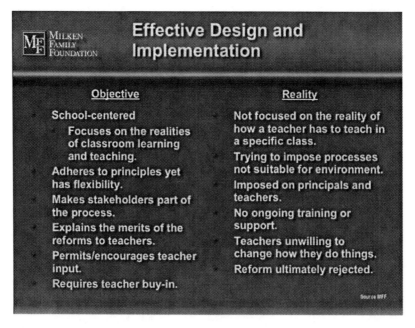

Chart 1.18.

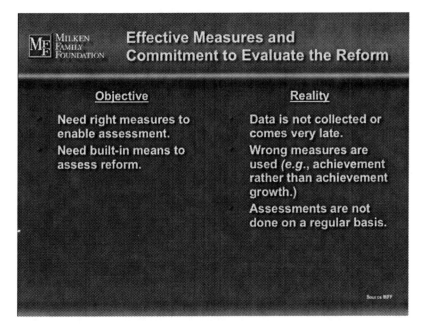

Effective Measures and Commitment to Evaluate the Reform

Objective	Reality
Need right measures to enable assessment.	Data is not collected or comes very late.
Need built-in means to assess reform.	Wrong measures are used *(e.g.,* achievement rather than achievement growth.)*
	Assessments are not done on a regular basis.

Source: MFF

Chart 1.19.

dents per classroom. The result was to double the number of emergency credentialed teachers 5% to 10% in one year.

The next factor that must be in place is a reform based on sound research (Chart 1.17). Another key element is effective design and implementation (Chart 1.18). So many reforms have not been effective because they were structured on top-down, where teachers were not consulted but yet expected to buy-in. The next element is implementing effective measures and commitment to evaluate the reform (Chart 1.19).

The final element is continuity and sustainability (Chart 1.20). All too often even the most promising reform will fail because of a lack of continuity in its application. With a changing cast of governors, state school chiefs and school district superintendents, it is often difficult for even a promising reform to remain in place for a sufficient time to yield results.

All of this brings me to my first question for our panel today. Why has 30 years of school reform yielded so little in terms of student achievement growth? What are the key elements you believe need to be in place to properly implement school reform that will have impact and be sustainable?

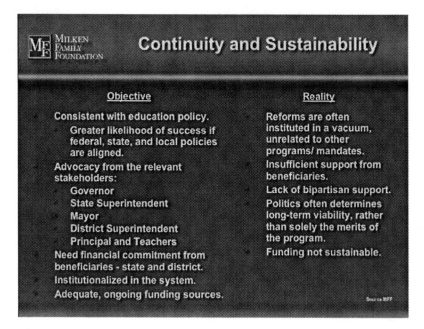

Chart 1.20.

Anthony Amato

Good morning, ladies and gentlemen. Lowell, in terms of the elements you put up today, they depict a very compelling story. And as much as I feel hopeful about public education, I share your sense of urgency. The next question concerning the little achievement yielded by 30 years of school reform falls on our implementation strategies. Over and over again, when we try to initiate reforms that are piecemeal or popped into a system, everyone is taken aback when the reform fails; we often fail to view the reform in terms of its contextual framework. We don't ask the simple questions: Where does this reform sit? Why do we have to do this? What's the bigger picture? Reforms that have been successful start with the big picture; we go up to the balcony, get a clear view about the context of the reform, and implement it following a comprehensive approach.

In terms of context, we must first have our school board, governor, mayor, and other power brokers understand that our children have multiple challenges. That is the context into which the new reform will exist. For the reform to be successful, we must first seek to obviate some of the emotional, social, and physical challenges that our children face every day. One of the many ways to do this, for example, is the creation of a community full-service school. We change the context of the reform when we place a library, clinic, emergency services and other supports into schools. But we must ensure our educators and partners understand that we must deal with the physical, emotional, and social context of our children for a reform to have any chance of success.

The flipside of the needs children have is the tremendous gifts they bring to the context of school. How we look at diversity, speakers of other languages, and cultures in a very positive way is crucial; we must realize that it is our problem if we don't know enough to maximize a child's talents and take advantage of those gifts. So the first thing we need for successful reforms is to look at the context of the initiative, obviate as many obstacles for the children, and maximize their strengths.

The second big issue for successful reforms is professional development. Everyone involved in the reform must receive some degree of training. For example, in the late '90s, when we reformed science and began using an inquiry-process science approach, the first thing we did in New York City (when I served as superintendent) was to take all the principals in my district of Harlem and Washington Heights, as well as all administrators, including myself, for a one-year course to study inquiry science. Once we were comfortable with it, we took another year to train the teachers. We just didn't put the reform into place and say, go ye forth and do inquiry. It took us two years of professional development before we launched the reform. To this day, I'm happy to say, inquiry science is alive and well in the district.

Lowell Milken

Tony, with all of the short-term growth that you achieved when you were in New York, when we look at the test scores today, it does not appear that the gains were sustainable in both reading and math. How do we explain this?

Anthony Amato

Reforms go through stages like everything else. The first stage is implementation where you have to focus on context and professional development, as I have already indicated. The second stage is the maintenance stage; this is where you work out the initial challenges and start settling in. But the most important stage for me—and this is where I think many of us, including myself, miss the mark with some reforms—is the adaptability stage. This is the crucial point where a reform has plateaued and needs revitalization to continue serving the children successfully.

As a quick example, I'll use the same inquiry science program I began speaking about before. Although it was highly successful, we reached a point where the program needed improvement. Teachers were complaining about missing elements to the course of study. For instance, assessments were embedded in the curriculum. They were so embedded that the teachers found the assessments useless. So we spent a summer with teacher teams extracting the assessments and creating performance-based assessments instead. Then the teachers went further the next summer. They created science journals to integrate all other curricular areas, including reading and writing, into science. Then, we came to the point where the children—I repeat, the children—started to have assessment fairs to create their own assessments. They actually had competitions for first grade and up, against other classes to see which assessment was the best for their grade. The assessments were voted on by the classes in a particular grade to determine the assessment most meaningful to all children. This is a way of keeping sustainability growing from within. The fire must keep burning. Once a superintendent, principal, or lead reform teacher moves out of an organization, a reform has a strong chance of vanishing unless sustainability is made part of the original plan. You must plan for evolution.

As a final thought, sometimes the need to sustain comes from external sources. Using the same inquiry science example, research is now showing that students who go through an inquiry-only science program don't do as well in college compared to more traditional approaches. It is assumed this happens because once you go to college, a more traditional textbook approach is followed. You no longer learn science the way scientists work. To sustain inquiry to the next level, we have to incorporate a fair amount of expository reading in the area without making it text-only driven. So that's yet another adaptation the program will need to survive as a reform.

As to why reading and math scores were not sustained in the New York district, I think that, unlike science, educators are too quick to try new reading and math programs. They all feel quite confident about their own methodologies, and new leadership usually brings new programs regardless of prior success. Science, however, is a subject often ignored in lower grades. I suspect the science inquiry reform survived because of its internal adaptability and the fact that it was not on anyone's agenda to change.

Lowell Milken

Paul, would you please address the sustainability issue. You've implemented what appears to be effective reforms in Chicago, but what happens when you're no longer there? How can effective reforms be sustained?

Paul Vallas

After 15 or 20 years of school reform, I think we've reached a consensus on what works and what doesn't. Some of the things that we thought were so innovative in the 1990s have really become commonplace. If you look at the research done by the Broad Foundation and by the Council on Great City Schools on a number of high-performing school districts, or if you look at the work that Kati Haycock has done at Education Trust, looking also at individual schools and poor-performing districts, you see certain commonalities that may exist.

You certainly see high academic standards embraced. You see a consensus reached on the most effective curriculum/instructional models to be used across the school district. You see an intense investment in professional development. You see a significant increase in the amount of instructional time on task. You see an accountability system using data-driven instruction, so that you're not just taking one snapshot a year, but rather you are following children's progress through benchmarks. In Philadelphia we do six-week benchmarking in the core subject areas so that the teachers and parents get feedback, multiple times during the year, on how children and schools are performing.

These commonalities seem to exist in school districts that have experienced dramatic success. The problems exist at the level of finance and operations. You can have a great vision, but if you can't figure out the financing—that does not always mean new money—or if you can't put the school district on a long-term financial plan that can sustain the reforms you're implementing, then you have these peaks and valleys where one reform sputters out and a new one takes its place.

The same thing can be said for operations. You can have a grand vision, but you need the operational capacity to deliver on that vision; you need the ability to bring people in who can do the curriculum, instruction, and professional development. The ability to organize yourself (like the military has with the War College and the Command and General Staff College) sustains the quality of their professional development and instruction by constantly adapting best practices.

Again, where these reforms fail is not in vision. I think the research points us in the direction of what we need to do, particularly in large districts where we have from 30% to 40% mobility. However, the trick is on the financing end, and the trick is on the operational end. If you can't tackle those two issues, then one incomplete reform just gets layered on another.

I like to refer to myself first as an educator and second as an archaeologist, because every single time I take over a new school district, I have to dig through four or five or six reforms, all of which are incomplete. It's like searching for Homer's city of Troy where there were seven cities built one on top of the other. That is what inevitably happens in school districts.

Work done by the Broad Foundation on this topic led them to set up not only a leadership academy for managers, but also a leadership academy for school board members. Also, the work done from the Council on Great City Schools speaks to the issue of governing boards that give the superintendent strong support and the latitude to implement reforms. Look at what's recently happened in San Diego, where I believe the superintendent there was making significant progress. He did an outstanding job, but he ran into problems when the make-up of the board changed. So, having stability in the governing structure is absolutely key. Everybody gives me more credit than I deserve for having some success with large urban districts, but I've always selected districts with very strong corporate-style boards, which had individuals with longevity.

You clearly need to have a governing structure that is going to give the superintendent the support that he or she needs to drive the school system forward. That's been one of the keys to success.

Thomas Payzant

Standards-based reform is really radical because it is based on the premise that all students have to meet certain standards to graduate with a high school diploma that will give them access to opportunity—meaning continuing education, a good job, responsible citizenship. This is what we would want for our own children; that means *all* students. What other country in the world with a public education system is making the commitment to *all* students? I would argue none, so that's where we begin.

Next, we have to ask what the balance is between our role in the schools and the rest of the society. What do you have to have? First of all, you've got to have a common set of goals. They must be focused on where the research tells us the leverage is—quality of instruction. That doesn't mean to go out and preach and tell teachers to do it. You've got to have a support system for teachers instead of one teacher per classroom in isolation trying to figure it out for himself or herself. You've got to bring the profession together, so teachers learn together and from each other, and make the school climate one of trust. When you look at student work, share a rubric for the type of work, and reflect on your practice with support from colleagues, it becomes easier to go next-door to see what's going on and learn.

The second variable is leadership. I don't think there is a more important leadership role, outside of the classroom teacher working with students, than the principals in schools. Over the past 10 to 12 years, we've asked principals to make a radical change in their role over the last 10 to 12 years, to move away from being operations people and managers. Years ago, the heads of schools were called masters because they were master teachers. And if they're going to lead the work just like any CEO who leads the work, they have got to know the work, and focus on sustaining human beings in the organization and helping them grow.

You have got to have clear goals. We've had the same goals in Boston for the last eight or nine years. It's all about achievement and getting students to proficiency. It's making continuous progress each year, and it's closing the achievement gap. I have a little triangle, the Boston people know, that I stole from Ron Ferguson at the Kennedy School at Harvard. Relationships are at the pinnacle of the triangle. Curriculum is on one corner, and instruction is on the other. That's what the focus of the work has to be.

I've been very privileged to have the opportunity in two districts, in San Diego for almost 10 and a half years, and in Boston it'll be 10 years in October 2006. When you get continuity of leadership on both the governing and the executive sides of the house, commitment to ongoing focus, coherence, and you begin to develop a climate where people who are out in the schools doing the hard work every day believe the work is important, it's going to happen.

In terms of sustainability—I worry about that a lot. You need to have people coming in as superintendents who don't always say, "Well, I've got to start over." Rather you need them to come in and say, "What has my predecessor been able to do that has worked and that the people in the school system have bought into?" You need to build on that and have the vision, along with the board, for going to the next step. So, it's a combination of building on what is good, what seems to be sustained, then improving it by perhaps taking on some new challenges.

Lowell Milken

Tom, I don't deny that there are good things happening in schools, but when we look at the number of young people in 2005 who by the fourth grade cannot read, it is clear that there are serious problems and they are not being addressed on a timely basis.

Thomas Payzant

Well, you've got to use data as a major source to understand what's going on. Aggregate data is dangerous. You've got to break it down and see what's going on underneath. We just completed a mobility study in

Boston, and probably most people in the room would predict what the outcome was. If you look at how many years a child has been in the same school in addition to his or her performance on the state assessments, you will see that the longer a child is in the same school, the better the performance on the state assessments will be. Now, the good news in Boston is we have, in the aggregate, an average 80% stability range. But the other 20% is in constant churn. And there are two impacts: one on the student and one on the teacher. If you've got 25 children in the class, with 20 of them there for the whole year but a constant churn with five, then it's having a dramatic impact on that class and what the teacher needs to do. I think we need more value-added types of assessments so that we can look at the mobility piece, look at the stability piece, and follow students over time.

We need to look at results by race, special education, English Language Learners, regular education, and then drill down more, in terms of how we've got to approach some of our strategies differently. So the picture is mixed: you look at the kids that are with us over time, and you get a different picture from what you get here.

Lowell Milken

Tom, I hear what you are saying but, once again, when we look at the results set forth on Chart 1.6, we're still seeing a low percentage of students at a proficient level. Wouldn't this suggest that we need to try some new approaches? For example, should more competition be introduced into the system? Jennifer, what is your view?

Jennifer Marshall

I wholeheartedly agree with you. It's been interesting that the human capital factor has come up so many times in this discussion. I think part of our problem is that too often we approach education as a system. We're very good at systems here in the United States, and we have been ever since the Model T. But now we're trying to apply that to education. I look at education from a federal vantage point here in Washington, D.C. There's a great tendency to talk about a monolithic education system and to try to inject the right strategies into this single system.

At times, this lends itself to all kinds of nonsense, shortcomings, and certainly over-politicization. If we have got a single system, then the control of that system is a political football. We've seen that, and both parties are guilty of that here in Washington, D.C. I think getting beyond this requires more radical solutions, as you're suggesting—the idea that we're going to deliver education through new means. What is public education? It's not cinder blocks. It's not a system of schools. It is the education of the public.

We should put that first and foremost, and we should put the true art of education, the art of teaching, first—which I believe to be a teacher assessing where a student is, envisioning their potential, and moving them closer to that potential. How can we organize education in a way that will free up that human capital to allow for variation on the local level? We've heard a lot about diversity already—the diversity of ethnic backgrounds and the high mobility in our country today.

There is always going to be diversity and variation. We need an organization of education resources that can accommodate that. I think that organization is going to be a variety of delivery methods and mechanisms, like charter schools, where there is a degree of autonomy. You've also pointed out the governance issues here, where there's a consolidation of the governance and interest at a school level—where those principals and teachers are empowered to do what works for the students they're serving. Charter schools have allowed that to happen to a greater degree.

Lowell Milken

Congressman, one of the most disappointing aspects of school reform is what I perceive to be the lack of urgency. In 1983, *A Nation at Risk* provided the warning, and since then we have had summits, Goals 2000 and many other attempts to reform the system.

What do you think the federal government can do to not let another generation pass through a system that some argue is at-risk?

Chaka Fattah

I think what we have in education is a selective amnesia. That is, in every single state we have high-achieving schools, and we have low-achieving schools. States seem to know how to create financing systems, curriculums, and teacher certification programs that work in our wealthy suburban districts. When we get to poor districts in rural and urban areas, where are those teacher certifications and regulations? They get waived. There are 501 school districts in Pennsylvania, but Philadelphia receives 50% of the waivers. You find this disparity all across the country.

The fascinating thing about your list of reforms is the one reform that has never, ever been tried in America: give to low-achieving students and schools the same resources you give to high-achieving students and schools. We tried all the other reforms. Now we want to experiment with these children and their lives, rather than to replicate what already works. We know how to make public schools work—they work in every one of our wealthy suburban districts in every single state in this country.

What we need to do, and what I think the federal government ought to do, is to be a referee, insisting that states should provide to children in their state the same quality of education that they provide those in their highest-achieving districts. We should measure the quality of teachers and the classroom size, because you won't find many 15-to 20-student class-rooms in Chicago, Philadelphia, or New York. In New York, 418 schools are without libraries—not without librarians, but without libraries at all.

In Roy King's affidavit in the Arkansas school finance case, he says that he was the entire math faculty at this high school, teaching 200 students. He didn't major or minor in math. His degree was in physical education, but he was responsible for teaching Algebra, Algebra II, Calculus, Geome-try, and Trigonometry. He had 20 textbooks for 200 kids, so he did a lot-tery about which ones get to take the textbook home on any given day.

What we're asking poor children to do is to demonstrate that they can swim in pools where there's no water. Then, we stigmatize them with high-stakes tests. Then we come along with another, usually one-word reform like "charters" or "vouchers." Really, these are just distractions. What we need to do is tell states, "Whatever you're doing in your highest achieving schools, whatever you decided is the upper tier of educational expecta-tions and resources, you should provide for the poorest children in your state."

You don't have to be a math major to figure that in Philadelphia, we're going to pay the lowest amount of any of the school districts at every level—if you get a master's degree, if you stay for 10 years, if you get a doctorate. In fact, at every level you can go out to suburban districts, teach half as many children, and get paid twice as much. The inverse logic here is that since we might have poor children who have more difficult challenges, what we've decided to do in this country is actually give them the least of every single thing that we know they need in order to get an education. We give them the most overcrowded classrooms and the least qualified teachers.

You talked about California. Forty-five thousand teachers, teaching out-of-field, are aggregated in the highest poverty districts. We can look around at this, and the only thing I would say to you is, you don't have to look very far. Look at the whole list of reforms, and the one thing you can't find is the thing that already works. That's what we ought to try, too; maybe that would be a great experiment.

Paul Vallas

First of all, suburban districts don't necessarily do as well as urban districts when it comes to educating poor children. This is why many of the suburban districts are probably leading the charge when it comes to explaining and, in some cases, filing lawsuits against No Child Left Behind, because the disaggregation of the data has put us all in the same boat. I like that boat, incidentally. I love disaggregating of data. I love the accountability.

The bottom line here is that disaggregating data has helped by putting us in the position where we have now lifted the curtain and find there's underachievement in many, many places where we never expected underachievement to be. I just want to make that point.

Do we have school superintendents who need more money? Yes. Do the federal mandates need to be fully funded? Yes. But we must acknowledge that we're probably getting more money than we've ever gotten before.

There were big increases in Title I at the federal level again this year. But at the end of the day, as a superintendent, I gave up expecting or hoping that I would get all the money I wanted. The bottom line here is that we have to work with what we have regardless of the level of federal and state funding; we're not going to be able to sustain our reforms unless we have a financial strategy to sustain those reforms.

That means we maximize the revenues that are at our disposal or the revenues that we can access. My approach in Chicago, which was much more refined in Philadelphia, has been to really take advantage of the market to help us sustain our reforms. If you look at what we're doing in Philadelphia, in many respects it's probably the most dramatic, market-driven reform that one has ever seen. We don't develop our curriculums in-house. We go out and purchase the best curriculum and instruction models around. We don't revitalize, lay out, or implement our technology strategies in-house. Rather, we work with the big technology companies, like Microsoft and others, and we bring them in to drive the technology reforms, whether it's on governmental operations, curriculum instruction, or professional development; to select the best curriculum and structural models, we look to the market.

The same thing is happening with our high school reforms. We don't have the capacity to dramatically transform our high schools into much smaller choice schools over the next four to five years with the resources we have in-house. So, what we've done is bring some of the top universities and educational consulting groups, like Kaplan and others, to literally take over management of a few of our small high school projects. This means by 2008, we will have gone from 38 high schools to 80 high schools. The average size of those high schools will be 800, and half of them will be between 400 and 500. But every single small high school that will be in operation will be a college preparatory high school with honors advanced placement courses and neighborhood-based magnet programs. So the market is there to be exploited, so to speak.

What's happened in the last 10 or 15 years is the push towards choice. What's happened with No Child Left Behind and its predecessor during the Clinton administration is that an education market has emerged. A private sector, for-profit, and not-for-profit industry is out there, and school districts that are strategic can access the type of resources they never could generate in-house at reasonable rates. So, if there's one thing that I've learned in my 20 years of public service and my 10 or so years as a big-city superintendent, it is that if public education plays its cards right, then the market may actually save public education, and the market is there to be taken full advantage of.

Lowell Milken

Paul, how many students are in charter schools in your district today?

Paul Vallas

This year it will rise to about 14%. We have 56 charter schools, and growing. We also have about 12% of our schools under private management. Last year we had double-digit increases. We've gone from 19% reading to 41% reading. And if we can sustain that number, we actually may approach the No Child Left Behind goal by 2014. For the last two years we've seen growth in our charter schools, our privately managed schools, and our public schools. We've literally seen double-digit growth in reading and in math.

Lowell Milken

What results in student performance have you seen in your charter schools?

Paul Vallas

Last year there was about a 5% to 6% growth in the charters, and among the privately managed schools, the growth ranged from 2% to

10%. For example, the Edison schools show 10% growth in their reading and close to 10% growth in their math scores.

I'm all for choice. I'm all for diversified management models. And in some cases, these models are very helpful to us because it allows us to sustain a broad reform at an accelerated pace. I don't want to build another layer. I don't want some superintendent, another archaeologist, to dig in and find my reforms half complete.

The key here is accountability. I love charters, but I also love holding charters accountable. So what we do is use the standards. We use the accountability goals set down by No Child Left Behind, and we apply them to all of our schools, whether they're privately managed or publicly managed. Our charters fall into three categories: About a third of them are terrific, and we're replicating those models—High Tech High, Mastery Charter, KIPP—we're giving them second and third campuses. Another third are treading water, and they could go either way. The last third are as bad, if not worse, than the worst of schools. Whether they're privately or publicly managed or are charters, we've got to be able to hold those schools accountable to the same accountability provisions.

If you have tough accountability and hold everybody accountable, then you can create choice, which creates competition, which I think improves the system. At the same time you can have quality across the board.

Lowell Milken

Ray, we have heard from everyone, and now I'm going to give you an opportunity. We have heard about the hundreds of school reforms over the past 30 years. Part of your responsibility is the implementation of No Child Left Behind and to assure that it has both impact and sustainability. Why is No Child Left Behind different from those other reforms? Why might we expect NCLB to yield different results over the next decade?

Ray Simon

When I first came to Washington, D.C., from Conway, Arkansas, the first thing I asked was, "When can I talk to a teacher?" I want to hear what teachers have to say about No Child Left Behind. I've heard what the associations and other groups have to say. So, partially through the help of Lowell and some other folks, we brought groups of teachers to Washington on three separate occasions.

These were Teachers of the Year and past and present Milken winners. We spent a day with each of those groups, listening to them tell us what they thought about not just No Child Left Behind, but also the same types of things we're talking about today. What is it that you need to do a better job? What is it that gets in your way? So, the short answer to your question is: it's the teacher being the center of No Child Left Behind that makes this different than any other initiative that I'm familiar with, (and this is my 40th year).

That's a component of No Child Left Behind that is really not understood well. The teachers told us they believe in the mission of No Child Left Behind. They believe it's absolutely imperative that every child be able to read and do math at grade level. They believe in the mission 100%. But they weren't sure they could pull it off, because in the past they hadn't succeeded in getting every child to grade level.

So, the teachers' universal request was to show them somebody who's doing it. We did; we went around the country and found what I've called 50 "Miss Bonkers". For those of you who have read *Hooray for Diffendoofer Day!*, Miss Bonkers is the teacher that No Child Left Behind was meant to support. We found 50 of those teachers and took them on a "summer of love" tour around the country. And we invited other teachers to come and hear from Miss Bonkers. Again, these are teachers that are doing every day what No Child Left Behind says should be done. They're teaching poor kids, kids of color, kids whose first language is not English, and special education children, all to 100% proficiency.

The highly qualified teacher provision of No Child Left Behind is meant to put a Miss Bonkers in front of every classroom in the United States. It's not right that a poor child does not have access to a Teacher of the Year every year, but they don't. I agree with the Congressman: statistic after statistic shows that our best teachers, our most experienced teachers, are not where they are really needed, and we must develop some system to get them there. No Child Left Behind is our single greatest hope right now to make that happen, because it meets the six criteria you need for successful reform (see Chart 1.14).

The top of that list is human capital, and it's got to start with the teacher. We're going to have to pay teachers more to go where no one dares to go. Back when I was state chief, we did a survey of the teachers coming into the profession that the colleges produced over a five-year period in our state—1,193 physical education majors and one physics major. The one physics major went to work in North Carolina, and eventually left teaching altogether.

Now, I love coaches. I have nothing against physical education. But very likely, the physical education teacher is going to make more money than that one physics teacher, because the coach is going to have the great privilege of working with kids after school and will get paid extra to do so. Coaches probably get an extra month or so of salary to work with the athletic teams in the summer, and that's why a number of people enter coaching. It is more financially rewarding than a pure classroom teacher who doesn't get out and get to breathe the fresh air every day.

We have got to change this pattern around. We have got to pay more to teachers who teach in a shortage area, such as math, science, foreign language, or special education. We're going to have to pay them to go to schools that need the best teachers where maybe there's no shopping around the corner, no movie theater down the street. We're going to have to get back in sync with what's important. And again, what's important is that very top one—human capital.

The second thing the teachers told us is to not let this go away. One teacher said, "For the first time, I see an initiative that's putting me at the center of things, which is where I need to be. Don't let it go away." So we've got to have continuity. It doesn't matter who the president is, who is in Congress, who is at the Department of Education, who is the superintendent or principal. We must sustain it. It's got to be bigger than any one administration.

Anthony Amato

I want to shift for one second back to competition and take a look at a few charts. The charts (Charts 1.21-1.22) clearly indicate why some competition works so well on the business side but not necessarily on the education side. Many times in my career I've seen charters, voucher systems, etc., that don't play by the same rules as the public school system.

Let's talk about when the Baby Bells in the telecom industry were created. The Baby Bells all had to function by the FCC rules, and that was fine. That competition really led to a lot of good things happening in America. But, we're not playing on the same field in education. I'm not against charters or vouchers or anything else, as long as the playing field is the same. And it would be nice if the public school system could play by those same rules that charters and others are afforded. For instance, in D.C., with the public charters—where you can obviate and eliminate a lot of those bureaucratic encumbrances—that's a perfect solution. We all know that the quickest way to get fired in education is to be a risk-taker. We have to start nurturing and rewarding risk-taking that results in student success.

Lowell Milken

Let's move to the issue of governance for a moment. Paul and Tom, what kind of governance structure would be best to enable you to accom-

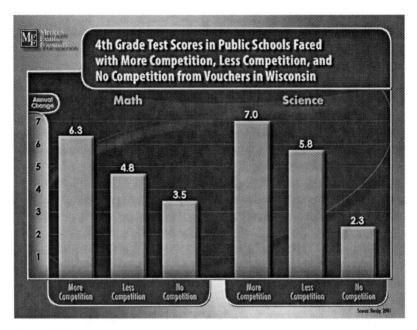

Chart 1.21.

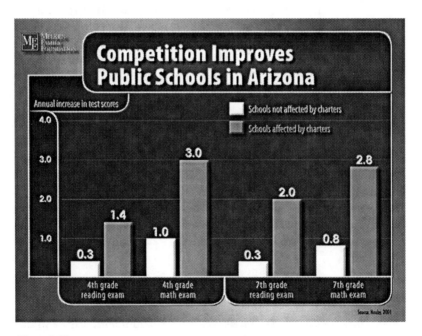

Chart 1.22.

plish your goals as a big city chief? Would it be best for the mayor to have "control" over schools?

Thomas Payzant

I've had five superintendencies in five different states. In four of them I worked for elected boards. When I refer to a school committee in Massachusetts, I mean it's a school board. My experience has been that both can work. It's context-specific. And it is continuity of leadership. When I was in San Diego in the 1980s, there was a five-member board. The entire board membership didn't turn over until I'd been there for about seven years. In addition, one new board member got elected at a time, so there was a group of four that helped acclimate the new board member.

In Boston, there is a mayor who, from day one, has said that he wants his legacy to be the improvement of the Boston public schools. If you look at the budget in Boston, you'll see its public safety and schools are at the top all the time. The mayor likes kids, and he's in schools all the time. We're joined at the hip; I'm on his cabinet.

In Boston at this point, I think it's the only way to go, and I think there are some other examples around the country too. But, if you had a mayor and a superintendent who were on a different page in that kind of system, one or the other or both would leave.

Paul Vallas

My experience has been with corporate boards. In Chicago the entire board was appointed by Mayor Daly. He and his father have been there for four out of the past five decades, so there's continuity. Secondly, in Philadelphia it's a five-person corporate board, two appointed by the mayor and three appointed by the governor. The members all have four- to six-year terms; so, even if it's an elected board, you can have lengthy terms and therefore continuity. There's a good chance that the board members who recruit a superintendent, and have buy-in with that superintendent, are going to be there for a while, and you won't have a sudden changeover and end up with board members without an investment in that superintendent's appointment. That's critically important.

Wherever I've gone, I've always insisted that in my contract I have complete autonomy over the selection of staff in all departments, in all the agencies, so no one interferes or slows me down. Regardless of whether the superintendent is empowered by the state, the school board or contractually, it is critical that they have the personnel control that enables them to build their own system.

Tom's had great success with elected school boards, and I have enjoyed my success with corporate boards. But, if there's been constancy, it's been in the continuity the governing boards' personalities as well as always having great autonomy and ability to recruit and appoint the best people.

Lowell Milken

Let's take questions from the audience.

Audience Question

I want to continue the conversation about what teachers need to be given. Being a teacher in an inner-city school, I've seen what works and what's not working, and I definitely don't think it's salary. It's more an issue of safety. Also, nobody has mentioned anything about outside sociological or cultural factors. I've seen many teachers having a hard time due to not understanding the children they're teaching.

Chaka Fattah

What the research shows is that if you have an effective teacher, if you have a qualified teacher, that nothing else—all the socioeconomic, demographic issues—will impact your educational attainment as much as the teacher will. Further, what it shows is that if you happen to be an African-American or a Hispanic kid in this country, you're the least likely person to experience a qualified, effective teacher at the front of your classroom. That's the only place where race and all this other stuff come in.

Access to a qualified teacher is inhibited by many of the things that we were talking about earlier. It's true that respect is important, working conditions are important, facilities are important, funding is important.

When the *Chicago Sun Times* went out and surveyed schools, they found that if you're an African-American student in the city of Chicago, you are 22 times more likely to have a teacher who failed all 10 or 11 basic skills tests for the Illinois teacher's exam. In Baltimore, when the *Baltimore Sun Times* went out and did a survey school by school, they found that twice as many city teachers were teaching out-of-subject than in those suburban districts.

Paul Vallas

I have a few points to make. First, my approach is to deal with the situation I have. I always feel that if I bring credibility to the system, it helps me. It helps me lobby in Washington for more money; it helps me lobby with the legislature for more money. Do schools need more money? Absolutely. Do mandates need to be fully funded, particularly the special education mandates? Absolutely. But at the end of the day, I can either gripe about it or make excuses, or I can get up and move forward.

Now, I'll talk about the issue of highly qualified teachers. For the last three years in Philadelphia, we've increased the number of recruits by 400 to 500. We're having tremendous success. The key now is to sustain those teachers who are coming in. You can make a qualified teacher a highly effective teacher, and that's where investment in a managed instructional system comes in.

I taught at a military officer's candidate school for about four years. I am not a military guy, but the superior curriculum and instructional models they gave me along with professional development, enabled me to deliver quality instruction. Now granted, I had 100% attendance and everybody was in uniform.

The bottom line is to equip teachers with the proper gear: a superior curriculum and instructional models. Provide teachers with the hours of professional development they need, as well as mentor and teacher coaches working in the schools to provide them with support. If you can't get their class sizes reduced or at least get a teacher's aide or a school support assistant in that classroom to help them, you can increase the amount of their instructional time on task. Thus, teachers who are teaching out of their certification can become highly effective. I think that's something you can do through investment in a quality managed instructional system and through investment and professional development.

Audience Question

I am a teacher who taught in Detroit public schools for 10 years in an inner-city school. I want to thank the Congressman for not being afraid to speak the truth. I don't think that people are hearing what we're saying. I keep hearing that we want to have highly qualified teachers in these inner-city schools. What we want you to understand is we'd all like to make more money, we'd all like to have that professionalism, but that's not why highly qualified teachers are either avoiding or leaving these schools. The fact is, we're put in a situation where we're not given supplies or resources; we're expected to teach to a certain level, and then we are judged with schools that have everything.

Then, when a new reform comes in, basically we're punished because we didn't do what the other schools did. We want you to understand that's the frustration. That's why you don't have qualified teachers in these buildings.

Chaka Fattah

There's been a lot said, especially by some of my conservative colleagues in this town, about how much we spend on education. First, no matter what we spend, ignorance is going to cost this country more. Secondly when Roosevelt was president, we were spending five cents out of every federal dollar on education. Now we're spending one and a half cents of every federal dollar on education. I sit on the Appropriations Committee, where I observed that we spend $400 billion on defense in this country—which is more than the rest of the world combined spends on military defense. The kids applying to be in the military who are failing the military access academic exam are coming out of Detroit, Philadelphia, and Chicago. We have a Cadillac military, in terms of this operation, but we can't fill the ranks, because the kids in these wealthy suburban districts are not signing up. So, we better really start to think. It's not just smart bombs; we need smart children. It's in our national interest.

Audience Question

I have worked at one of the top schools in the nation, and I've also been principal at one of the poorest high schools in the nation. I'm familiar with No Child Left Behind, and as I listen to everything that was said here today, it makes me ask why in No Child Left Behind are we still measuring percentage of kids working at national norms. Should we not be considering something like individual growth? A year's growth for a year's schooling across the board for rich schools, poor schools, everyone.

When the teacher walks into the classroom in September, there's baseline data for what those kids are achieving in both reading and math. Let's wait a year. After they've had the year's instruction, let's come back and see the percentage of kids who have made a year's growth for a year's schooling.

Lowell Milken

Ray, it is argued that No Child Left Behind should be measuring student achievement growth rather than absolute levels. What is your view?

Ray Simon

Number one, the measure of proficiency under No Child Left Behind is not a national norm, it's a state standard. Although we use NAEP as the national exam to make some comparisons, it's not at the heart of No Child Left Behind, in terms of adequate yearly progress.

There is an opportunity for measuring growth currently under No Child Left Behind in something called Safe Harbor. If the children in a particular school or grade level do not make the absolute standard, then there is an opportunity to show growth and to get credit for that. But there are others who want to look at growth in a broader sense, and the Secretary has indicated that growth models would be something we're going to take another look at.

We want to make sure that we still don't lose sight, that every child must be proficient by 2014. We don't want to set a different standard for a poor child or a child whose first language is not English.

Audience Question

I am a fourth-grade teacher from Wyoming, and I am quite fascinated with educational change. I noticed that several times it was mentioned how, over the past 30 years, educational reform has failed. And I would like to share a quotation that I find quite powerful, which I think may be the missing link as to why educational reform is failing. The quotation comes from Michael Fullan: "However noble, sophisticated, or enlightened the proposals for change and improvement might be, they come to nothing if teachers don't adopt them in their own classrooms."

If teachers don't translate them into effective classroom practice, educational change that does not involve and is not supported by the teacher usually will end up as change for the worse or as no change at all. In the end, it is the teacher in his or her classroom who has to interpret and bring about improvement. Leadership that neither understands nor involves the teacher is therefore likely to be leadership that fails. And the reason I say that is because of the accountability movement, which I feel is good for kids and will bring a lot of good.

However, as a teacher, sometimes I feel beaten down by it. I feel that people don't understand how frustrating and difficult it is to face a group of students each day, to help your second-language learners and your diverse students learn. Every teacher wants every child to succeed. The question is how can you support us and help us accomplish this goal?

Professional development needs to be put across in a way where teachers actually learn and can use it in their classrooms. We want to attract highly effective and highly qualified people to the profession. But frankly, highly qualified people have to choose between sitting in a comfortable office and earning $300,000 a year, versus facing 35 hyper kids who cause a lot of stress, so it's obvious why lots of people choose other professions. I feel the key is to find ways to help your existing professionals become better and thereby grow your expertise within your existing school. That's how you will solve the problems.

Lowell Milken

We keep coming back to teacher quality as a key issue for effective school reform. When we focus on teacher quality, we need to consider not only those who entered the teaching profession, but the many highly qualified people who decided not to pursue teaching as a career. In order to entice greater numbers of talented graduates to enter the teaching profession, we need to restructure the teaching profession to offer strong opportunities for career advancement, professional growth and competitive pay.

In developing the Teacher Advancement Program (TAP), we conducted extensive focus groups with Milken Educators, with inner-city teachers, and with teachers who once taught in the inner city but left for the suburbs. What's particularly revealing is that compensation does make a difference. The vast majority told us that there should be greater opportunities for increased compensation for taking on additional roles, such as a mentor or master role.

When we spoke to many outstanding teachers who had left the inner city to go to the suburbs, I asked different groups of educators, "What would it take to get you to move back and teach in the inner city"? The first response was not "money." Instead, the focus was on having a principal with leadership and vision and a "critical mass" of other talented teachers willing to change school culture and practice.

Chaka Fattah

About a year ago, *The Washington Post* had a story about some students from a suburban high school visiting an inner city school, with the inner city kids visiting the suburbs. One school had a full chemistry lab with microscopes and an operating bank that the students ran. It had three gymnasiums and an Olympic-sized pool. It had a library with thousands of volumes of books. Anyway, I won't tell you which school was which. The other school had nothing—no equipment in the science labs or anything like the other school had. So, I'm going to get to the point: when we talk about resources, it's not always teacher's salary.

The shame is that *The Washington Post* story could be about any city and suburban high schools in our entire country. Right now there are adequacy lawsuits in 48 states. Nobody wants to pay any attention to this issue. In Topeka, Kansas, where Brown vs. Board took place, 300% more is being spent in the suburban school district than in the city of Topeka. We're right back at the beginning again. If we really want to do something to have these children move forward, we have to create an equal opportunity for them.

Jennifer Marshall

We have heard this fiscal theme a lot, so I just want to offer another perspective on it. I think we have all agreed that we should provide adequate resources to education. But as much money as we've pumped into the system over the years, we've seen no narrowing of the achievement gap. So something else is going on here, and we've got to figure out what that is. If we take the essence of what you're doing in the Teacher Advancement Program, some of those same theories, and use them not just for teachers, but widen them to the whole education environment, the whole system, then we will start having market-driven concepts come in, just like you have in TAP.

If we have performance-based evaluation results, I think what we will get is something like Tony's answer to an earlier question—a public school system where all public schools are charter schools, where a teacher can be in sync with the leadership at his or her school, and where the school can be in sync with the district.

Take a look at a Michigan charter school's performance (Chart 1.23). Michigan addressed school finance issues at the same time it permitted charter schools to form. Every school on this page is getting more money. The white bars represent schools that are not experiencing the competition of charter schools, while the gray bars represent schools that are. So, what we have here is a win-win situation. Those teachers and students in the charter school are performing better, and we see a rise in the public schools themselves. Carolyn Hoxby, an economist at Harvard, did this research as well.

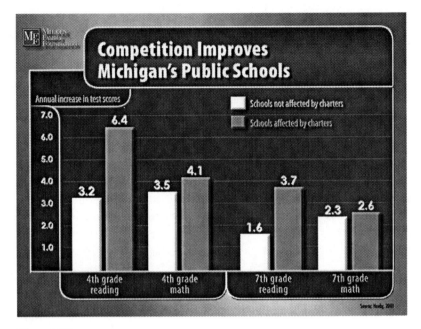

Chart 1.23.

I think it's because we're taking education back to the human scale. We're getting back to the smaller issue of what education is really about, cutting through the system bureaucracy that really makes things sticky in our inner cities today.

Lowell Milken

As we move to a close, are there any final statements our panelists would like to make?

Ray Simon

We just have to do business in a different manner than we've done in the past. Part of the President's agenda is eliminating some 48 programs that we believe have not had a track record of success, and putting that money in No Child Left Behind and further improvements up to the high school level. It's a matter of saving what works and throwing away what doesn't work. My encouragement to the states is support your state departments of education. I admire the state chiefs who are here. They have a real capacity issue to deal with schools and districts and teachers that really want help. Now is not the time to be cutting back on technical assistance for schools.

Thomas Payzant

I think we need to really focus on what we know works: helping teachers create a climate with the support of administrators, and schools that focus everybody on how to support and improve what goes on in every classroom for every child; having the tough conversations about the achievement gap and what we're going to do to work together; and thinking with our supporters and providers about the bigger picture to coordinate policies that affect our kids beyond education. That will make it better for kids and families.

Jennifer Marshall

Thank you very much for the opportunity to be here, to interact with you as master teachers, and the influence you have on the next generation. Much of the credit is due to you for thinking outside the box. In the same way, we in the policy arena have an obligation to think outside the box and to think outside the scope of the federal budget. A dollar spent here in Washington doesn't mean an extra dollar in your classroom or in your paycheck. There are other ways to spend that dollar, and there are other places it can be spent. That's where we need to think creatively. I think there are a number of things for us to learn from TAP and from the strategies that you all have used to become great teachers who can influence policy on a larger scale.

Anthony Amato

Let's push heavily on community full-service schools, where each school is imbued with a passion of having clinics, crisis intervention centers, and all the things that take the challenge off the teacher and put it back into society but are embedded within the school itself. Let's really, really look at this issue of teacher performance, and really start supporting risk-taking. We all know the quickest way to get fired is to be a risk-taker in education. We have to start rewarding severe risk-taking.

Lowell Milken

A special thank you to each of our panelists. Your participation is a powerful statement of your commitment to improve public education. And with the nation's attention now focused on student achievement and the need for high quality teachers, we have the opportunity to make a meaningful difference.

CHAPTER 2

PRESENTATION BY CONGRESSMAN RALPH REGULA

Ralph Regula

Introduction by Michael Milken

It's my pleasure to introduce Congressman Ralph Regula, who has had a distinguished career in public service, one that has spanned more than four decades. One of the most senior members of the U.S. House of Representatives, Mr. Regula is serving as vice-chairman of the Appropriations Committee and is chairman of its subcommittee on Labor, Health, and Human Services and Education. He's also the dean of the Ohio Congressional Delegation.

As subcommittee chairman, Mr. Regula oversees the largest, nondefense spending bill, providing federal funds for education, health and labor programs. He also serves as a member of the Smithsonian Board of Regents, the governing body of the Smithsonian Institution. Prior to his service in the U.S. House of Representatives, Mr. Regula was a teacher and a principal in the public schools, which explains his tremendous knowledge and interest in education and in all of you. He's also been a lawyer in his own private practice, a member of the Ohio Board of Education, a member of the Ohio House, and later, the Ohio Senate.

The Challenges of School Reform: Implementation, Impact, and Sustainability, 43–47
Copyright © 2006 by Information Age Publishing

Congressman Regula was instrumental in helping the Teacher Advancement Program in its initial federal funding, and he continues to be a huge help and strong advocate of the program. I'm continually impressed by his dedication and understanding of the nuances of a wide range of educational issues. Please help me in welcoming one of the strongest supporters of teachers in Congress and a man of great vision, Congressman Ralph Regula.

Congressman Ralph Regula

Well thank you very much. I just met our two Ohio Milken Award winners, who are in the kindergarten field. I started out teaching sixth graders. Then, I was in a school where we had a combined total of four teachers for eight grades. I was the principal, occasionally the bus driver, basketball team coach, and had a combined seventh- and eighth-grade class. During the last three years of my career as a principal, I had a 20-room school. When I had a teacher that was ill, I would try to substitute, so I went through all the grades. I learned how to put galoshes on first graders. And you couldn't give them busy work—you had to teach all day long.

You're precious; I have to tell you. Some of you may think you don't make a difference, but I have two grandsons who are in schools where there are three teachers in each grade. They knew which teacher they wanted; they had that figured out long ago. That's just a little background.

I'm on the Appropriations Committee, and I'm chairman of the committee that funds the Labor Department, the Health and Human Services Department—that's the National Institute of Health (NIH) and Center for Disease Control (CDC). They tell me one of the problems that challenges them is getting skilled researchers. The bottom line is: everything goes full circle back to education.

The Teaching Commission was put together by Lou Gerstner, who retired as president of IBM. He understood how important it was to have people who were educated and could develop their machines. He really had a top notch committee, including former governors, Barbara Bush, and the former secretary of education. A quotation by Lou Gerstner says it all: "If we don't step up to the challenge of finding and supporting the best teachers, we'll undermine everything else we are trying to do to improve our schools. That's a conscious decision that would threaten our economic strength, political fabric, and stability as a nation. It's exactly that clear cut." It's all about the importance of teachers.

Thomas Friedman from *The New York Times* is traveling around the world. He's basically a foreign policy expert, but he said, "I came home one night and said to my wife, 'After having visited many parts of the world, the earth is flat.'" Now what did he mean? He meant that in this age of communication, there are no barriers. He points out in his book, *The World is Flat*, that this year, 100,000 Americans will have their income tax returns done in India. It just so happens that the wife of my district director is a CPA with a pretty big firm, and one of her jobs was to teach Indians how to do the Ohio state tax returns.

Another thing Friedman points out is that one of the major auto companies is designing a new car. They have an engineer in China, an engineer in India, an engineer in the United States, and perhaps some where else; in real time, they're designing the car. Why? Because we can communicate so easily. They can be in all these different places, and yet be putting together a new car.

What really it all boils down to is education, and that's what we ought to make the highest priority in the United States today. In essence he says that if we don't make education our highest priority, then in 15 years, we're going to be behind—because around the rest of the world, the competition is getting tough. China will graduate 40 million college kids this year. I gave a speech back home, saying that I feel like Paul Revere, in that I believe the rest of the world is coming. And they are; they're coming. They've suddenly discovered that education is where it is. That's the sum of what this book says in the final analysis, and I recommend it to you. The world is flat; how true that is.

You're all my heroes and heroines because you are the future. As chairman of the committee, and as I've said to my other committee members, I have three goals. Number one: put a good teacher in every classroom. I would add to that, a good principal and superintendent in every school. Number two: every child should be able to read by the third grade. This leads me to my third goal: lower the drop out rate in the United States. Thirty-two percent of students that start high school do not finish. That's a terrible, terrible waste. In some of the big cities and states, they plan their prospective prison population and how much space they'll need on the dropout rate, because there's a correlation between the two.

I remember I was on the Ohio Crime Commission when one of its speakers did a study years ago and reported 10 years later. He said that by the sixth grade, he could identify which of these kids were going to be successful and which ones were going to be in trouble, which, of course, points out how important education is. The way you deal with the dropout rate is that you've got to teach reading. I say the dropout decision is not made at the ninth grade, it's made at the third grade. If you don't learn to read by then, the inclination when you get to high school is, to heck with it.

We have challenges as a nation, and it's so clear in Tom Friedman's book. I keep coming back around to it—whether it's National Institutes of Health (NIH) that needs researchers to develop new cures or whether it's the Center for Disease Control (CDC) serving as the watchdog to keep the avian flu and all these other esoteric problems out of the United States— they need people with skills. These skills cannot be acquired unless you start out early in the education process. Again, teachers truly are the nation's greatest resource. That's why I am so partial to educators and people involved in the education world. I think that we in Congress need to make every effort to support that. I was sort of flabbergasted when my party had a list of priorities for this year. They included immigration, tax reform, and a whole host of things. Education wasn't even on the list. I said that it has got to be at the top of the list because all the rest of the things start with education.

I think it's great that the Milken Family Foundation recognizes outstanding people. To those of you that are winners, that you take on a responsibility beyond getting the accolades here this week. Others will look to you. You're like the pebble dropped in the pond, and that's true of all teachers. You put the pebble in the pond and it ripples out. One of the things I ask when I speak to Rotary and Kiwanis is "How many had a teacher that made a difference?" Everyone raises their hand. Now if I said five teachers, it's not as likely there would be as many hands.

I can remember so clearly my seventh grade teacher, and I can remember a couple of college professors that made a difference. In fact, I wrote a letter to them about 10 years after I had been out of college, after I got to Congress. I said in the letter that every time I vote, a little bit of my experience in Mount Union College with them goes with me.

I grew up on a farm. As you might expect, out in a rural community, there were 24 in my graduating class from high school. We had 100 in the whole high school. We were deprived and didn't know it, but I didn't know much about social programs at the time. I had this teacher who opened my eyes to the challenges, and to this day, I remember some of those things that he said to me. The other teacher I remember was my speech teacher. I'd never given a speech in my life, and the first time I did she said to the class, "You know, I think he has a little potential." It gives you encouragement. Those two teachers, and of course, a couple of my grade school teachers, made all the difference in the world for me.

Teachers can have such a tremendous influence, and that's why it's so important that we have good teachers in every classroom. That's one of my goals. It's so important that we have good principals and good superintendents because the future of this nation is being shaped in the classrooms of today. We are working towards this goal. We have a math and science programs. Friedman talks about the need for more math and science. Some of the other countries are putting enormous emphasis on math and science. When we write the bill for this year, we're going to put more emphasis on the math and science partnerships. We're going to put more emphasis on the programs to upgrade the quality of teaching. We're going to try as much as we can with the $60 billion, to target and stimulate.

We fund the young people with Teach for America. I love that program. It gets bright, young teachers into classrooms. We've worked with Susan Zelman in the Troops to Teachers program. We have a lot of people discharged at Wright Patterson Air Force Base, and these individuals are retired in their early or middle 40s. Most of them have traveled. They've managed people as corporals or sergeants. Get them to the classroom. We want to get the best possible people in the classrooms, so that my grandchildren don't have to say "I want that one." Instead they can say that any one of the three teachers would be great.

I love all of you because you mean a lot to the future of this nation. And I think the Milken Educator Awards is a great program. I'm sure there are many others that deserve recognition, but you will be role models. You will probably be invited to go and speak to other groups, to be that pebble that goes in that pond and just ripples out and changes the course of human events and the course of this nation in the future.

I thank you for all that you do, and I thank you for what you mean to all of us in the United States today. You know, President Reagan used to say that we're the shining city on the hill, and we are as a nation. This is a wonderful country. This is a country that makes sure that the disabled have access to every building. This is a country that has Individuals with Disabilities Education Act (IDEA). We said every child, whatever their limitations, ought to have a chance, and we want to keep it that way. Thank you for all that you do.

PART II

NO CHILD LEFT BEHIND (NCLB)

CHAPTER 3

PRESENTATION BY MARGARET SPELLINGS, SECRETARY OF EDUCATION, UNITED STATES DEPARTMENT OF EDUCATION

Margaret Spellings

Introduction by Lowell Milken

Reforming American education is an enormous challenge. It has been and it will continue to be. It is a task our speaker today has tackled with great enthusiasm, talent, and success.

Earlier, during our panel on the "Challenges of School Reform: Implementation, Impact and Sustainability," we surveyed the decades of reform that—however well-intentioned—have not met the challenge. These are reforms that have left generations of Americans with inadequate education and opportunities, reforms that have perpetuated a system that has left all too many children behind.

Education is the primary concern of the Milken Family Foundation. Systemic reform to assure that every child is afforded a high-quality edu-

The Challenges of School Reform: Implementation, Impact, and Sustainability, 51–57
Copyright © 2006 by Information Age Publishing
51

cational experience is our goal. Programs with exponential impact are our means. The first is the one that brings us together today—an awards program that focuses on excellence in the teaching profession and makes recognition of excellence a means to elevating the profession in the minds of teachers, students, parents, and communities.

The second—the Teacher Advancement Program (TAP)—also focuses on the crucial role that effective educators play, but does so by restructuring the profession to attract far greater numbers of talented people to teaching and then to create an environment—by means of powerful opportunities for career advancement, professional growth, and competitive compensation—so that this talent will stay in education.

But reforming American education, to repeat, remains a great challenge. To succeed requires fundamental and, yes, difficult-to-achieve change. It therefore requires responsible officials of particular vision and courage.

The individual we're about to hear from is a key architect of what I believe to be the most visionary and courageous federal education reform in the last half century. No Child Left Behind (NCLB), which passed with overwhelming bipartisan support three years ago, is the first education reform to focus the nation's attention on achievement with consequences and to require that every child be prepared by a highly qualified teacher. That these goals should require federal legislation is indicative of the magnitude of the challenge before us.

Until NCLB, of course, the debate had focused on access. Access is essential. Access is laudable. But what good is access if 60% of Black and 56% of Hispanic fourth-graders in our nation can't read? What's the point of access if, after 30 years of intensive reform efforts, the achievement gap between rich and poor, suburban and inner city, and among ethnic groups is as wide as ever? As Secretary of Education Margaret Spellings recently observed: "Returning to the pre-NCLB days of fuzzy accountability and hiding children in averages will do nothing." Later in this book, we will be discussing NCLB, and I predict that you will hear that even at this early stage of implementation, promising results are being achieved.

United States Secretary of Education Margaret Spellings brings a diverse capital of experience to her latest position. As assistant to the president for domestic policy in President Bush's first term, she had responsibility for development and implementation of health, labor, transportation, justice, and housing policies—as well as those in education. Before coming to Washington, as then-Governor Bush's senior advisor on education policy, Ms. Spellings' achievements included the Texas Reading Initiative and the Student Success Initiative to eliminate social promotion.

Her most inspiring achievement, though, is likely one she has just attained: she is the first mother of school-age youngsters to serve in the top national education position. Ladies and gentlemen, a true friend of every child and every parent, too—United States Secretary of Education Margaret Spellings.

Margaret Spellings

Thank you. I want to thank Lowell Milken for that kind introduction. He's been a real friend to America's schools. We're all thankful for your commitment to improving education.

One magazine called the Milken Educator Awards the "Oscars of Teaching." The only difference is the speeches here are a bit shorter. As I look around the room though, I do feel the urge to start thanking a lot of people, and I haven't even won anything!

I want to thank all the chief state school officers here today. We've seen a lot of each other lately, and that's a good sign because we must work together to achieve the promise of No Child Left Behind. It's also great to see Michael Milken. Thank you for all your generosity.

Finally, and most importantly, let me thank the teachers and principals here today. There's no harder job in the world than being a teacher. And as you well know, there's no more rewarding job either.

I know you didn't choose this profession to win accolades. You didn't choose it to make the cover of magazines. You chose it because you wanted to help children and serve your communities. In truth, I know most of you didn't choose this path at all. It chose you. As President Bush likes to say, teaching is a calling. And I want to thank you all for answering that call.

That's why these awards are so important. They give us a chance to say thank you and to reward you for your hard work. That's something we don't do often enough for teachers in this country. And it's something we must change if we want to realize the promise of No Child Left Behind.

Looking around this room, I see a hundred reasons to honor teachers. Take the example of Chris McAuliffe from Oxbow Community School in White Lake, Michigan. When Chris first came to Oxbow, only around 20% of the school's fifth-graders were passing Michigan's statewide science assessments. Last year, over 90% of Chris's students passed. Chris's secret is combining science and math with technology and art. This year, he and his students studied simple machines and circuits by making a miniature amusement park out of old VCRs. Good for them—I barely can program my own VCR!

One of Chris's newest students is an 11-year-old boy named Mahir from Iraq. When Mahir arrived in Chris's classroom last December, he spoke no English, and he had only known a world of violence. Just five months later, Mahir can read English well enough to write all of his assignments down in his daily planner, and he's holding his own in math.

As the father of three children, Chris also goes out of his way to keep parents involved in the classroom. That's something I can appreciate as a mother. And by the way, in his spare time (don't ask me how he finds any!), he works the night shift at the local fire department. After the September 11 attacks, he went to New York City to help. Chris, thank you for your service to your students and your country, particularly in its time of greatest need. You're an inspiration.

And you're in good company today. You all have inspiring stories to share. When someone says a child can't learn, you see a child who only needs a chance. Where many people see an impossible challenge, you see opportunity and hope.

It's the same spirit that led President Bush and representatives from both sides of the political aisle to pass the No Child Left Behind Act three years ago. The law says that all children have the potential to achieve high standards in school. And it says we must measure student progress each year to make sure they all do.

In the years before No Child Left Behind, the performance of minority, low-income, and special-needs students would get lost in meaningless averages. We allowed the performance of the top students to overshadow the struggles of those at the bottom of the pack. No Child Left Behind forced us to confront this achievement gap and to do something about it. The law holds schools accountable for making progress among all groups of students.

And that starts with annually assessing every student and breaking down the results by student groups. We don't insist on annual assessments because we like to test students. We do it because we know this data provides teachers and principals with a valuable tool. It shows you which students need extra help and where. As the saying goes, "What gets measured gets done." When we assess every student, we make sure every child counts. And as a result, test scores are rising, and the stubborn achievement gap is starting to close.

No society has ever made such a commitment, and to most people, it was a revolutionary idea. But to the outstanding teachers here today, it was nothing new. You have brought that same attitude to work every day of your professional lives. And as a nation, we're learning what you have always known: every child can learn.

Studies show that nothing helps a child learn as much as a great teacher. That's why No Child Left Behind says that by 2006, every classroom must have a highly qualified teacher. The president's new budget includes almost $3 billion to help states meet this goal.

Unfortunately, the schools that could most benefit from highly qualified teachers often have the hardest time attracting them. Our high-poverty schools face a real teaching crisis. To fill vacancies, they often must resort to emergency and temporary hires. Recent data shows that students in high-poverty secondary schools are far more likely to have teachers not certified in the subjects they teach.

And we have a system that doesn't give the teachers who want to help these students the support they deserve. While most professions reward those willing to take on the hardest assignments, the public school system often does the opposite. Teachers with the skill and desire to close the achievement gap find themselves drawn away from the schools that need the most help. Many school systems even offer *de facto* incentives for teachers to leave these schools.

It makes no sense, but that's the way the system has worked for decades. The results are devastating. Students often don't receive the best instruction possible. The achievement gap claims new victims, and many of the most energetic teachers find their dedication and talents underused. That's not fair to our students. And it's not fair to our teachers.

We must treat our teachers like the professionals they are. That means we must reward teachers who make real progress closing the achievement gap in the most challenging classrooms. That's why the president has proposed a new $500 million Teacher Incentive Fund. This fund will provide states with money to reward teachers who take the toughest jobs and achieve real results.

According to a study by the bipartisan Teaching Commission, 76% of Americans and 77% of public school teachers support extra financial rewards for teachers willing to work in high-poverty schools. It's simple economics. When you have excess demand for a highly skilled position, you need to raise salaries to meet that demand. That's the way every business in America staffs its workforce. Why shouldn't we do the same for teachers?

The Teacher Incentive Fund will help align the way we reward teachers with the goals of No Child Left Behind. If we expect results for every child, we must support teachers who are getting the job done in America's toughest classrooms. There are a lot of different ideas for how these incentive systems could work. And we'll give each state the flexibility to design its own system for rewarding teachers. We recognize these decisions are best left to states and districts.

We'll also reserve some of this money to help states and districts develop new performance-based teacher compensation systems. Right now, most districts use pay models based on credentials and seniority: the longer you work, the more money you make. We want to help states develop pay models that reward not just experience but also results and hard work in challenging environments.

Across the country, states and districts have already started using these new systems with great success. For example, in 1999, Denver public schools worked with the local teachers union to develop a four-year pilot program for performance-based pay. Under the program, teachers received bonuses for meeting different classroom goals.

A study of the Denver program found that when teachers set high objectives, students responded with higher test scores. In other words, when you challenge low expectations, you can achieve big results. The program was so successful that Denver voters are now considering making it permanent.

The Milken Family Foundation has also been on the forefront of this issue. They recognized that teachers face a horrible choice between advancing their careers and staying in challenging classrooms. No teacher should have to face this dilemma.

Their Teacher Advancement Program, or TAP, has given over 2,000 teachers in nine states a new path to follow. TAP lets teachers move up a career ladder while staying in their classrooms. Each year, teachers have the opportunity to improve their skills and take on more responsibilities such as mentoring younger teachers. The program also rewards teachers who make a real difference in the classroom by improving student performance.

Of course, teachers aren't the only ones benefiting. In Arizona and South Carolina, student achievement in TAP schools outpaced achievement in similar schools two-thirds of the time. The message is clear: when we treat teachers better, students perform better.

We want to encourage more states and districts to make these reforms. I know Governor Tim Pawlenty of Minnesota is working to give teachers in his state the compensation and respect they deserve, and the Teacher Incentive Fund will support similar efforts across the country.

As we work to make the teaching career more attractive, we also must tear down the barriers that have kept many of the best and brightest out of our nation's classrooms. The Teaching Commission estimates that over the next decade, our nation's public schools will need to hire around two million new teachers.

The president's budget includes almost $100 million to help schools meet this demand, including $40 million for a new Adjunct Teacher Corps Initiative. This money would help bring talented professionals from other walks of life to high school classrooms. These nontraditional teachers can bring valuable real-world experience to subjects, like math and science. Imagine a NASA scientist teaching high school physics.

We're also working with the Department of Defense to support the Troops-to-Teachers program. The program has helped thousands of soldiers find jobs as teachers in high-poverty schools. These teachers bring a special can-do attitude to our neediest schools.

Now let me close with an old story about a famous soldier who left quite a mark on my hometown of Houston, Texas. During his life, Sam Houston served as the president of the Republic of Texas, as a U.S. senator, and as a Texas governor. But looking back upon his life, he remarked that his experience as a teacher in Maryville, Tennessee stood out above the rest. Houston told a friend, "I experienced a higher feeling of dignity and self-satisfaction than from any office or honor which I have since held."

The president and I believe every teacher should go to work with this same feeling of dignity and accomplishment. You are true professionals, and you deserve credit for the good work you do.

We knew when we passed No Child Left Behind that the hard work of closing the achievement gap would fall on your shoulders. We also knew that you wouldn't want it any other way. You never give up on a child. It's the same hope that drew you to teaching in the first place. And it's the same spirit that will lead us to the promise of No Child Left Behind. Thank you.

CHAPTER 4

MEETING THE REQUIREMENTS OF NO CHILD LEFT BEHIND

Lewis C. Solmon, Antonia Cortese, David P. Driscoll, Nina Shokaraii Rees, and Andrew Rotherham

Lewis Solmon

The panel today will discuss No Child Left Behind (NCLB): where we are with the law, what's happened so far, and what we think will happen in the future. You've already heard about many of the issues surrounding No Child Left Behind; Lowell's panel earlier talked about reforms that work and the prospects for No Child Left Behind. I'm going to present a couple of charts. Some of these are going to be repetitive, but as all you teachers know, it's good to go over yesterday's work to start the next day.

Chart 4.1 shows that we're teaching kids, but most of them are not learning very well. Sixty-nine percent of fourth-graders and 68% of eighth-graders are not proficient in reading. Not only are the general levels of proficiency low, but when we look at the proficiency levels of the kids eligible for free and reduced lunch vs. not eligible for free and reduced lunch, there's a huge difference. However, even those kids *not* eligible for free and reduced lunch scores are nothing to write home about

The Challenges of School Reform: Implementation, Impact, and Sustainability, 59–89
Copyright © 2006 by Information Age Publishing

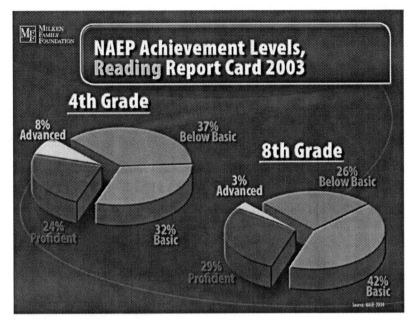

Chart 4.1.

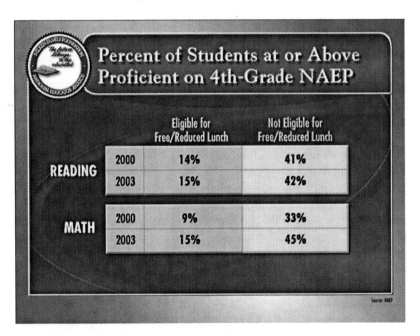

Chart 4.2.

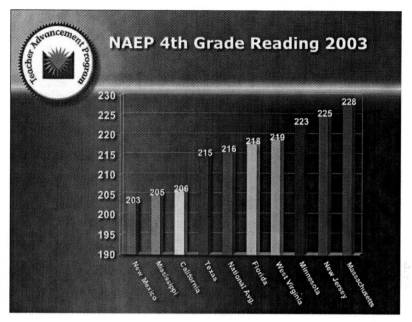

NAEP 4th Grade Reading 2003

Chart 4.3.

(Chart 4.2). The fact that less than 15% are proficient in fourth-grade reading is terrible. Now you've seen a lot of other gaps in achievement, but I developed a new kind of gap. I call it an interstate gap. These are the scores on 2003 fourth-grade National Assessment of Educational Progress (NAEP) reading by select states (Chart 4.3). I wanted to show this because one of our panelists is the commissioner in Massachusetts, and as you can see, Massachusetts' score is 228 compared to some of the other states.

Ten points on the NAEP score is a year's growth, so if you look at New Mexico's score of 203 versus Massachusetts' 228, that's about a two-and-a-half-years difference in fourth-grade reading between those two states. (Chart 4.4) shows the achievement results for Latino students, and you can see that the national average in eighth-grade math is 276. You can also see the difference in states: Texas has a score of 267, and California scored 250. So again, this signifies two-and-a-half-years difference between eighth-grade students in math in California and the national average. Additionally, we have gaps not only by race, but also by income. We also have them regionally.

We have a great group of panelists to discuss how in the past, present, and future, No Child Left Behind has helped or will help alleviate some

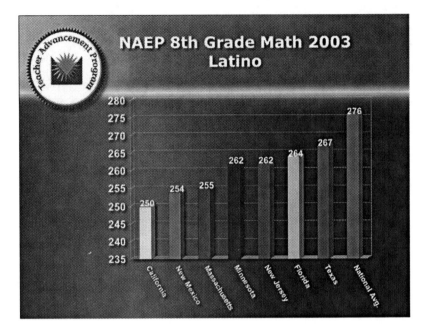

Chart 4.4.

of the problems that I've presented. What will it take to make No Child Left Behind effective?

I will introduce the panel, and each of them will briefly comment on the state of No Child Left Behind today. These comments will include what its effects have been, what needs to be done next, and what each panelist's experiences with No Child Left Behind have been. Then I'll ask some questions, and finally we'll open it up to audience questions.

Our first panelist is David Driscoll, the 22nd commissioner of education for the Commonwealth of Massachusetts. David has overseen the implementation of the Massachusetts Comprehensive Assessment System (MCAS), which is the school and district accountability system. He has also overseen the Educator Certification Test, Special Education Reform, and the historic High School Graduation Requirements instituted in 2003. Already nationally at the forefront of education reform under David's leadership, Massachusetts was named one of the first five states in the country to have its No Child Left Behind accountability plan approved by the federal government. Currently, Dave is the president of the Council of Chief State School Officers.

He'll be followed by Andy Rotherham, who's director of the 21st Century Schools Project at the Progressive Policy Institute and editor of the education blog, www.eduwonk.com. During the Clinton Administration, he served at the White House as special assistant to the president for domestic policy and led the White House Domestic Policy Council's education team. He recently was appointed by Governor Mark Warner to the Virginia State Board of Education, and he's working on his doctorate in political science at the University of Virginia.

Toni Cortese is the executive vice president of the American Federation of Teachers (AFT). She served as an officer of the New York State United Teachers, which represents more than 500,000 people in New York's public schools, colleges, universities, and health facilities. Toni began her education career as a fourth-grade teacher and school social worker. Among her many professional activities, she serves as an appointee of the U.S. Department of Education to the National Assessment Governing Board. She's also served on the New York State Education Department's Task Force on closing the performance gap.

Finally, making her first appearance since coming back to work after having her baby is Nina Rees. Nina is assistant deputy secretary for innovation and improvement in the Office of Innovation and Improvement. Nina oversees the administration of approximately 25 competitive grant programs, working with the office of elementary and secondary education. She also coordinates implementation of public school choice and supplemental service provisions of No Child Left Behind. Prior to joining the U.S. Department of Education, Nina was one of four aides to Vice President Cheney, advising him on domestic policy issues. Before that she served as an education advisor to the Bush Campaign, helping draft the No Child Left Behind blueprint for the Bush-Cheney transition team. From 1997 to 2001, Nina served as chief education analyst for the Heritage Foundation.

We will start with each panelist commenting on where they think No Child Left Behind is, what they think will happen next, and what their experience with NCLB has been. We will start with David Driscoll.

David Driscoll

In many ways, Massachusetts is the "poster state" for No Child Left Behind. We had started our system of accountability and reform back in 1993 with a very comprehensive law. We had looked around the country at various systems of accountability for schools and districts. We had the graduation requirement, and, as Lew said, we implemented it beginning with the class of 2003. To those that predicted the world was going to end, it didn't. Instead we've been administering it ever since.

Looking at school and district accountability, we liked the Texas system. In fact, we had a representative named Susan Sclafani, who was an assistant superintendent in Dallas, who later to went with her superintendent to the U.S. Department of Education, and she explained the Texas system, which was basically looking at disaggregating data and then meeting goals over time. We established our own Annual Yearly Progress (AYP) system before No Child Left Behind. It was a little different. It went out to 2020, and I'll spare you the details. When No Child Left Behind came along, the only thing we needed to do was to add grades. Additionally, because we tested only in grades four, six, and eight; we had to add grades three, five, seven, and so forth. So for us, it wasn't anything new.

In fact, most of our schools are still focused on the MCAS and our own accountability system, rather than what No Child Left Behind has brought. This is because that's been driving the system for awhile. So let me just show you what's happening in Massachusetts (Chart 4.5). We have drawn a straight line. In some of the states, I call the pattern a field hockey stick: they start out small and then go up. Instead, we drew a straight line of improvement. I call it the "Great Hypotenuse in the Sky." If you're below the line, you haven't made adequate yearly progress. If you're at or above the line, you have. The two dots show where we are. You can see that in both mathematics and in English, we have made AYP as a state in the aggregate. This is great because we have among the highest standards in the country.

My local people like to say we're the highest in the country. Because they like to complain, they ask, "Why don't you set lower standards so we can easily make AYP?" I think it's supposed to be about getting kids to proficient, but I'll leave that argument aside. There are many other states that have equally high standards. Our standards are geared to NAEP. As you can see, our scores so far are good, in the aggregate.

We also have this thing called a Composite Perfromance Index (CPI), which is a proficiency index. You get points if you move kids along. If you go from a low basic to a high basic, we actually give points for that. You obviously get a lot of points for getting kids to proficient, so we call that a CPI. The interesting thing is that every single subgroup has made progress. Every number in the CPI change is positive, which means there's been growth. You'll see in the case of limited English proficient, special education, and free-lunch kids—even though they've made a lot of progress in English, language arts, and mathematics—they have not made AYP as subgroups.

So, that's our system. We think, "so far, so good."

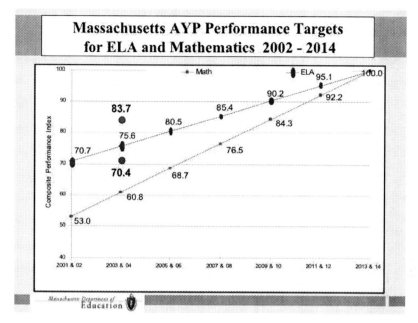

Chart 4.5.

Andrew Rotherham

I am a state board member from Virginia. I want to briefly talk about No Child Left Behind in general terms, to frame some of the backdrop for what you're reading about—and particularly if you happen to read *The New York Times*. In terms of the overall punch line, NCLB is a work in progress. I think it's enormously premature for people to ask the question of whether it is working or not.

When large-scale federal policy shifts like this occur, you often don't know if they're working for a decade, or in some cases, a generation. If you think back to federal education policies like the original Elementary and Secondary Education Act (ESEA) in 1965, for example, you wouldn't have wanted to decide whether we were going to keep it or not, based on what was happening in 1968 or 1972. In fact, Mike Kirst, who's now at Stanford (but was previously a federal official) makes the point that it really took two reauthorizations of the original ESEA to even start working out the kinks and getting it to work smoothly. If you take a look at the Individuals with Disabilities Education Act (IDEA) we're now a generation later and still ironing out a lot of problems in IDEA. However, I think very few people would say that IDEA hasn't been an enormously important step forward for children with special needs.

In terms of where we're going to be in the next generation with No Child Left Behind, it's probably going to be in a similar scenario. We're still going to be dealing with headaches, working out kinks, and so forth. But at the same time, people will say that for minority children, this was a really important step.

Because it's a work in progress, I think there are a lot of kinks that need to be worked out. Some of them were actually foreseen by the drafters and the crafters of No Child Left Behind. They were keenly aware that this was a law with a long time-horizon and that it was going to be modified multiple times. Some problems, as with any federal policy, were unintended, unforeseen, and that's just the nature of policymaking.

In the public debate, No Child Left Behind should not be the only federal law that is held up and expected to be perfect from its inception. They all take changes. The politics of this shouldn't really surprise anyone. I think too often that we look at education politics as though they are somehow unique from the politics we see around other issues, but they're really not. You have to look at the education issue through the exact same analytic framework that you'd want to look at any other issue.

What I mean by that is that education reforms are generally what you would call a "general interest" reform. If they're good overall, we all benefit. If we address some of the achievement gap issues that Lew was showing earlier, we all benefit as a society. There are all sorts of very positive externalities in doing that. However, to do so, there are going to be specific costs. Let me give you a micro example of this. If a school district wants to build a new school, there are going to be costs to local property taxpayers, so you're going to get antitax groups who are upset. You may want to implement a new reading program, so you're going to possibly have to raise taxes. You're going to get the same kind of resistance. Likewise, a charter school opens and it takes some students away from the local school. All of these things may or may not be in the "general interest," but even assuming they are, there's no doubt that selected constituencies bear the costs as a result.

That's exactly the case with No Child Left Behind, and it's complicated by the fact that some constituencies are well organized. They know how to access the political process. They know how to access the media process. They're going to make themselves heard. The intended beneficiaries of this law—particularly low income and minority kids—are not well organized. They don't know how to access the political process. You don't hear from them, so it's front page news when the National Education Association (NEA) is suing the federal government.

These politics aren't unexpected; I don't think they're anomalies. If you look across issue areas, every decade in Washington we reform the tax code. Then every following decade, we reform it again because it has gotten cluttered. That's because it's in the general interest to have a simplified tax code, but special interests want their little thing in the code. It's the same reason we can't deal with agriculture subsidies. Some are a drain on all of our pocketbooks, but there are people who are very interested in keeping them. The politics of education are no different. Interest-group politics are interest-group politics, regardless of whether you're talking about sugar subsidies, Angora sheep or school kids.

Now in terms of where I think we're going, I think "No Child Left Behind II" is going to have to include some repairs. There obviously are some technical problems that need to be addressed. I think we're going to have to do a lot more on the supply side of this law.

Whether you want to talk about getting better equalization of where high quality teachers are teaching or more options for kids, it costs money. We've got the demand side; we're starting to get it right. But schools need a lot of help with the supply side, and that includes instruction. We need to incorporate into more public sector activities the kinds of things the Milken Family Foundation is doing. I think that's the direction we're ultimately going to go with "No Child Left Behind II."

We'll talk about the high schools, but the focus is much more on getting the K-8 policy right, before running off and expanding it into high schools.

Lewis Solmon

I had written something some time ago, called the *Lags in Effect of Education Policy* (Chart 4.6). In economics, which is my discipline, macroeconomists often studied the question: when you increase the money supply, how long will it take to actually make the economy boom again?

They talked about lags. What I did is thought out what the lags are in education reform. This speaks to Andy's point that it's too early to decide whether NCLB is effective. First of all, you've got to recognize a problem, then you've got to decide on what policy is needed to address it. Next, you have to legislate it, write the regulations, and appropriate funds. Then somebody's going to litigate, and then it's going to take some time to implement it. Some people are not going to like it, so you have a buy-in time. Then there's a learning lag, and then it'll take some time for the reform to make an impact.

And then you have to measure it and collect data. You have to report that data, and if you don't like the results of the data, you interpret the

Chart 4.6.

data differently. Ultimately, if none of that is to your liking, you criticize the methodology of the study. By that time, there's another reauthorization.

So, I agree that it does take time. One of the questions that we'll talk about later is the difference between the short and long term.

We will now hear a representative from the teachers' union whom I don't think is suing the federal government at this time.

Antonia Cortese

No, we're not suing the federal government. I guess that when you're third in line, people get to steal some of your lines. So, if you saw me using my pen, I've been crossing out some things that have already been said. I do want to underscore the fact that this is the 40th anniversary of the Elementary and Secondary Education Act (ESEA). When ESEA was passed, it wasn't without its kinks and problems and things that had to be worked out. When you pass legislation, that's one thing, but when you're working to achieve the goals of it, you sometimes run into problems.

With the complexity of NCLB, it would probably win a prize for being the thickest piece of legislation ever developed, so it's going to take some time to get it right. My remarks are really in the context of what do we do to get it right and how. Our experience is that there are some fundamentals that really need to be changed, not just some things around the edges.

One thing that's become extremely clear to us is that, under NCLB, we have schools that are performing poorly, and we have students that are significantly behind academically. The evidence that has come out has made this absolutely clear. We are faced with a greater challenge for working with schools that are at the bottom versus schools that are missing AYP by just a little.

We need to look at how we're going to accelerate the learning for the poorest performing students because, as we know, even if the kids at the lower level are learning at the same rate as the kids who are in the schools that are doing better, they're never going to catch up. There's always going to be that gap. Regardless of the progress of the poorest achieving students, they will always be behind. That's extremely important to keep in mind.

One of the biggest problems that we see (and this is something that would have to be corrected in the law) is inadequate yearly progress. First of all, closing the gap requires extraordinary progress, as I just mentioned. Bear in mind, this means schools that are the poorest, have the least resources and parental involvement, and the worst school buildings and the worst working conditions, are the ones that have to be accountable for accelerating the learning of their students.

If we're ever going to meet the goal of 100% proficiency by 2014, and I think 100% proficiency on any test is debatable—something has to change so that there isn't just progress there's also acceleration. The second thing is that despite the "P" in "AYP" the formula does not actually measure the progress of students over time. It certainly does not give credit to those schools that have been doing very poorly yet make considerable progress over time. So, if you don't meet some arbitrary standard, you haven't made progress. I think AYP fails to recognize real progress. I think there was a song about how there are 50 ways to leave your lover. Well, there's only one way to achieve AYP. However, if you come from a school where you have a great deal of diversity, a great deal of poverty, and a very large school, there are at least 50 ways to make sure that you get on a list indicating your school is in need of improvement.

That creates a particular vulnerability for those schools. It is more based on statistical grounds than on common-sense educational grounds. We think AYP ought to be overhauled into a system that sets progress goals and makes them attainable. It should be a system that produces accurate accountability decisions, without excluding certain groups of students, and maintains reporting on student achievement by subgroup, without giving schools dozens of ways to be declared failures.

The use of tests and other assessment measures that are valid, reliable, and actually aligned with state standards and the curriculum has been overlooked. I also think that it is extremely important to create assessments and accountability, for our English language learners (ELL) and for our special education students, that are fair and address students' specific needs.

The second topic I wanted to touch on very quickly is the whole issue of Supplemental Educational Services (SES). There's no research base that says this is going to be effective in helping our students. I also want to ask a practical question: why is it so important to have highly qualified teachers between the hours of 9:00 a.m. and 3:30 p.m., and use research-based programs between the hours of 9:00 a.m. and 3:30 p.m. and have strong accountability measures between the hours of 9:00 a.m. and 3:30 p.m., and yet we have supplemental educational providers who do not have to use certified teachers and who have questionable research bases for their programs? Even those states that try to keep track of SES providers find it very difficult to know if they're actually teaching to the state standards. I think we've got an unfair set of accountability measures working here.

I want to sum up by saying that I've pointed out a lot of negatives, but I think that our agenda should really be to have those schools that are serving our poor students, the students who are furthest behind, become beacons of excellence within the public school system. I think that what those schools need are the resources of smaller class sizes and more adults in the classroom. They need a safe learning environment; I'd even go so far as to say, a pleasant learning environment. They need to have the materials necessary and the highly qualified teachers so that some day those students who have the least will have the most to work with. Thank you.

Nina Rees

Thank you very much for having me. I also want to take this moment to congratulate all of the teachers who were recipients of the Milken Educator Awards. I've been to this event now for three years, and I think this is probably one of the greatest and most fun events that an educational organization has put together. So I hope you've enjoyed your stay in Washington.

Since Lew mentioned the fact that I just had a baby, I want to make an analogy to NCLB as a medicine. If NCLB were a drug that was administered to a patient, I would say that after three years and some odd months, this patient is actually in a pretty good shape. You're going to have certain parts of her body aching. You have some states that are complaining about the law. But overall, when you talk with the school chiefs around the country, they are definitely in sync with the spirit of the law. If you look at how they're implementing the law, by and large, they're all meeting the letter of the law. There are going to be some glitches along the way, but we feel that NCLB is on the right track.

As Andy mentioned, the fact that the National Education Association and other organizations are unhappy with this law is not a surprise. In fact, if they were not complaining, we would worry that the law was not really an effective law.

Think back to the reauthorization of ESEA in 1994. Many of the pieces in NCLB were actually put in place first in the 1988 reauthorization then in the 1994 reauthorization. Unfortunately, what happened eventually was that those laws were not as rigorously implemented. We feel that one of the reasons we're hearing some noise is because we are taking the job of implementing the law seriously, and states are responding positively.

Building on what the secretary of education mentioned in her speech at Mt. Vernon, we recognize that after three years we need to go back and reevaluate the law, and in some cases we should be open to offering some flexibility to those states that are making the needed progress toward closing the achievement gap. She has opened the door for some negotiations, and we think this is going to get states even more focused on the goal of closing the achievement gap. What she has outlined, basically, is that you need to be able to show that you are closing the achievement gap. You must have a testing system—a method to measure adequate yearly progress by student outcomes, and so forth. But the rest of the components of the law are things that she's willing to discuss with the states, to see whether there are ways for us to meet halfway. Again, we are meeting the goals, while at the same time, being flexible. So, that's something that I think everyone should look forward to and be open to talking with the secretary about.

One of the ideas she also mentioned in her hearing before Congress was that she really wanted to reduce the number of horror stories or the unintended consequences of the law. So again, we have a new sheriff in town, and she's open to discussing the details of how this law is being implemented. We all look forward to working with states on the details of what this flexibility entails, so long as the goal is to close the achievement gap.

In terms of the challenges that we face, I'm going to focus a little bit more on the innovation aspect of NCLB. Because I manage the Office of Innovation and Improvement, I figured that would be an appropriate place for me to focus. I think it's important for us to work very closely with school officials, teachers, and principals to make sure they are not compromising the innovations that they are bringing to their schools and classrooms in an effort to focus only on testing and closing the gap. They should focus on testing, but at the same time, they need to make sure their schools are involving students and all the other aspects of life that turns them into productive adults one day.

So, the goal is to maintain the innovative components of an education system, while at the same time, trying to reach AYP. In terms of the consequences that are supposed to kick in as the timetable progresses, it's extremely important for us to take those consequences seriously, but also to recognize a few issues at the same time.

First, in the area of public school choice, we have noticed that some districts have capacity challenges. The reason we wanted to be serious about public school choice, and why our regulation actually has a component that prohibits districts from using capacity as an excuse not to offer public school choice, was to get the states to pay more attention to the districts' need to create more schools. However, as long as we haven't helped the states in the process of creating a climate conducive to building new schools and finding innovative ways of reforming schools that may not be performing well, this component of the law will not be implemented very well.

The other component of NCLB, which is not talked about that much but that we should focus on a little bit more, is what happens after public school choice and supplemental services occur. Eventually the law requires districts to restructure schools that have failed AYP for five years. These efforts are actually matters we don't know that much about. Therefore, I think the key thing to focus on and scrutinize is any effort to build a new school or to turn an existing school that's not doing well into a new school. The last thing you want is an effort whereby an old school is simply labeled as a new school. School doors open, everyone's excited that they have a new school, but the school is actually not that different from the previous one.

In the immediate future, you're going to see some excitement. Parents are going to feel that they have a brand-new school they can send their children to, but you definitely want to make sure the school is one that is able to close the gap. That's going to be a really challenging task ahead of us—one that all of us should focus on—because we don't know that much about how to overhaul a school that's not performing well.

Last, if you look at the studies that have been done on accountability and efforts that have put consequences in place when a school has failed to make adequate yearly progress, one of the glaring things we have noticed is that once the job gets politically difficult, most of the efforts also fall by the wayside. Again, it's very important for us to keep the momentum and not just look at the consequences as ways to raise student achievement. We think it's important for the students to be doing well academically, thanks to those consequences. But more importantly, we need to be focused on efforts that states and districts should be putting in place in order to avoid the consequences. Those are the efforts that I think policymakers and everyone should be thinking about as they look into the future about the implementation of No Child Left Behind.

Lewis Solmon

The order in the law is public school choice, supplemental services, and then restructuring. The question I am constantly asked is: "Why didn't they put the supplemental services before choice?" In other words, wouldn't it be better to tutor kids to get them up to speed and, if that doesn't work, let them move, rather than telling them to move?

Nina Rees

When the bill was being drafted, people at the table felt that when you implement public school choice, you're keeping funding within the school districts. So they felt this would be less of a sanction compared to supplemental services, which entails potentially offering the money to private providers.

But again, in practice, because of the experience that a lot of school districts have had with the 21st century after-school programs, I think they've been used to contracting out these services. We are noticing a lot of interest in switching the order of supplemental services with public school choice. However, there are some districts that are ahead of the curve in implementing public school choice, and Milwaukee is one of them. When you talk to them, they prefer having public school choice before supplemental services.

Lewis Solmon

Because they have choice already.

Nina Rees

Exactly.

Andrew Rotherham

Lew, I want to add something. I think Toni makes some very good points about supplemental services. I agree with some of them, and some I don't agree with. I actually have a more fundamental problem with supplemental services, though. I think it's a function of a problematic part of the law, and the reason is that the law is intended to get our house in order so we can deliver much more powerful instruction to many more children than we do now.

Part of that battle was a long-fought battle on Title I, to move away from Title I programs that pulled kids out, and these programs often weren't aligned to the mainstream curriculum and so forth. I really worry with supplemental services, that as a matter of delivering powerful instruction in coherent, instructional programs, we're now moving right back towards pull-out programs that may or may not be aligned with what's happening elsewhere in the curriculum.

Obviously, there are things states and schools can do to guard against that, but there are only 168 hours in the week. We need to focus our efforts. I worry that we've opened up a whole can of worms here that we may well regret down the road.

Antonia Cortese

It's also an issue of resources, because you have to set aside 20% of your funds in order to finance both the choice and the supplemental educational services. There was a study done in Fairfax County, Virginia that said most of the SES were actually being delivered to the higher achieving students in those schools identified as "in need of improvement." That's a little disturbing because you're not really hitting your target audience. I know that some SES providers give free tickets to sporting events, iPods, or other things, so that kids attend after school. I guess it goes back to what Andy said: perhaps that's not the most effective way. If there could be other intervention programs offered during the regular school day, using small groups of kids and extra teachers, that might be a much more effective and proven way of getting kids up to proficiency.

David Driscoll

I think we have to go back to the context. This is a law that passed with overwhelming support on both sides of the aisle. I think we have to recognize that most people in Congress haven't read the law and don't really know what's in it. Instead, they have relied on a key group of legislators on both sides and the administration to really hammer out the details. But don't kid yourself, it had overwhelming support across the board because of frustration.

Congress was looking at billions and billions of dollars being spent particularly through Title I, yet not seeing any results. I think we have to keep that in mind. When we get into the various provisions, you're going to see some of the provisions hammered out by some parts of leadership in Congress. You had Ted Kennedy on the one hand and John Boehner on the other, so you're going to see some philosophical differences here.

Supplemental services and choice are based on the idea that we do not want to trap a child in a school that is not getting results and that is really failing its kids. Therefore, there is the answer of giving them a choice; let them go to another school that's doing better. Then, if the school is not getting the job done, maybe there's somebody else who can do the job better.

Now, you can argue with that. I think there are a lot of flaws with the implementation of supplemental services and, by the way, that's the state's fault. It's our job to implement that. It's our job to see to it that those providers are getting results. In our case, many of our districts such as Boston are providing those services. They do very well, but I think we need to remember the context.

This is where it gets simplistic; people get frustrated and say, "Well it's not working, so we've got to do this and we've got to do that." I think they're simplistic answers. In a lot of cases, supplemental services aren't going to solve the problem, either. But it's a way to at least provide competition. And in some instances where the supplemental service providers have done a great job, it's helping kids who aren't being helped during the regular school day.

Lewis Solmon

Nina?

Nina Rees

I think the Commissioner answered the question better than I would. Do you want me to just go after some of the criticisms, Lew?

Lewis Solmon

If you want.

Nina Rees

We have done a lot of work in my office on supplemental services, particularly in trying to make sure we're offering as much technical assistance as possible to states and school districts on this particular topic. We gave a grant to the American Institutes for Research to conduct a series of workshops with state education agencies, to help them take the job of monitoring and evaluating supplemental service programs a little bit more seriously and to really use this as an opportunity to inject some real reform at the district level.

In terms of some of the criticisms, you're going to have a few glitches on the road. This is probably one of the most innovative aspects of NCLB. We firmly believe that nine times out of 10, when you empower the parents with the option of picking something for their child, they're going to make a better decision than someone who doesn't know their children.

Some parents, however are not going to be that engaged. We have to be cognizant of that. That's why we've placed the real emphasis on having the school districts work closely with local and community-based organizations, so that parents are making educated choices about the program they're enrolling their children in. The number of students benefiting from supplemental services has doubled from the 2002-2003 school year to the 2003-2004 school year.

We feel there is a healthy climate at the state level to monitor this program more carefully. We also think that there are a lot of district officials who are doing a fantastic job of offering services and incorporating the spirit of SES into their programs.

Antonia Cortese

One of the difficulties I hear about from teachers is that they're not getting feedback from the supplemental educational service providers. It raises the questions: Well if you're not getting feedback, then how do you know the student is making progress? And what should you be working on while the student is in your classroom? Quite frankly, I think that still begs the larger question: What do we know now that could be effective in raising student achievement? I want to go back to things that we've talked about for 20 years, which is early childhood education. It makes a lifelong difference for students. Studies have followed people in their 20s and 30s and where they ended up. It's proven effective. That seems to me to be research-based. That ought to be the place where we put our money.

The second is that I heard a presentation yesterday by Dr. Joe Torgeson, who serves as the director of the Florida Center for Reading Research, about what he was doing at the Center. I think it is great. The frustration you feel is—why can't what he's doing be universal? What that calls for is an adult-to-student ratio that provides more time and explicit instruction.

We need to be able to find some way to disseminate that information and have a school organizational structure that can accommodate that kind of intervention for our students, so that we don't worry that, once they're up in high school, they can't read. I really think we need to concentrate on what we know works.

Lewis Solmon

It seems to me that No Child Left Behind is a goal: have people making progress each year. It doesn't preclude doing Reading First or having smaller classes. I mean, we talk about No Child Left Behind or the alternatives. Are Reading First or smaller classes alternatives? I don't think they are.

Antonia Cortese

No. I think it's the emphasis. I think it's the resources.

Lewis Solmon

David?

David Driscoll

I think the complaint is legitimate and rests at the state level. It is our responsibility to oversee supplemental services. If the school district has a provider, and the district isn't getting any feedback, then yell at your chief. The district should have a system to see to it that they get feedback. Clearly, we're going to get to the more comprehensive issues, but No Child Left Behind gets blamed for everything.

Lewis Solmon

Right. That's my point.

David Driscoll

By the way, No Child Left Behind brought us Reading First. However, I do agree with Andy; it's a little early. The first phenomenon that's pretty amazing is that all 50 states submitted accountability plans that were approved by the United States Department of Education (USDOE). That's the first time. I never thought 50 states could agree on anything, so the fact that they submitted plans and got them approved under the requirements is pretty remarkable. Now we'll see what happens when they have to actually implement them.

One of the pre-NCLB weaknesses was the fact that states didn't know what was happening in other states. The new sheriff is taking care of that. The plans are all posted, and we're talking to each other. So, lo and behold, now everybody knows that Massachusetts has a growth model. I didn't know it was so unique. In our plan, we take care of this issue of schools and/or districts that are way below the line. As Toni said, they have to make huge progress.

In our system, if you are a school or a district way below the big hypotenuse, but made enough progress over a two-year period—such that if you kept going, you would hit the big hypotenuse in the sky—then we say that you have made adequate yearly progress. To me, that's progress, and we take you off all the sanctions and labels.

The USDOE finally came to an agreement with us that they would accept our model under the safe harbor provision, as long as there were some confidence levels. So there's an example, and I think the secretary wants to include that kind of flexibility. We're not going to see any legislative changes to No Child Left Behind. Of course, it's going to reauthorize in 2007 anyway. But in the meantime, I think the thing that states need to do is work with each other and figure out how to make it work.

The secretary has indicated that she's already made some adjustments for special education kids. She's also talking about English language learner (ELL) kids and growth models. I think there's a great opportunity now to get some flexibility and at least to make the law work pretty well. We can argue about the results and so forth, but we have 50 plans that have been approved. It's pretty remarkable.

Lewis Solmon

You mentioned flexibility. Let's go to that for a minute. A lot of people are saying isn't it great? But then there are some people, like Chairman Boehner and George Miller, who issued a statement saying that flexibility is good but don't be too flexible. Don't be so flexible that you give up the fundamental principles of the law. I think other people are saying that the flexibility is a smoke screen and there's really been no change. Andy, what do you think? Is flexibility good, bad, real, or unreal?

Andrew Rotherham

In terms of the department-specific approach to this effort, it remains to be seen. I think one of the biggest problems that they've had is that their communication with states has been dreadful. There are a lot of state officials around the country, superintendents, and deputy superintendents in a number of states who are just outraged at the way they've been treated.

If you scratch beneath the surface at some of the problems—for example, in Connecticut—some of it has to do with exactly this. It's less about the substance of some of these requests, and I think people would be OK if certain requests got turned down. The department cannot change the law. People would often be OK if it were done in a faster manner with more explanation.

I think that some of these problems are in process. In terms of the flexibility in particular, they actually have it kind of backwards. In general, I'm with Boehner and Miller on this; you have to be very careful here; otherwise, we start creating all kinds of loopholes that kids fall through. For example, in a lot of communities, the 1% rule on alternate assessments for disabled students was too low. They needed a higher cap. There was a waiver process, though, because this is a locality-by-locality, state-by-state process. People didn't know how to use or access the waiver process because of a lack of information. Now they've gone to a cap, which is 3%. This will work in some communities, but it won't work in others. In some communities, it's going to be too high, and special needs kids, who should have access to the mainstream curriculum and so forth, are going to fall through those cracks; in others, the cap will be too low.

In going back to the politics of this, I really think it's a tragedy that, as we talk about this, the child with Down's Syndrome gets trotted out. That child is not the average child in special education. Over half the children in special education are there because of learning disabilities. A lot of those students shouldn't be there in the first place. It's not so much a learning disability as an instructional one, in terms of reading instruction. I wish they would show more flexibility around provisions like that, and I'm worried that we've opened the back door to whittle away some of these issues.

I want to say very clearly that the American Federation of Teachers (AFT) has been a great actor on this, so it is unfortunate that they get lumped in with a broad brush. They have tried to be thoughtful about alternative accountability systems and so forth, and they deserve credit for that. However, I worry that while we talk about kids in education and how much kids matter, as soon as we start talking about accountability, we immediately slip into a discussion of schools. The law is not called No *School* Left Behind. Sure, schools have greater challenges under this law. However, the children in those schools didn't elect to go there, and they don't deserve to have any less attention paid to them under an accountability system than do the kids who go to more homogeneous schools.

There are going to be sharp edges. There are always going to be. However, it depends on where you sit. In a country where we lose half of our African American and Hispanic kids before they finish high school, or they're trailing four grade levels behind by the time they finish high school, we simply cannot afford to have any unit of analysis other than kids. That's why the accountability system is so important.

Lewis Solmon

Do you feel a little like you're damned if you do and damned if you don't? Last year, people were accusing you of being too rigid. Now, you're too flexible.

Nina Rees

Well, all I have to say is that we should give the new secretary and the agency some time. She just made the announcement two weeks ago, and what she basically said is, "I'm open to discussions. If your program or what you have in place at the state level seems to be working, and if you have the data to prove that you're closing the gap, I'm willing to listen to your cause for more flexibility dealing with certain components of No Child Left Behind." I think we just have to give her a chance to see how this plays out.

As for Andy, you wrote a paper a few years ago calling for this kind of flexibility in allowing states to have more freedom to do different types of things, so long as they're closing the achievement gap. It's good for people, watchdogs, and members of Congress to keep us honest, but at the same time, I think we need a little bit of time to figure out how we hope to administer this flexibility, what types of things we are going to accept, and which things we won't.

Lewis Solmon

I have put up this as a chart (Chart 4.7) because some of the staff worked so hard to find this data. What this shows is the percent of schools that made AYP by state, and some of the states at the top in 2004. I don't think anybody's actually looked collectively at this data. Previously we just got them from the state reports.

States like Kansas, North Dakota , Wisconsin, and Wyoming are all over 90%. In the bottom we have, Alabama, DC, Florida, Hawaii, and South Carolina. To me, it appears there are a lot of schools making AYP.

The Northwest Regional Educational Laboratory just released a study from which *The New York Times* took particular findings, and not others. They said that achievement has gone up, but the rate of increase in achievement is declining. It's sort of the second derivative for a calculus teacher. What that's saying is that if the growth and test scores went up by 20% last year, and this year it only went up 15%, then that's a decline in

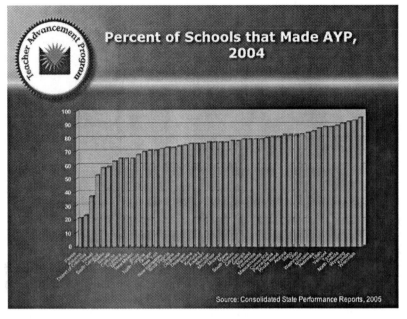

Chart 4.7.

the rate of growth. They also said that if the change in achievement of this magnitude so far continues, it won't bring schools close to the requirement of 100% proficiency by 2014. Is that a concern? This is the whole realistic versus unrealistic issue. Is it a concern that we've set the standards so high that we're just never going to do it? Is it something we can do? David, you're doing well now. Do you think you're going to be OK in 2014?

David Driscoll

I think people like to jump out to 2014, particularly those people who don't like the law. It's sort of its illogical consequence that 100% of kids are going to be at proficient. They say, "Now look, we're not going to get this, so let's forget it." I think the hunt is worth it, so I think the idea of it was to start where we are and try to move forward. I think that's, in essence, the system. Again, it's not just conservative Republicans. It's Ted Kennedy and others who buy into the system. They do feel there should be more resources, and there are a lot of other issues. The basic system relies on taking us where we are and moving to get as many kids as we can to proficient. I don't know if we can, but we ought to go for it and try it, and we're seeing some movement.

This whole idea of allowing states to decide their own systems so that some states set higher standards than others is seen as a weakness. But I think that's a strength, because some people are starting at different places. Eventually it will be noted that they're way below NAEP. However, the system is supposed to force people to look at themselves and say, "We are where we are, and that's not good."

Look at high-stakes tests. In my own state, 68% passed the first time they took the test. This past year, 83% passed the first time. Well over 90% of the kids are passing the test, and our drop-out rate has not gone up, despite what everybody says. It's stayed about the same. So it's a question of whether you can engineer the system externally. I think it's way too early to say the answer is no. I think we ought to go for it.

Andrew Rotherham

I agree completely. This is a question that really bears on people in this room; what Lew's chart doesn't show is that this year, to make AYP in 28 states, only 50% of students had to be at grade level. As a profession—and this is really my concern with the NEA strategy—we need to be really careful about planting our flag right now in 2005 and saying that is unfair, it's impossible, or that we can't do it. I think that in the long run, it's destructive to building and sustaining support for public schools.

Antonia Cortese

Also, I think that chart might change when the number of schools comes out in August because the target is constantly moving. It may be sufficient enough, and it may be with some hard work you can get a student here. But then, with little vocabulary and comprehension skills, it's going to be harder to lift it even further.

But that's not an impossible problem. There are lots of instructional strategies out there and programs that can be used to help students do that. But it means a certain intensity that has to happen in those schools. It's not just business as usual.

Nina Rees

Making these predictions on what's going to happen in our schools is like predicting the weather 10 years down the road. There are so many things that are going to happen between now and then that I don't know how you can make a good prediction. I also think they didn't take into account the consequences that are supposed to kick in, such as restructuring and what kind of affect those consequences are going to have on the well-being of our schools. I'm not quite sure that I would buy their prediction.

Lewis Solmon

I would like to have a one-word answer on the next question, and then we'll move on. Should we extend No Child Left Behind to the high school now?

David Driscoll

Not now. That's two words.

Andrew Rotherham

No.

Antonia Cortese

No.

Nina Rees

Of course, yes. I mean, it's a natural progression. We feel that if kids are not graduating, capable to go on to college or get a job, then you haven't really accomplished anything.

Lewis Solmon

OK, let's open this up to audience questions.

Audience Question

I'm a teacher from North Carolina. My question is twofold because my first question has to do with when we offer up the choice to parents to take their children elsewhere. I understand the premise behind that, but inherently my understanding, at least being in the trenches of No Child Left Behind, was for quality instruction. What I begin to think about when we look at choices and offering the choice to go to other schools, at least in my state, is that even if students leave, you still have teachers who were not enabling students to learn and to meet the qualifications. Regardless of pointing fingers or not, those teachers don't disappear. They take those kids to other schools, while those teachers still have jobs. Is there something built into No Child Left Behind that I'm not aware of?

Secondly, what I see happening is that if you take your child to a school with low performing teachers, and there aren't enough children for them to stay at this school, guess what? They get moved somewhere else. Their abilities that were hindering learning before are now transferred to another location, where again they're impacting children, but just in a different setting. My question really is, at this point: without having accountability built in at the teacher level, won't the problem really spread more?

David Driscoll

Well, again, I think this plays out all the way along the line. Remember, if nothing else, this law came out of some frustration. So, there are these simplistic things which say, "Hey look, if you're trapped in a school," and I think we would all feel this way if it were our children, "you have the right to move them." Now, does that solve all the problems you're talking about? No. It at least says, "Hey look, system, we're not going to trap kids." Now that doesn't get to all of the issues that may be occurring in that school that's underperforming. It's not meant to solve all of the problems of the world. It's meant to be simplistic and say, "Look, we're going to move because they're failing, and the issues you talk about are much more complex."

Lewis Solmon

Anybody else want to talk about that?

Antonia Cortese

Well, I've heard this complaint many times. Let's remember that all tenure represents is a due- process procedure, which is really embodied in our constitution. This means that one gets to hear the charges against them and to represent them. It is not a job for life. Having said that, I think there are also other responsibilities that schools must take on—and maybe this is a good benefit of NCLB—that there should be a lot of professional development going on in schools.

You should be able to work it out with your testing company, to be able to get the test scores early enough for teachers to sit down and analyze the data, and see what needs to be done. To me, that's a different level of accountability for teachers than ever existed before. Now, when you begin to look at that data, and if a particular educator isn't participating in doing that, then maybe you've got some grounds to move on.

I think the important thing is to focus on the positive. What can we do in the system to focus on the instruction of students and keep a narrow focus? What tools do teachers need to be able to address the needs of the students? I think that's a much more productive way to go.

Andrew Rotherham

You ask a terrific question. We don't do a very good job of hiring in education. We are not a talent-sensitive profession right now. Like any other walk of life, the very best dismissal policy is a sensitive hiring process that you deal with on the front end. The second is culture. I think there are some problems; some of the due processes create a deterrent effect. However, the larger issue is not the differences between states' procedures. The larger issue is that we are a profession that tolerates mediocrity. We move people around rather than deal with low performers. We are not a profession that likes to fire people. We have to create a culture that does not tolerate mediocrity. That's something that's going to have to come from within the schools, not from within the state house.

Lewis Solmon

One of the things that we found is that these processes are very transparent. When you actually see that teachers are associated with kids not making progress, you don't need the protection of tenure to keep people there, because they're going to leave when the light is shined on them.

Andrew Rotherham

That's culture.

Audience Question

Hi, I'm a teacher from Idaho. One of my concerns was what Toni talked about. If AYP does not give credit to those who make gains but are still below proficiency, we have a problem. My children graph their fluency and their math CBMs, which is a curriculum-based measure on math computation, and look at their growth. I have a little boy who came into my class reading about 45 words a minute. Now he's reading about 95 words a minute. He is so excited. He has gotten the extra services he's needed, but he still does not meet state standards of reading fluency. Therefore, he got a two and not a three.

He came to me in tears, saying, "What am I doing wrong?" I said. "You're not doing anything wrong. Look at all that growth." But he does not feel the success and celebration because he is not "meeting the standards by the state." Therefore, I am not a good teacher because I don't have my child to a three. It's very frustrating because you're not looking at the individual child. I just want to know how we can address that in No Child Left Behind so that we look at the growth. That's really important.

Nina Rees

There's nothing in No Child Left Behind which prohibits a state from having this kind of growth model in addition to the benchmark set under No Child Left Behind. I think perhaps looking at what Massachusetts has done may be one way for your state to deal with this issue.

Lewis Solmon

The superintendent of Georgia.

Kathy Cox

Just to quote a local superintendent in Georgia about NCLB, he said that this law's allowing him to do for children that which local politics had never allowed him to do before. Clearly, our state embraces this law and what is happening because of it. However, there are two train wrecks: One is special education, which I think the administration is trying to address (but I'd like to hear the superintendent from Massachusetts and some of the others). The other train wreck is unsafe school choice.

I see inflexibility on the part of the people looking at how states are implementing that law. It's one thing, as a parent, to get a letter that says my school is not making adequate yearly progress or one that says the teacher is not highly qualified. It's quite another thing to get a letter that says my school is persistently dangerous.

This inflexibility is a huge train wreck. That's a death sentence for a school. It seems to me that the administration's out there, trying to find a scapegoat for not making AYP and point a finger at states and schools if we don't find one. I see that as a major, unintended consequence of this law; we're going to have principals turn their head to discipline issues because it's a disincentive to report and to do something about it.

David Driscoll

I couldn't agree more Kathy, but it's part of a law that should be talked about a lot more than supplemental services, which I agree is the state's responsibility to make sure those people are getting results. Again, the theory is that you shine a light on them. As you know, anything can happen in any school, but there are schools that seem to suspend students at a minute's notice. These schools do not have good discipline or good rules and regulations.

If you look at any of the major incidents, it's not just one kid. For example, if you look at Columbine, there were so many tell-tale signs there, over a period of months, that adults should have picked up. I think that's the spirit of the law. I hope that the USDOE will spend some time talking about how this is going to be implemented in a good way.

Otherwise, it becomes game playing. By making us report schools where there have been knives, excessive fighting, or whatever, you're shining a light on an area that we need to pay a lot of attention to. Bullying is a big problem that we deal with in our schools. We're asking teachers to help these kids move academically, and they're being bullied on the way to school. It's pretty hard for a kid to learn if they've been bullied on the way to school. So I think it's a huge issue we need to pay attention to.

Andrew Rotherham

I think it's a silly provision. The reason I say that is not only because it's unworkable and ridiculous, but also because parents should be able to choose from among public schools, period, not only if their school happens to be dangerous or not doing well. This is a principle. Parents should be able to choose from among various public schools.

If we, as a profession, continue to resist that sort of public school choice and continue to sort of fight to maintain basically what's the last legal monopoly, I don't think we're going to like where we end up. We're going to lose our public in the next 10 or 15 years.

Antonia Cortese

Well, certainly, dangerous schools are unacceptable. I do think that defining what is persistently dangerous is important. I guess my background comes from New York, which is the upper tier of danger. The thing that I worry about is that schools also need to concentrate on creating a culture that makes them serious places for serious learning. There are a whole lot of behaviors other than carrying knives that get in the way of learning. I think that school districts ought to be looking at their codes of conduct and their consequences, and not just leaving that until somebody carries a rifle or a knife into school.

Lewis Solmon

Notifying parents about the condition of a particular school is merely an attempt at keeping them informed. I think, by and large, most parents know if a school is not safe. This is just an attempt at notifying other parents who may want to move into a district and are making a selection about whether there are some schools within their neighborhood that are safe, or not. Now, where the states are doing a great job of implementing this piece of the law is questionable, but I think it's another data point that we need to have in order to offer parents more information.

We can go on for another hour, but we have reached our session's ending. Let's thank our panelists.

PANEL CONTRIBUTIONS

CHAPTER 5

NCLB

Its Problem, Its Promise

Antonia Cortese

Editor's Note: Submitted for reprint by Antonia Cortese, executive vice president of the American Federation of Teachers (AFT).

The AFT has long championed the principles underlying the No Child Left Behind Act (NCLB), the reauthorized Elementary and Secondary Education Act: high standards for all children, with appropriate tests to measure whether the standards are being met; disaggregation of student achievement data; "highly qualified" teachers and well trained paraprofessionals in every classroom; and, extra support for students and schools performing below proficient levels.

Title I, the cornerstone of NCLB, represents the federal government's commitment to raising the achievement of students in high-poverty schools . NCLB was passed in 2001 with broad bipartisan support, largely

The Challenges of School Reform: Implementation, Impact, and Sustainability, 93–104
Copyright © 2006 by Information Age Publishing
All rights of reproduction in any form reserved.

based upon the administration's promise of significant increases in funding. But President Bush has reneged on that promise, and experience has shown that the goals of NCLB cannot be met without changes in the law, proper implementation and the necessary funding.

Threats to NCLB's Promise

While the AFT is committed to the core goals of NCLB, there are serious flaws in the law and its implementation that must be fixed. The AFT is committed to assuring that NCLB is amended and appropriately funded to accomplish them. Problems include:

- The adequate yearly progress (AYP) formula does not give schools sufficient credit for improvements in student achievement. Its implementation does not allow schools to present valid and reliable evidence of student progress and the mandated interventions for schools not making AYP are not based on scientific research and are sometimes punitive rather than constructive;
- The highly qualified teacher requirements, as currently implemented, are unworkable for some teachers and do not apply to all individuals who teach public school students;
- Paraprofessionals are not being provided with the range of options necessary to demonstrate that they are qualified nor the financial support necessary to meet the requirements;
- The public school choice provision is designed in a way that can undermine schools rather than improve student achievement; and
- Supplemental educational service providers (other than school districts) are permitted to discriminate by ignoring the nondiscrimination provisions of the law.

This policy brief discusses these problems and suggests legislative and/or regulatory remedies.

Accountability, Adequate Yearly Progress, Assessments

Adequate Yearly Progress

With each additional analysis of how the AYP formula is working in states across the country, it is increasingly clear that expert predictions about the unintended and arbitrary consequences of AYP were accurate.

AYP, despite the word "progress" in its title, does not give appropriate credit for progress (see AFT paper, "Eight Misconceptions about AYP").

The issue is not that many schools and districts are failing to make AYP; ineffective schools should be identified. The problem is that many of these so-called failing schools and districts are being identified more for statistical than educational reasons, and more because their students were starting further behind than for the lack of progress their schools and districts are making with them. Indeed, as the Council of Chief State School Officers' State Collaborative on Assessment and Students Standards noted ("Making Valid and Reliable Decisions in Determining Adequate Yearly Progress," Dec. 2002), being faithful to the AYP formula means being forced to break substantial faith with the law's mandate that states define AYP in a valid and reliable manner.

Recommendation

While recent accommodations in rules regarding assessment of limited English proficient (LEP) students and students with disabilities (SWDS) will relieve some of the egregious difficulties with implementation of the current law, the conceptual flaws in the AYP formula cannot be fixed without changes in the law. New formulations must be developed that allow states to use measurements that are valid and reliable and that permit schools and districts to demonstrate the progress they are making with their students.

Assessment of Students with Disabilities

Although the U.S. Department of Education has revised its Title I regulations pertaining to the assessment of SWDS, the regulations are still problematic for two reasons. First, the revised regulations require that, except for the 1% of students with the most severe cognitive disabilities, the scores of students taking an alternate assessment must be measured against grade-level standards. This policy means that students who are performing well below grade level, but who do not fall into the 1%, will almost certainly be rated as not proficient. These are students who may be improving, but the regular assessment, even with accommodations, does not accurately measure their academic progress. Typically, the Individualized Education Program (IEP) team recommends that such students, often referred to as "gap students," take an out-of-level assessment because it is considered to be a better, more accurate, and more humane way to measure the progress of these children toward meeting grade-level standards. The way the revised Title I regulations are written, out-of-level tests, for AYP purposes, will only count for the significantly cognitively disabled, not the "gap" students. Districts and schools are left with no sound options for appropriate assessment of these students for AYP purposes.

Second, the revised Title I regulations allow states and districts to include in the calculation of AYP the proficient scores of students with severe cognitive disabilities who take alternate assessments measured against alternate standards, only if they don't exceed 1% of all students in the grades tested. Proficient scores that exceed the 1% cap may not be included in AYP calculations. Setting a cap on the scores that may be counted is extremely arbitrary. Preliminary evidence suggests that the cap may be particularly unfair for urban districts, which tend to educate more students with significant disabilities.

Recommendation

Amend NCLB so that the IEP team is responsible for determining how SWDS are assessed. This change would conform to assessment requirements under the Individuals with Disabilities Education Act (IDEA). IEP team members work directly with the student and therefore are best able to determine the manner in which the student should participate in state assessments. If the IEP team recommends an out-of-level assessment, that assessment should count for AYP participation and proficiency purposes. States should be required, as they are under IDEA, to establish clear eligibility criteria for IEP teams to use in determining how students with disabilities participate in state assessments, including alternate and out-of-level assessments. Districts should be required to train IEP team members in how to apply the criteria.

Assessment of Limited English Proficient (LEP) Students

The law requires states to offer academic assessments to LEP students in their native language "to the extent practicable," but many states have failed to do so. Furthermore, due to the way AYP has been calculated, most LEP students would never be proficient because these students are often removed from the LEP subgroup once they master English. While the U.S. Department of Education has recently offered new policies that offer some flexibility in this area—allowing states to exempt students who are new to this country from some testing during their first year of enrollment and allowing states to include students who have attained English proficiency in the LEP subgroup for up to two years—more needs to be done.

Recommendation

Require states to develop native language and linguistically modified tests and to provide guidelines for school districts on appropriate accommodations for LEP students so that their academic performance is accurately measured. In addition, permit states, for the calculation of AYP, to not count the scores of LEP students on content area tests who have less than three years of instruction in English and to include students who have attained English proficiency in the subgroup calculation for three years.

Teacher Quality

Options for Veteran Teachers To Demonstrate That They Are "Highly Qualified"

The law indicates that veteran teachers may demonstrate their qualifications by means other than a test, that is, by meeting a "high, objective uniform state standard of evaluation" (HOUSSE). The U.S. Department of Education's most recent guidance, however, suggests that states are not required to offer this option. Some states have not yet developed the HOUSSE, which will make it more difficult for teachers to meet the requirement to be highly qualified by the deadline in the law.

Recommendation

Clarify that states are required to develop the HOUSSE in order to ensure that veteran teachers have an option other than a test for demonstrating their qualifications. Provide veteran teachers with an extension to the law's deadline for becoming highly qualified in states that have delayed defining the HOUSSE. Teachers should have three years from the time the HOUSSE option is made available to meet the highly qualified requirement.

Definition of "Highly Qualified" Special Education, Bilingual, and Vocational Education Teachers

The requirements that special education teachers must meet to be considered highly qualified in subject areas are unworkable. Under current interpretations by the U.S. Department of Education, special education teachers who are fully certified in their field are also required to meet separate subject-matter requirements for each core academic subject they teach. This requirement is simply unrealistic, particularly in the case of those who teach multiple subjects in self-contained classrooms. The unreasonable burden placed on special education teachers is likely to exacerbate the shortage of teachers in this field.

A teacher who is fully certified as a special education teacher by the state should be considered highly qualified under NCLB. Fully certified special education teachers have a solid base of understanding in the content areas of math, reading, English/language arts, science, social studies, and the arts. They command a core body of knowledge in the disciplines and draw on that knowledge to design and deliver instruction, facilitate student learning, and assess student progress. Such teachers also draw on their specialized knowledge of specific disabilities and the instructional issues such disabilities pose in order to set meaningful goals for their students and appropriately instruct them in the core subject areas.

The situation is similar for bilingual education teachers. Teachers of LEP students who are certified in bilingual education or similar areas (English as a Second Language or English for Speakers of Other Languages, for example) should be considered highly qualified under NCLB. In addition to meeting the requirements of the core curriculum in education, teachers that obtain bilingual certification and licensure have completed a specialized course of study in language acquisition, culture, and pedagogy specifically designed to address the various instructional needs of linguistically and culturally diverse students. The qualifications include demonstrable proficiency in linguistic skills and core subject content, as well as an ability to teach in cross-cultural settings.

Vocational education teachers who are fully certified should also be considered highly qualified. Fully certified vocational education teachers command a core body of knowledge about the world of work in general and the skills and processes that cut across industries, industry-specific knowledge, and a base of general academic knowledge. Such teachers foster experiential, conceptual, and performance-based student learning of career and technical subject matter, and are able to integrate them with academic disciplines.Vocational education teachers also develop student career decision-making and employability skills by creating opportunities for students to gain understanding of workplace cultures and expectations.

Recommendation

Amend the law to permit special education, bilingual, and vocational education teachers who are fully certified by their state to be considered highly qualified.

Definition of "Highly Qualified" Middle School Teachers

In previous guidance the U.S. Department of Education said that middle school generalist exams could not be used to meet the subject-area requirements of the highly qualified definition. This policy is unfair to veteran middle school teachers who have already demonstrated their competence in subject areas by passing the generalist test that was offered when they received their license. More recent guidance has modified the U.S. Department of Education's position somewhat, but does not adequately clarify the issue.

Recommendation
Amend NCLB to state that veteran middle school teachers who passed state-approved middle school generalist exams when they received their license shall be considered "highly qualified."

Qualifications for Charter School Teachers

Under NCLB, teachers in charter schools are not required to meet all the requirements of the highly qualified definition. Specifically, they are not required to be certified if the state's charter school law does not require certification of charter school teachers. Charter schools are public schools, and their teachers should be required to meet the same standards as other public school teachers. Students in charter schools deserve to be taught by fully certified teachers.

Recommendation
Require teachers in all schools that receive federal funds to meet all the requirements of the highly qualified teacher definition.

Qualifications for Teachers in Supplemental Services and Extended Learning Time Programs

NCLB and the Title I regulations do not require supplemental service providers to employ highly qualified teachers, and the regulations go so far as to prohibit states from requiring that they do so. The U.S. Department of Education also has said that third-party contractors and teachers in extended learning time programs are not required to adhere to the highly qualified provisions in the law. The requirement that public school districts ensure that every classroom has a highly qualified teacher is a core component of the law's goal to guarantee that every child receive a high-quality education. The U.S. Department of Education sends a contradictory message by prohibiting states from requiring providers of supplemental services to hire only highly qualified teachers, and indicating third-party contractors and extended learning time programs need not employ highly qualified teachers. Excusing these providers from having to hire highly qualified teachers will undermine the quality of the services provided to students participating in these programs.

Recommendation

Require supplemental service providers, third-party contractors, and extended learning time programs to employ highly qualified teachers.

Paraprofessionals

Paraprofessional Qualifications

The law provides three options for paraprofessionals to demonstrate that they meet the requirements of NCLB with respect to their qualifications: (1) completing two years of study at an institution of higher education; (2) obtaining an associate's degree; or (3) meeting a rigorous standard of quality and demonstrating, through a formal state or local academic assessment, knowledge of, and the ability to assist in the instruction of reading, writing, and mathematics (or reading, writing, and mathematics readiness). Unfortunately, many states and local school districts have not yet provided paraprofessionals access to the third option required under the law. This delay will make it difficult for paraprofessionals to demonstrate their qualifications by the deadline specified in the law and could force dedicated, experienced paraprofessionals out of classrooms where they are needed most.

Recommendation

Clarify that states and districts must provide paraprofessionals with all three options outlined in the law for demonstrating their qualifications, including the option for an assessment. Provide paraprofessionals with an extension to the law's deadline for meeting the new standards in states and districts that have delayed developing or approving the required assessment. Paraprofessionals should have three years from the time the assessment option is made available to them to meet the requirements.

Funding to Assist Paraprofessionals to Meet the New Requirements

NCLB allows LEAs to use Title I funds to assist paraprofessionals to meet the new NCLB requirements. However, many states are not providing the needed financial assistance to help paraprofessionals who cannot afford to meet the new requirements without financial support.

Recommendation

Require states and districts to fund the costs of any education, training/professional development, or assessments required of paraprofessionals to meet the NCLB requirements.

School Improvement, Public School Choice, and Supplemental Services

Funding for Public School Choice and Supplemental Services

Under the law, districts are required to set aside an amount equal to as much as 20% of their Title I funds to pay for choice-related transportation and supplemental services. Requiring schools to use scarce Title I funds to support public school choice and supplemental services funnels already limited classroom resources toward often unproven interventions. Districts should not be required to divert scarce Title I funds from classrooms to finance these programs. States, districts, and schools must be able to use all available Title I funds for research-based interventions—such as early intervention, intensive professional development, and/or reduced class size—that have proven effective in improving student achievement.

Recommendation

Permit districts to propose to the state that they be allowed to use a different, research-based intervention for schools in school improvement instead of choice or supplemental services. Provide a separate authorization of funding for choice and supplemental services and other research-based interventions.

Public School Choice—Capacity

The regulations do not adequately address capacity problems in the choice program while requiring districts to offer more than one choice of school to transferring students. School capacity must be a factor if public school choice is to be successful for the students it was intended to benefit.

Recommendation

Amend the law to make clear that overcrowded schools with class sizes that surpass state averages should not be required to accept additional students under the public school choice regulations. Codify the U.S. Department of Education's guidance that districts may provide public school choice by creating schools—within-schools. Indicate that districts may offer transferring students the choice of one or more schools.

Public School Choice—Desegregation Plans

The U.S. Department of Education's regulations indicate that if a desegregation plan interferes with a district's ability to offer school choice, the district must go to court to get the desegregation plan changed. This policy raises serious constitutional issues and places an unrealistic and unfair burden on districts that are grappling with other responsibilities under NCLB.

Recommendation

Amend NCLB to say that nothing in the section on school choice shall be construed to override the requirements of a desegregation plan.

Supplemental Services—Civil Rights Protections

The U.S. Department of Education is permitting supplemental service providers to discriminate by ignoring the nondiscrimination language in section 9534 of NCLB and by declaring that supplemental service providers are not recipients of federal funds for purposes of the application of civil rights laws. This interpretation is simply wrong. In addition, the U.S. Department of Education makes it clear that providers are not required to serve students with disabilities or English language learners.

Recommendation

Clarify that supplemental service providers are recipients of federal funds subject to federal civil rights laws and that they may not discriminate with respect to employment or provision of services on the basis of race, color, religion, sex (except as otherwise permitted under Title IX), national origin or disability. Providers should be explicitly required to accept all students, regardless of disability or language limitations.

Restructuring

The sanctions to be imposed on schools that have reached the restructuring phase include several options that experience and research tell us are unlikely to improve their performance, such as converting the school to a charter school, turning the school over to a private company, or to the state. Other research-based alternatives are more likely to prove effective in turning these schools around. For example:

Pilot Schools

During the 1993 contract negotiations, the Boston Public Schools and the Boston Teachers Union created pilot schools as in-district charter schools. These schools are semiautonomous with full control of their budget. They make all educational decisions at the school site, and staff are employees of the district, covered by the contract for the purposes of salary and benefits. Schools determine the working conditions, including length of school day and year. Still within the district, these schools have the advantage of being supported by both the district and union.

Community Schools

Community schools offer nonacademic resources to students while supporting the academic mission of the schools. In such schools, community-based organizations provide mental health, social and recreational services to students and the community at-large. These organizations become part of the school improvement or site-based management team, which provides continuity of programs and generates support from the community. Beacon Schools in New York City, Communities in Schools and the Children's Aid Society's programs are examples of community schools.

Schools-Within-Schools

Schools-within-schools are schools that operate independently from the rest of the school, including separate administration and programs. They can establish small learning communities with the focus or mission that best meets the needs of the students, based on the school's data. Many districts, such as Cincinnati, Minneapolis, and New York City, operate small learning communities or schools-within-schools as part of the district offerings.

Small Schools

School districts across the country are breaking up large, comprehensive high schools into smaller learning communities. With help from a number of large foundations—Annenberg, Carnegie, and Gates among them—small schools provide structural and curricular changes designed to improve student achievement. Generally, small schools are designed around a particular focus such as business, law, arts, science, and technology. Many creative ideas exist that can serve as models or starting points for redesigning large high schools. For example, the Knowledge Works Foundation, the Gates Foundation, the Toledo Federation of Teachers, and the Toledo Public Schools are collaborating together to create small learning communities within large high schools.

Recommendation

Include options to reopen a school as a magnet or theme school or to restructure a larger school into a series of smaller schools. These are significant restructurings that the evidence demonstrates will be more likely to result in improved performance than the options currently in the law.

AFT's Commitment to High-Quality Education

Increasing student achievement, especially for disadvantaged children, is a central educational goal of the American Federation of Teachers. AFT will continue to address the problems with NCLB and to work tirelessly to achieve the necessary change in the law. AFT will lobby Congress and work with parents and other groups to secure the funding promised for our students. We will lobby the U.S. Department of Education to amend regulations and issue new guidance to clarify areas that are not aligned with the letter of the law and lobby Congress to make the necessary changes. We will call for a Congressional hearing to address the many problems associated with AYP and other aspects of the law and its implementation.

AFT will also assist state and local affiliates by creating tools to help them: respond to the law's shortcomings; communicate with elected officials and others about the law's strengths and weaknesses; navigate its requirements to mitigate its punitive effects; and, negotiate effective interventions and corrective actions.

CHAPTER 6

REMARKS BY NINA S. REES BEFORE THE MIDWEST EQUITY ASSISTANCE CENTER OCTOBER 4–5, 2005

Nina Shokaraii Rees

As we approach the fourth anniversary of the enactment of the No Child Left Behind Act (NCLB), I am pleased to talk with you today about the progress we have made under the law and some of the new flexibilities the Department is offering. Like most four-year-olds, the law has experienced growing pains, and is continuing to develop. I am sure that all of you with children know that it's a good idea to have them seen by a physician for regular check-ups. And I am also certain that you have seen the latest diagnosis of our nation's educational system: The long term trend results of the National Assessment of Educational Progress (NAEP), commonly called the "nation's report card." This report card, or "check-up," gives us reason to believe that our four-year-old law is developing well, and helping to positively influence the learning of all children.

The most recent NAEP shows that students are performing better and that achievement gaps are closing. According to the NAEP, our nation's students have made more progress in the last five years than in the previ-

The Challenges of School Reform: Implementation, Impact, and Sustainability, 105–110
Copyright © 2006 by Information Age Publishing

ous 30 years combined. Progress before 1999 had been incremental, with a general pattern of student achievement improving by just a couple points at a time. For example, from 1971 to 1999, nine-year-old reading scores gained only four points overall. Then suddenly in the last five years, the score jumped an unprecedented seven points, by far the highest score yet. The reason: around those years America made a commitment to leave no child behind. This commitment is helping students from every race and background to succeed in school and ultimately in life.

As Secretary of Education Margaret Spellings likes to say, we have learned a new equation, that in education, "accountability plus high expectations plus resources equals results." We have seen such great progress on the NAEP from students in the early grades because No Child Left Behind has helped channel resources to our younger students.

Let me give you more numbers to demonstrate why we are confident. I will start with mathematics. Nationally, math scores for nine- and 13-year-olds have reached all time highs. For example, in the last five years, Hispanic nine-year-olds raised their scores by 17 points, while African American nine-year-olds raised their scores by 13 points. As for our 13-year-olds, every subgroup has made significant gains. Since 1999, scores for White students increased five points, scores for Hispanic students increased six points, and scores for African American students increased 11 points.

We are also seeing vast improvements in reading. The gap between White and African American nine-year-old students is the smallest it has ever been. Since 1999, African American students have improved their reading scores by 14 points, which is a huge jump.

Additionally, individual states are bringing up the test scores of students who have often been overlooked by the education system. In Maryland over the last two years, 16% more African American third-graders have become proficient in math, and 24% more Hispanic third-graders have become proficient in reading. In Wisconsin, 87% of the state's third graders are reading at or above grade level. This percentage is a 13-point increase over scores in 2002, and represents the highest mark Wisconsin has reached yet for reading proficiency. A little farther south in Georgia, over 8% of the schools met state standards for Adequate Yearly Progress (AYP) for all groups of students. This number sounds even better when we realize that it was reached in a year when Georgia actually *raised* its academic achievement standards. Local examples of success are just as impressive. In Georgia's capital, the aptly named Capitol View Elementary School has a student population that consists of 90% minority students. Over 90% of the students are also low-income. Let me add another 90%—*over* 90% of the students are meeting state standards in *both* reading and math.

All of these statistics represent real students in real schools, taught by real, hard-working teachers. The students' progress is a testimony to the efforts of state and local educators and administrators like you who are dedicated to making sure that in every classroom students are engaged and learning.

Now as you know, this past month has proven to be a real challenge toward ensuring that goal, with thousands of children in the Gulf Coast displaced by Hurricanes Katrina and Rita. We all want these students to continue to meet their educational goals and reach state standards like the students who have made incredible gains in Maryland, Wisconsin, and Georgia. At the U.S. Department of Education, we believe that the principles of NCLB can ensure that Gulf Coast students do not fall behind in school.

We also realize that certain flexibilities need to be put in place to accommodate the needs of districts, schools, students, and families that have survived these two disasters. Secretary Spellings has mailed states several letters outlining the flexibilities at their disposal. We are providing maximum flexibility in the administration of federal education programs, including those regulated by NCLB, and are requesting that Congress grant the department broad waiver authority to reach out to more states, districts, and schools.

Just last week Secretary Spellings offered two flexibility options that will give schools impacted by Hurricanes Katrina and Rita flexibility for one year on particular aspects of the law's AYP provision. Both options require that all students still will be tested, and that the results of these tests will be made public, so that schools are held accountable for educating their newest additions. Under the first flexibility option, schools that take in displaced students can report those students' test scores as a separate subgroup, or they can opt for a second option that is based on a provision of the law that is already in place. This provision involves "exceptional or uncontrollable circumstances, such as a natural disaster." With this provision, districts and schools can be temporarily exempt from showing improvement results on the statutory timeline. The new part of this provision is that schools and districts affected by Katrina and Rita will not need to submit an application for a waiver to the department.

The department also has launched a "Hurricane Help for Schools" Web site to connect the needy with corporations, organizations, schools, and individuals who can donate supplies. So far, over 150 matches have been made on the Web site, enabling books, clothes, backpacks, and other materials to be sent directly to Gulf Coast victims who need them. Most importantly, we recently asked Congress for up to $2.6 billion in support for families and areas hard-hit by Hurricane Katrina.

In the last few weeks it has become clear that States and districts that are providing services to displaced students are dealing with myriad logistical issues and unexpected costs. In order to assist with these costs, the president has proposed that Congress provide up to $7,500 per student in federal funds. Therefore, for one year only, and for students who have been displaced by Hurricane Katrina, the federal contribution to a state's per-pupil expenditures for elementary and secondary education would increase from about 9% to 90%.

Thus far, we have been working on an individual basis with states that are requesting flexibility for certain provisions of the No Child Left Behind Act. This approach is being used to ensure that children who have been affected by the hurricane will not be additionally set back by lowered standards and weak accountability measures. These latest flexibility measures ensure that the immediate needs of the people who are dealing with the natural disasters are met, and that the principles of NCLB, which have been proven to work, remain intact so we can ensure that all students are proficient by the 2013-2014 school year.

Now let us go back to what we have done and hope to do next to ensure that the states and districts not affected by the hurricane have what they need to meet the goals of the law. Based on the positive NAEP results, the latest AYP determinations, and students' scores on state tests, we know that the basic tenants of NCLB can help us close the achievement gap. Strict accountability for results based on annual assessments, disaggregated reporting of results, and a focus on closing the achievement gap can get us there. These are the bright-line principles of the law.

A major part of Secretary Spellings' administration is based on implementing NCLB in a common sense fashion. All of us also know that common sense often requires us to be flexible in order to make things work. As a result, the secretary and the Department of Education have been committed to giving flexibility to states and districts that share the main principles of No Child Left Behind. Over the last few months, the department has announced flexibility in a few areas. One key area concerns the assessment of students with disabilities. New research tells us that students with disabilities need extra time and intensive instruction in order to reach grade-level proficiency. These students often do not meet grade-level targets at the same time as their peers. Consequently, the department is working to develop regulations that would allow states to implement modified standards to measure the achievement of students with disabilities. States would be able to count proficient scores on tests based on these modified standards for up to 2% of the total student population in determining AYP data. Because these regulations have yet to be fully developed, the department has permitted states to use a proxy to achieve similar flexibility in calculating AYP. So far, 31 states have applied.

Because all students must be accommodated and special needs take many forms, the department also has granted flexibility with regard to limited English proficient (LEP) students. States may now count former LEP students in the LEP subgroup on state assessments for up to two years after the students have become proficient in English. The secretary also has put together a special working group that is exploring appropriate ways of measuring the academic progress of students who are not native English speakers. Because we want to serve the needs of these students while still holding them to the high expectations of their peers, the secretary's working group will find ways to include English language learners in state accountability systems. The working group consists of researchers, practitioners, and educators who are experienced in working with ELL and LEP students.

Perhaps one of the most innovative provisions of No Child Left Behind deals with supplemental educational services (SES). SES is a critical example of one of the choice options that students and parents have under the law. Low-income families can enroll their children in supplemental educational services, or, free tutoring programs, if their children attend Title I schools that have been designated by the state as "in need of improvement" for more than one year. Unfortunately, current data suggest that only 10 to 20% of eligible students are participating in SES. As a result, we are providing new flexibility to ensure that more students are able to take advantage of the benefits of these services.

Our new flexibility agreement with the Chicago Public Schools (CPS) allows CPS to serve on a pilot basis as an SES provider. This flexibility was granted despite the fact that the district has been identified as in need of improvement, which would normally take it out of contention as a provider. Allowing CPS to provide supplemental services is expected to both increase the number of students participating in SES, and improve access to district facilities for other providers. As part of the agreement, CPS will provide early notification of SES eligibility to parents, extend periods of enrollment, and provide district facilities to nondistrict providers for a reasonable fee. In line with Secretary Spellings' mantra, "In God we trust, all others bring data," CPS also will provide academic performance data to evaluate the effectiveness of its supplemental services programs.

Another way in which the department has provided SES flexibility is through a series of pilot projects in which districts will be permitted to reverse the order in which they provide SES and public school choice for students in schools that have been identified as underperforming. The initial pilot involves four districts in Virginia. One of the key goals of this project is to collect data on SES effectiveness that can be shared with other states to improve SES quality and implementation nationwide.

One other area of possible flexibility concerns growth models, which will give schools "credit" for improving student performance over time. However, as with all of the other recent flexibility decisions, this option will be consistent with the basic tenants of NCLB, which include annual assessments, and a commitment to closing achievement gaps and educating all of our nation's students.

In closing, the No Child Left Behind Act will officially turn four years old in December. We have had much reason to celebrate, but we also know that there is much work yet to be done. Hurricanes Katrina and Rita have let us see that NCLB is a "living law"—one that continues to develop and change. Since the inception of the law we have also seen that with high expectations, resources, and flexibility, all students can achieve positive results.

CHAPTER 7

HOPES AND HAZARDS

No Child Left Behind and
Low-Performing Public Schools

Andrew J. Rotherham

In January 2002, President Bush signed the No Child Left Behind Act (NCLB) into law. The law is equal parts culmination and inauguration. It represents the culmination of work by a chorus of voices across the political spectrum demanding greater accountability for poor and minority students in federal education policy.

Simultaneously it is the inauguration of an unprecedented effort to improve the quality of schools serving poor and minority students. At its core, however, it is a law about tackling the problem of schools not succeeding with some or all of their students. That's why it raises a host of political and policy challenges at the national, state, and local levels that are substantially more complex than bromides about "no excuses" or faddish reforms.

The Challenges of School Reform: Implementation, Impact, and Sustainability, 111–120
Copyright © 2006 by Information Age Publishing
All rights of reproduction in any form reserved.

This article first appeared in the Summer 2003 edition of the *State Education Standard,* the journal of the National Association of State Boards of Education.

The ugly truth is that while there are excellent public schools serving high poor and minority enrollment, nowhere have we been able to achieve this success on any scale and even in affluent communities troubling achievement gaps persist. Advocates claiming all that is needed to do so are "proven strategies" like smaller classes or after-school programs are selling the same snake-oil as those willing to bet it all on school vouchers as way out of this morass.

Substantial research indicates that the basic ingredients of a successful school are excellent teachers and leadership, a challenging curriculum, sufficient resources, and parental and community commitment. Yet, even assembling these building blocks is an enormous challenge. Throw in the political complexities and the educational intangibles that researchers cannot quantify and multiply them by more than 8,000 public schools (serving more than four million students) already identified as needing improvement, and the scale of the challenge begins to become clear.[1]

The New Deal

But however daunting, this is a challenge we cannot afford to shirk. For most of the last century American public schools delivered on the basic deal they were charged with. They educated a minority of students very well, and the rest sufficiently, for the era. Educators did not ask very much of government and government did not ask too much of the schools. This deal worked because for most Americans a "middle class" lifestyle was within reach almost regardless of educational attainment.

The losers in this deal were poor and minority students who were systematically undereducated. But even these students could find work in an economy essentially structured around producing goods and moving them around. In former Urban League President Hugh Price's characterization, it was an economy where a strong back was as important as a strong mind.

Now, social and economic circumstances have changed and the old deal is obsolete. Demographic trends demand that all Americans, not just a privileged few, are afforded a chance at economic mobility and self-determination. As a practical matter this is less an issue of economic necessity than social equity. The American economy is resilient and has historically adapted to ebb and flow in the demand for high skilled workers. The adaptability of American society to continued inequities in life chances because educational opportunity is essentially allocated by zip code and race is more of an open question.

Addressing the achievement gap and modernizing the delivery of public education to ensure greater customization, responsiveness, and performance is a struggle that plays out in many areas of education policy but is converging around NCLB. The framework the law lays out—quantifiably examining school performance and intervening in inverse proportion to success—is akin to Churchill's famous characterization of democracy: The worst system except for all the others. It is laden with a host of technical, policy, and political challenges but is the most promising attempt yet to ensure that disadvantaged students are well-served by public schools.

This is why it is frustrating that many traditional progressives oppose the NCLB framework, often for reasons no more substantial than because it is associated with a president they do not like. Moreover, despite pious claims of fidelity to the goals of NCLB, the reactionary posture of many education interest groups makes clear that the needs of the "system" and concerns about "fairness" and "due process" for schools rather than fairness and equity for children are paramount.

Some critics of NCLB claim that the law is a plot to undermine confidence in the public schools. For example, National Education Association President Reg Weaver argues that it "sets up children and public schools to fail." This unserious charge will become self-fulfilling if the public perceives educators as only bellyaching and unwilling to do more than demand greater funding to attack the achievement gap. It's ominous that constituencies traditionally strongly loyal to public education are increasingly signaling serious frustration with the status quo and a willingness to walk away if the problem of low-performing schools is not seriously dealt with.

The law will doubtless need some changes and modifications; it would be amazing if a law of this size, scope, and complexity did not. But the not-too-subtle foot-dragging and lobbying for major changes is likely not only futile but also counterproductive.

This framework represents a hard-won centrist consensus and the nation's political dynamics are such that if it moves substantially it will be toward the Right. This is presumably not what the loudest NCLB critics seek.

Low-Performing Schools

Those are the macro currents swirling around NCLB. As a policy matter NCLB's linchpin and most visible manifestation is efforts to improve low-performing schools or providing other public options. The success or failure of this effort depends on five key changes happening in tandem over the next several years. Although each entails complicated hurdles, educators, and policymakers must:

- Move beyond existing ideological and political constraints;
- Engage social entrepreneurs to help address vexing challenges and complement public sector activity;
- Ensure that accountability systems are reliable;
- Substantially upgrade the ability of state departments of education to assist low-performing schools as well as enhance the capability of the U.S. Department of Education to deliver assistance and leadership to states, school districts, and schools; and
- Provide adequate resources to leverage new reforms and support change.

Ditch the Ideological Constraints

America's public schools labor under a stifling set of ideological and political constraints. It's rare for localities to pay teachers willing to work in the hardest schools more because the teachers unions do not like this idea. Despite being accountable for their school's performance, most principals have limited latitude about whom they can hire, how to spend most of their budget, or even the hours their school is open to serve children. And the notion of opening new public schools and charter schools to meet the diverse needs of students in a standards-driven environment is frowned upon as a "conservative" idea. The common refrain of "we can't do that because" stifles all manner of new ideas.

The goals of NCLB simply cannot be met within these existing constraints, which squarely stand between public education as we know it now, and a more performance-based, customized, and child-focused system.

A recent analysis by Ron Brady, a seasoned educator with experience helping low-performing schools in multiple districts, converges with other evidence indicating that where interventions happen, policymakers should reasonably expect a successful school turnaround rate of only around 50%. In some ways the low-performing schools environment will be similar to welfare reform where the sharp policy change created positive results for the easier cases but simultaneously increased the challenge of dealing with the hardest ones. This means that in addition to a willingness to innovate in terms of school interventions, policymakers must also look to public charter schools and other strategies to increase the supply of public schools. This, of course, also bumps up against ideological constraints.

Likewise, research demonstrates the how important teacher quality is to student learning. Yet existing political constraints about teacher licensure and pay hamstring efforts to attract and retain enough high quality teachers in the most challenging schools (or to meet NCLB's mandate on teacher quality). This is inexcusable at a time when getting into Teach For America is more competitive than most elite graduate and professional schools and the success of "teaching fellows" programs in several cities demonstrate that talented people want to go into teaching, even in the hardest schools. But Teach for America and these initiatives run afoul of orthodoxy too.

It's a cliché to point out that teacher collective bargaining agreements add to the constraints. In too many communities they absolutely codify pernicious practices, put the needs of adults before those of children, protect incompetence rather than foster professionalism, and tie the hands of educators.

However, it is simplistic to assume that their absence would unleash a wave of rapid change because there is also a risk-aversion constraint that governs much of public education. We reward educators for compliance, incremental change, and caution. The sort of modernizing change that is desperately needed in many low-income communities means that risk-taking rather than risk-aversion must be the norm. This necessitates a realignment of political and policy incentives.

As efforts to turn around low-performing schools become more substantial and sophisticated, additional issues requiring fresh and creative thinking will certainly emerge. But educators will be chasing their tails if the political and policy landscape remains as narrowly banded as it mostly is now.

Unleash the Social Entrepreneurs

Even in a more reform-oriented political environment, the public sector alone cannot meet the educational demands placed on it by NCLB. The need for new, high quality, public schools in many communities, more and better teachers and school leaders and innovative solutions to data management, analysis, and use are a few examples of opportunities for social entrepreneurs to help states and school districts improve low-performing schools.

At a time when many school districts complain of a dearth of high quality candidates for principalships, the nonprofit New Leaders for New Schools received more than 1,000 applications for 70 principal training fellowships in urban schools. Likewise the Broad Foundation was inundated with more than 250 applicants for just six administrative fellowships. And Teach For America received nearly 16,000 applications from America's most academically qualified students for 2,000 teaching positions in the nation's most challenging schools.

Meanwhile, nonprofit organizations like Aspire Public Schools, KIPP Academies, and Green Dot Public Schools are opening excellent public schools in the neediest communities. Aspire boasts a 99% reenrollment rate for students, a 97% retention rate for teachers, and terrific student performance. And despite myriad political problems, the for-profit Edison Schools has, on average, produced noteworthy gains.

Social entrepreneurs are also helping states and school districts meet the challenges of using and reporting student achievement data and other information. Organizations like Just for the Kids, GreatSchools.net, StandardsWork, and even companies like Standard and Poors are providing platforms to manage and use data increasing the analytic leverage of educators, parents, and policymakers.

All these initiatives share a common trait. They are the vanguard of a new way of thinking about delivering public education which values performance and views public education as an essential public good but one best delivered through a variety of publicly accessible and accountable contexts rather than only "the one best system" that characterized most of the last century.

Get the Accountability Right

Efforts to improve low-performing schools will be ineffective if the mechanisms for identifying these schools are inadequate or unreliable. That does not preclude using test scores for accountability. On the contrary, research, most recently studies by Martin Carnoy and Susanna Loeb as well as Erik Hanushek and Margaret Raymond, indicate the benefits of accountability, especially for poor and minority students.

NLCB requires that all schools make "adequate yearly progress" (AYP) by making the AYP provisions from the 1994 law more stringent. Although the new provisions introduce unprecedented transparency and accountability for low-income and minority students, they also carry substantial technical challenges. Not surprisingly, assessment and accountability provisions for more severely disabled students and English language learners are presenting difficulties for most states.

Each state must design its own accountability system, and doing so is complicated and demanding. States must ensure that the measurement system is technically rigorous, that rules for measuring subgroup performance are reliable, and that state and school district officials are able to accurately and clearly communicate information about school performance to the media and the public. NCLB gives states considerable flexibility to design accountability systems that are statistically robust, but not all states are taking full advantage of the law. Subgroup sizes that are appropriate for score reporting (to protect privacy) often are not appropriate for accountability measures so the law allows flexibility about subgroup size and makeup, and scores can be averaged over several years. Still, substantial challenges remain and the U.S. Department of Education must now balance enforcement with reasonable accommodation for legitimate problems that arise in various states.

The adverse consequences of underidentifying schools where subgroups of students are not making progress are readily apparent but inappropriately identifying schools as needing improvement, particularly as a result of technical problems is also a problem. Most immediately, state resources to intervene in low-performing schools are limited and overidentification can dilute the impact of state efforts. And accountability systems that are not reliable threaten to erode confidence in reform efforts and reenergize the unproductive debate between apologists for broken systems and those ready to give up on public schools.

Even within a well-designed accountability system state policymakers must have a triage process for, and discretion about, school interventions. The transparency that AYP offers means that even schools with overall high test scores can be designated as "needing improvement" because of one or two subgroups of students not doing well.

"Needs improvement" cannot be a monolithic category in terms of public communication or public policy at the state and local level. Schools will be identified as needing improvement for different reasons and will require varied interventions. What is appropriate for a school where few or no students are making AYP is wholly different than a school where only one subgroup is behind. Similarly, state and school district officials have to communicate these distinctions accurately and understandably to parents and the media.

Lastly, this is a human endeavor and even the most well designed accountability systems cannot substitute for sound judgment. Mistakes and miscalculations are inevitable. The flip side of being prepared to communicate effectively about legitimate designations is having a real and reliable process for schools to contest a designation believed to be in error.

Modernize Departments of Education

Marc Tucker recently observed that no state department of education in this country has the "staff, legitimacy, and expertise" to provide sustained services to schools as their analogous counterparts in westernized democracies do. Our state departments of education are for the most part set up to give out money and monitor compliance not provide services and expertise. NCLB turns this on its head by asking them to become the managing partner in the effort to fix low-performing schools.

As a result, states will have to increase both overall numbers of staff and their expertise under NCLB. The technical challenges presented by President Bush's annual testing plan and NCLB's accountability requirements necessitate increased capacity inside and outside of state departments. According to the Education Commission of the States (ECS), only seven states currently meet NCLB's testing requirements and almost every state is making substantial modifications to its accountability systems to meet requirements about including subgroup performance, gapclosing, and proficiency targets.

But the magnitude of the challenge is far greater. A recent analysis from NASBE (The National Association of State Boards of Education) found that only 39 states tracked teacher shortages at a statewide level and the quality of their data and reporting varied markedly. ECS and *Education Week* data indicate that only 28 states are positioned to provide support to low-performing schools.

This is in part why U.S. Department of Education analyses show that under the previous ESEA (Elementary and Secondary Education Act) law 41% of principals in schools identified by states as needing improvement were unaware of the designation. Lack of state capacity to address this problem is also why only 50% of schools identified for three or more years reported receiving any assistance from their state or school district.

Successfully addressing the myriad problems plaguing low-performing schools means that states must compile, manage, and use more data than ever before. Rather than just funding and compliance, their new role is to collect data, monitor accountability and performance, support promising initiatives, actually help struggling schools and districts, and perform their traditional role of dispersing funding.

The federal government also has to change. It too has been focused on distributing money and monitoring compliance at the expense of building substantial capacity to help states and school districts. NCLB continues the precious federal responsibility of looking out for low-income and minority students but the Department of Education cannot only demand more of public schools. Federal support for research and promising initiatives must increase and the department must substantially upgrade its own capacity to help states and school districts. Thus far the Bush Administration has rearranged the organization of the department and turned it into an effective public relations vehicle, but done little to effect more systematic changes in its mission.

More vigorously enforcing the new ESEA law than its predecessors also demands smart and flexible enforcement. There is a happy medium between a policy that liberally grants waivers and one where even legitimate, and often creative, efforts to comply with the spirit and intent of the legislation are rebuked because they do not meet a strict reading of the letter of the law.

Money Matters

Fixing low performing schools or providing alternatives is not cheap. For example, four years ago Fairfax County Public Schools superintendent Daniel Domenech launched a focused initiative to raise achievement and close gaps in the twenty lowest performing schools there. Domenech recently wrote a short essay for washingtonpost.com pointing out that none of these schools has subsequently been identified as needing improvement under Virginia's Standards of Learning or NCLB. He also noted that it cost an additional $500,000 per-school for professional development, full-day kindergarten, and bonuses that helped drive the improvements.

Similarly, public school choice and charter initiatives carry transition costs and ultimately are proving to be at best revenue neutral alternatives. Because these initiatives help provide publicly accountable options for students in low-performing schools they are a worthwhile expenditure, but an expenditure nonetheless.

Fixing low-performing schools and saving money will be an elusive goal. As a basic matter of political economy, it is easier to drive change in education with new resources but even in absolute terms the demands of NCLB carry a hefty price tag.

Of course just as NCLB places these demands on states and localities, states collectively find themselves in their worst fiscal shape of the post-war period. Even though substantial shortfalls in a few states distort the overall picture and some of the problems are self-inflicted, the picture is pretty grim. According to the National Council of State Legislatures, 19 states are facing FY2004 budget shortfalls of more than 10% of their general fund.

However, instead of just rhetorically badgering Washington for more money states and local school districts must also demonstrate that they are aligning existing education funding with NCLB's goals. There is significant accretion from previous initiatives and long-standing programs. More funding is needed but privately most superintendents and state level officials also acknowledge that some existing resources can be used more effectively than they are now.

Finally, although the Bush Administration has made a series of unfortunate fiscal policy decisions resulting in less funding for NCLB than many supporters had hoped, calls for delaying NCLB until it is "fully funded" are disingenuous. The policy goals embedded in NCLB should not be held hostage to the vagaries of Washington budget battles.

Conclusion

As with any piece of major legislation to emerge from Congress NCLB contains annoyances and bureaucratic hassles but they are far overshadowed by the promise of the law to shepherd our energies toward the most disadvantaged students and move us further down the road to educational equity than where we are now.

NCLB has laid bare a longstanding, often embarrassing, and too infrequently addressed social problem: The appalling educational disparities that separate poor and minority students from others. Will NCLB eradicate this problem? Of course not, although as a practical matter even moderate success would yield enormous social benefits. That doesn't mean progress is not costly, both fiscally and politically, but the larger question is not whether we can afford to attack this problem but whether we can afford not to.

NOTE

1. As of when this article went to print. These figures are based on the previous ESEA and likely to increase.

PART III

TEACHER QUALITY

CHAPTER 8

THE TEACHER ADVANCEMENT PROGRAM

Tamara W. Schiff

I am pleased to be here today to talk to you about some issues that have become more common in today's educational jargon—teacher career advancement opportunities, relevant and directed professional development, rigorous accountability, and performance-based compensation. Today I will give you a sense of what we have been doing at the Milken Family Foundation regarding these issues.

The Milken Family Foundation was founded in the early 1980s to focus philanthropy primarily in the areas of education and medical research. In 1987, we started the Milken Educator Awards, which is now in 48 states and the District of Columbia. Over the years, we have researched educational issues such as the early accountability and standards movement, preschool education, and various small-scale reforms. However, what we soon realized was that without a high quality teacher in the classroom, no piece of technology, no program of study, no standard, and no accountability system can be used effectively to impact student achievement. Thus in 1998, we began focusing on developing a comprehensive model that would attract, develop, motivate, and retain talented teachers in the profession.

The Challenges of School Reform: Implementation, Impact, and Sustainability, 123–143
Copyright © 2006 by Information Age Publishing
All rights of reproduction in any form reserved.

In many ways, we were leading the pack in education. Not long after, national policy caught up to us, and No Child Left Behind (NLCB) was signed. Having a highly qualified teacher in every classroom is the cornerstone of this legislation. The federal government defines a highly qualified teacher as someone who has the following characteristics: fully licensed or certified; no waivers or emergency credentials; at least a bachelor's degree; demonstrated subject matter knowledge; state test; major, graduate degree, or advanced certification in subject area; and teaching skills demonstrated through state test.

While these criteria provide a framework for what a highly qualified teacher is, we also know that *certified* doesn't necessarily mean *qualified* since certification may be neither necessary nor sufficient. There are many outstanding teachers with undergraduate degrees in private schools across the country who might not have completed a traditional teacher education program. And we always joke at our office, that the Director of TAP, Lew Solmon, has a Ph.D. in economics from the University of Chicago, has taught introductory economics at the college level, and was the author of a book used as a primer for college economics instruction; however, in order to teach economics in a public high school today, he would have to get a teaching credential. That doesn't make sense.

I think we all can agree that excellent teachers must know the subject matter they are teaching and must have instructional expertise, but as you can see on (Chart 8.1), there are other characteristics that we all use to describe highly qualified teachers.

The work of Bill Sanders in Tennessee shows that after one year, low achieving students with effective teachers outperform those with ineffective teachers (Chart 8.2). His longitudinal work demonstrated that students who performed equally well in math in second grade showed enormous performance differences three years later, depending upon the quality of the teachers (Chart 8.3). Similar results have been found in Boston (Chart 8.4).

June Rivers' longitudinal work in Tennessee (Chart 8.5) also showed that average achieving students who were assigned to four years of ineffective teachers had only a 40% chance of passing the Tennessee high school exit exam, while similar students assigned to four years of effective teachers had an 80% chance of passing.

All of these data demonstrate that teacher quality does matter. The key question, though, is how can the money available for education reform best be spent to improve teacher quality? Many people will argue that we need to pay all teachers more in order to attract better ones to the classroom. However, in order to bring the states with the lowest average teacher salaries up to the mean, it would cost roughly $6,000 per teacher in 30 states. This additional money would neither be adequate to really

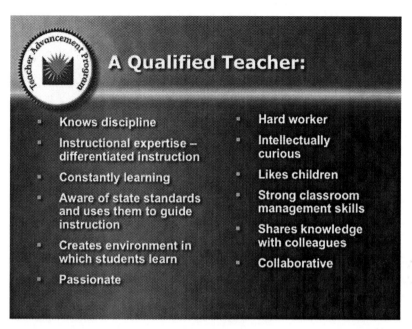

Chart 8.1.

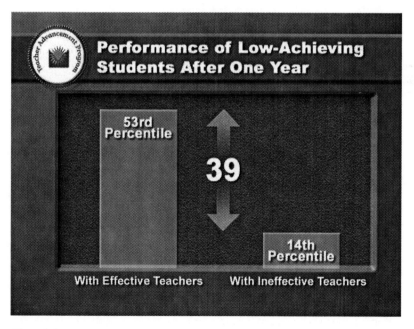

Chart 8.2.

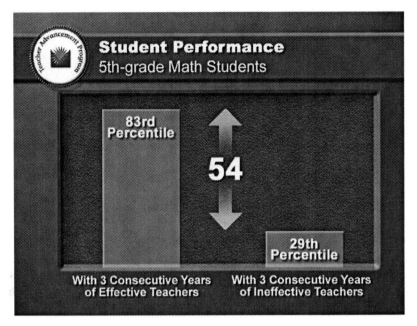

Chart 8.3.

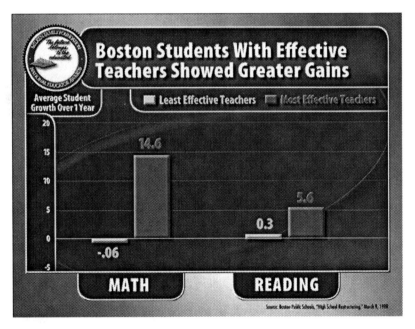

Chart 8.4.

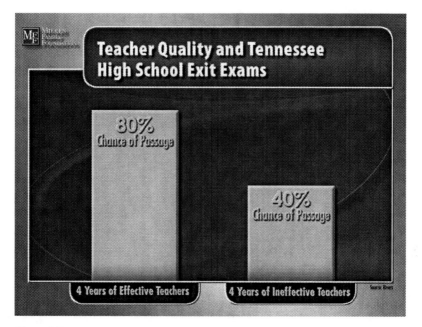

Chart 8.5.

change who comes into teaching, nor would it be financially viable. In the past, many states and districts have attempted to implement teacher career ladder programs to reward those teachers who do extra work. However, inevitably these programs have failed or have had limited impact, because the bonuses or rewards were not sufficient.

Instead of reforms such as this, there must be a reform that addresses more than just a single element, such as incentive to go to a particular school, or an add-on for teaching a hard-to-staff subject. This is why we developed the Teacher Advancement Program (TAP) as a comprehensive school reform that impacts professional development, teacher accountability, and teacher career advancement and salaries, all with the goal of improving student achievement.

We see that those who choose teaching are often not from the most academically selective groups, nor are they necessarily well trained. Work by Richard Ingersoll (Chart 8.6) finds that a significant proportion of secondary school teachers do not have either a major or minor in the subject they are teaching, and the figures only get worse when we look at our nation's high-poverty schools. But it's not just a quality shortage, it's also a quantity shortage (Chart 8.7). We have estimated that we will need 870,000 teachers over the next 10 years. The recent economic turn in

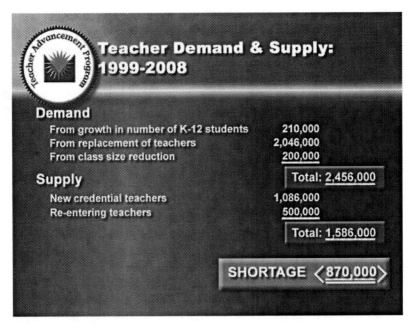

Chart 8.6.

Chart 8.7.

many states has led to fewer retirements and an influx of people in a mid-career change entering the teaching profession. However, this is a short-term phenomenon, and as the economy improves, these newer entries into teaching will also be the first to exit as other opportunities emerge.

Already, too many teachers leave within their first three years of teaching. Only one of every three new teachers is still in the profession after three years of teaching, and teachers are twice as likely to leave the profession if they do not go through an induction program. Further, those who score at the top of high stakes exams are the first to leave. We need to create an environment that helps retain teachers, support their ongoing professional development, and motivate them to continue in the profession.

All of us are familiar with some of the reasons why people don't choose to teach: salaries are usually not competitive; the cost of training is not warranted by the salary; teaching or nursing are no longer the only professional options for women; there is often little collegiality; there is minimal respect from the larger community; in the urban areas there is often an unpleasant or dangerous work environment; and teaching is one of the only professions where everyone with the same experience and credits gets the same pay, regardless of quality.

There are many ideas out there on how to attract more quality people into teaching, but there are significant drawbacks to many of these efforts (Chart 8.8). Most are small-scale, isolated efforts. They are not school centered, often poorly designed and implemented, and rather than being systemic reforms, they often solve one problem only to cause another. Bottom line is that if these efforts do succeed to attract new people to the same old profession, retention will remain a major problem.

The only way to attract, develop, motivate and retain high quality people into the teaching profession is to make it a typical profession. All of this information and statistics led us to create the Teacher Advancement Program (Chart 8.9). We looked at many reforms that were in the field, from class size reduction to technology. Some of these reforms, though well-intended and supported by many, actually led to additional problems. For example, class size reduction in California led to the hiring of so many under-qualified teachers, simply to have one adult in every classroom of 20, that student achievement growth was not realized several years later.

There are four essential elements of TAP: multiple career paths, ongoing applied professional growth, instructionally focused accountability, and performance-based compensation.

In most schools, teachers begin their career as a teacher, and 30 years later upon retirement, they end their careers with no advancement, no job title change, and minimal to no change in roles or responsibilities. Through TAP's multiple career paths, teachers have the opportunity to

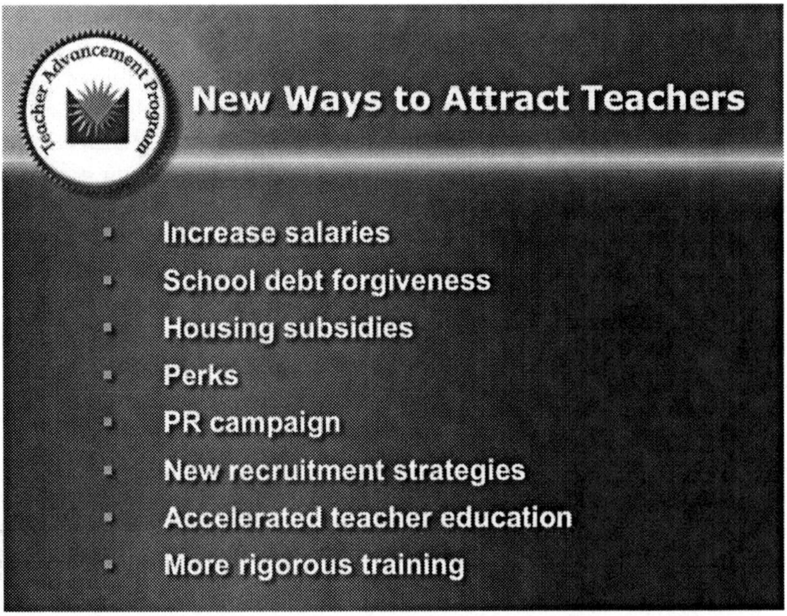

New Ways to Attract Teachers

- Increase salaries
- School debt forgiveness
- Housing subsidies
- Perks
- PR campaign
- New recruitment strategies
- Accelerated teacher education
- More rigorous training

Chart 8.8.

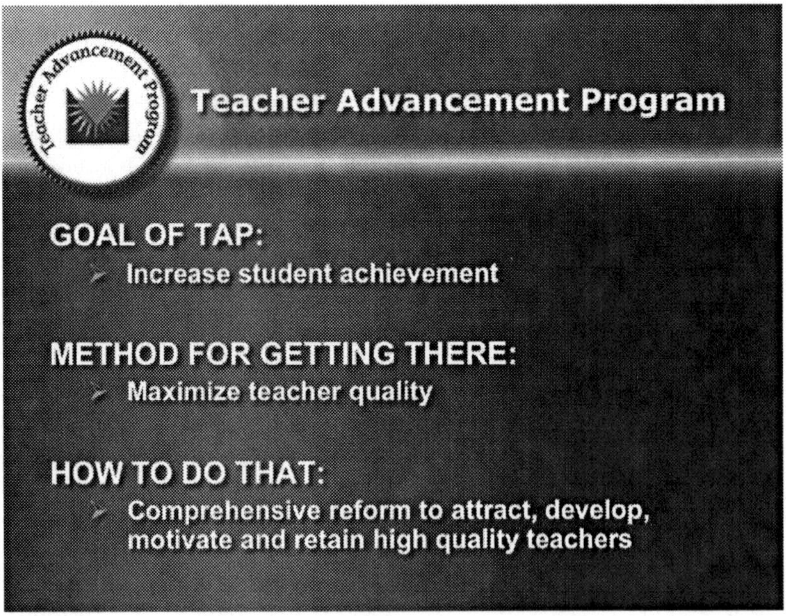

Teacher Advancement Program

GOAL OF TAP:
  ➤ Increase student achievement

METHOD FOR GETTING THERE:
  ➤ Maximize teacher quality

HOW TO DO THAT:
  ➤ Comprehensive reform to attract, develop, motivate and retain high quality teachers

Chart 8.9.

increase their roles and responsibilities along a career continuum from career teacher to mentor to master (Chart 8.10). Master teachers work closely with career and mentor teachers in the classroom to improve learning and instruction. They model lessons, team teach, and have an impact on many teachers and students. Advancement is based on desire, as well as demonstrated expertise and professional qualifications, and compensation is commensurate with the level of responsibilities held by each teacher.

Next, TAP provides an instructionally focused accountability system (Chart 8.11). In traditional schools, there is uneven accountability. Evaluations are often idiosyncratic, and rewards and sanctions are unrelated to evaluation outcomes. Further, support is provided only when deficiencies are noted. TAP provides clearly defined standards, procedures, and performance rubrics so teachers know what to expect when they are evaluated. Hiring and advancement, as well as compensation, are connected to evaluation outcomes, and there is support provided for the growth of strong teachers and refinement of teachers who have weaknesses.

The TAP accountability system goes beyond just classroom practice and includes school and classroom achievement gains. Teachers are evaluated on their classroom performance four to six times per year, by multiple, trained and certified evaluators. The evaluation system is supported

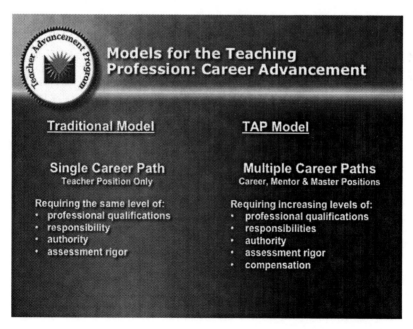

Chart 8.10.

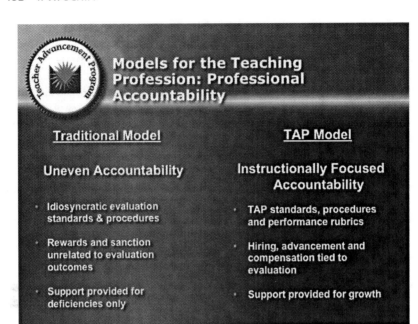

Chart 8.11.

Chart 8.12.

by a strong professional development structure that builds upon good practice as well as helps teachers who need additional refinement. Finally, the TAP accountability system ties teacher performance to compensation.

Though the TAP accountability and performance pay components often get the most attention, the ongoing applied professional development element is really central to a TAP school (Chart 8.12). Roughly 96% of American teachers participate in some form of professional development each year that they teach. However, few rate these experiences as productive or useful for improving classroom instructional performance or impacting student achievement. Further, there is rarely, if any, follow-up in terms of sharing what was learned in these classes with colleagues back at school, or implementation of new ideas. TAP restructures the school schedule to provide time during the regular school day for teachers to meet, learn, plan, mentor, and share with other teachers so they can constantly improve the quality of their instruction and hence, increase their students' academic achievement. This allows teachers to learn new instructional strategies and have greater opportunity to collaborate, both of which will lead them to become more effective teachers. Ongoing applied professional growth in TAP schools focuses on identified needs based on instructional issues that specific teachers face with specific students. Instead of trying to implement the latest fad in professional development, teachers use data to target these areas of need.

The element of TAP that seems to be most controversial is our performance-based compensation plan. We do not believe that the current step and column salary schedule in most school districts provides the necessary incentive to attract, develop, motivate, and retain talented individuals into the teaching profession, and we are not alone in these thoughts. Currently, teacher compensation means low salaries that are determined by years of experience and units earned, both poor indicators of student achievement. In TAP, higher pay is provided for the master and mentor teachers who take on new roles and responsibilities, as well as for excellent teachers as judged by both classroom performance and the achievement gains of students (Chart 8.13). Our model also supports higher pay for hard-to-staff schools or subjects, as well as for teacher training such as National Board Certification; however, these are not required as part of TAP implementation.

There are many characteristics of TAP's performance-based compensation system that make it unique. To begin, it is not a stand-alone program. Performance pay is supported by a strong, transparent, and fair teacher evaluation system where teachers are well aware of the standards they are being held accountable for. Further, when needs are identified through evaluation, TAP provides support to make improvements. Finally, the additional pay that teachers earn for their performance or their new

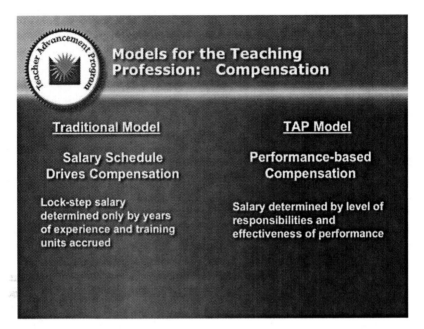

Chart 8.13.

responsibilities is sufficient enough to make the additional work worth the effort.

A common argument we hear against pay for performance among teachers is that it will encourage competition and discord among teachers. However, in our annual survey of teacher attitudes, we have found the opposite to be true. Teachers in TAP schools report high levels of collegiality and satisfaction, and in the vast majority of our schools, these levels have only increased since the inception of TAP. We believe these results are a natural outcome of TAP's ongoing applied professional growth structure. Whatever concerns teachers have over the shift in culture to performance-based compensation and rigorous accountability is tempered by the cluster groups that naturally facilitate collegiality.

Let me briefly go into a little more detail about how the TAP performance awards work. First, all teachers are eligible for a performance award in the form of a bonus. It is not cumulative year-to-year, but an add-on to one's current salary. The amount of the bonus is constrained by available funds, but we recommend at least $2,500 per teacher to be contributed to an award pool. Again, since this money is an add-on, no one will earn less money than they did prior to TAP. Also, all teachers have the opportunity to earn a bonus of some amount. If all teachers meet proficient levels in their classroom performance, and there are student achievement gains, then all teachers will receive bonuses. Further, if students' test scores do not improve, but teachers score well on their classroom performance, they can earn bonuses, or vice versa.

Fifty percent of the bonus goes for classroom performance as measured by teacher skills, knowledge and responsibilities. This is evaluated by multiple evaluators four to six times per year based on clear standards and rubrics. While this process has no room for nepotism or favoritism, there is a possibility that grade inflation can interject itself into the system. Evaluators may give higher scores than are merited because the traditional school culture is not to critique colleagues. In the past, there was often fear of reprisal for someone who might be critical. This is why oversight is a key element to ensure a fair evaluation system. The school leadership team, which comprises the principal, master teachers, and mentor teachers, must understand and apply the TAP Teaching Standards and scoring rubrics in the same way. All evaluators go through training and become certified after passing a test. Further, the data for each evaluation is monitored to maintain inter-rater reliability and scoring consistency across evaluators.

The other 50% of the bonus is based upon student achievement gains. This is the value that teachers add to their students in terms of student learning as measured by standardized test score gains. Twenty to 30% percent of this portion is based on school-wide achievement for all teachers, which gives teachers the incentive to help each other improve, and the remaining 20%-30% is based on achievement gains of individual teachers' students.

There is a big difference between pay for individual performance and pay for school-wide performance. In school-wide performance pay, the performance of a few can often carry the performance of many. In TAP, performance-based compensation provides incentive for all teachers to focus on student learning gains, but it also holds teachers accountable for their direct impact on their students.

Finally, TAP uses a value-added system. We don't measure absolute levels of achievement—for example, we don't say that you get the bonus only if you reach the 80th percentile. Rather, we look at where students started and where they end, and measure the value that the teacher adds to achievement growth. This is a methodologically complex concept to explain, but it means that teachers with all levels of students have the potential to show growth.

TAP also provides for a salary augmentation or stipend for the master and mentor teachers who take on new roles and responsibilities in the school. Augmentations are impacted by funds available as well as the average salaries in districts.

So there you have the TAP model. Some of its features may seem somewhat familiar, and this is because we looked at promising reforms from the past and tried to formulate them in a sustainable, impactful way. While TAP has career ladders, we also provide enough additional compensation to make it worth the effort. TAP's ongoing applied professional development supports the improved accountability system, is focused on learning and instruction and on issues identified through school and cluster group goals. Professional development is not an external activity in TAP schools, but rather an internal, ongoing, cohesive program. The TAP accountability system is instructionally focused, and is based not only on the research of others, but on the input of our own teachers and on best practices. Finally, we built upon the work of many who develop compensation models, but our performance pay plan does not function in a vacuum. Instead, it is closely linked to professional development and the accountability system, so teachers do not feel they are being evaluated on arbitrary or unrelated measures.

There are several research-based recommendations that guide a reform's success within a school. First, the reform must be well-matched in terms of the school's needs and the staff's desire. Given that teacher buy-in is an essential prerequisite to TAP, by definition, this match occurs. The program must provide professional development and support from the design team in how to implement the reform. The central office in Santa Monica and state-based TAP staff provides this support. Each state has an executive director who spends roughly 80% of his or her time in schools helping teachers and principals implement the program. We provide training during the year for the leadership team and are available to schools for support and guidance throughout the process.

Another key factor in successful comprehensive school reform is that fiscal resources are critical for implementation. We address this by looking at funding in the early stages of TAP and working with schools to identify funding sources and to create a sustainable program. We also look at accessing grant funds that are available for teacher quality reform.

The next issue that's essential for successful reform is district and school leadership. TAP works closely with all the stakeholders to build capacity and support for the program, from the state department to the teacher.

Finally, the ability of the reform to help meet state accountability mandates is crucial. While TAP is closely aligned to the basic tenets of No Child Left Behind as well as other state level accountability initiatives, the program provides a mechanism that allows schools to meet many of their more specific mandates.

Certainly, a challenge of TAP is the cost, because the traditional salary schedule remains in place, and no teacher can earn less than he or she did prior to TAP. As a result, additional funds are needed to provide salary augmentations and to develop a bonus pool that offers greater pay opportunities. We estimate that the average incremental costs associated with TAP are roughly 6% of the school budget, or about $400 per student. However, this amount can be significantly less if certain things are already available at the school such as specialists, literacy or math coaches, and professional development training days.

The bulk of the costs associated with TAP are personnel related. Master and mentor teachers must be paid more, and they also participate in additional training that requires compensation. When a master teacher is hired from within a school, that teacher must be replaced by a new classroom teacher. New specialists are often needed to cover classes while teachers are participating in cluster meetings. The last additional cost associated with TAP is that in some schools, additional tests must be given to assess every grade level, which comes at a cost, although this is less prevalent given the testing requirement of NCLB.

While the money seems to be an obstacle to implementing TAP, funds are being found. However, to sustain the program it takes a serious commitment to TAP that may require ending ineffective programs that have been in place for a long time. The bottom line is that TAP, or any other reform, can't be effective if we just add reform on top of reform on top of reform.

Many states have been going through tough economic times, so funds are not overabundant for education. It is most politically viable to spend education dollars on higher quality teachers—those who demonstrate their effectiveness. And education dollars are available if you know where to find them. For example, existing budgets often include funding for programs that are ineffective or no longer used. Calcasieu Parish in Louisiana is combining existing Title I and Title II funds, class size reduction monies, and other federal funds and putting that toward implementing TAP in 25 of its schools. Other potential sources of funds are from new state appropriations, ballot initiatives, private foundations, or federal grants.

In our current TAP schools, funds have come from Title I and Title II funds, foundation grants, federal grants, local business funds, state appropriations, as well as district or school and operational budgets. There have been provisions made in state legislatures that allow schools in need of technical assistance—low performing schools—to use their NCLB Title I funds to support TAP. This is happening in South Carolina and may happen in other states as well. Other states have passed legislation that provides specific funding for the implementation of TAP.

The growth of TAP has been steady. We have gone from five schools in Arizona in 2000-2001 to over 80 schools in nine states this past fall. Two new states and the District of Columbia will start this coming fall, while schools in several additional states are seriously considering joining the program.[1]

Of course, the question everyone rightfully asks is, what have been the results? When it comes to educational reform, we always want quick answers. But the reality is that reform takes time. The work of Michael Fullan tells us that student achievement results in elementary schools are not usually seen for at least three years. In middle and high schools, it takes even longer. School size, leadership, quality, and also support are all essential elements in seeing impacts.

We are expecting the report from our 2003-2004 school year to be completed next month, but many of you may be familiar with some of our early results from two years in Arizona and South Carolina. When we compared year-to-year changes in student achievement in 25 TAP schools compared to controls, our schools out-performed the controls nearly 70% of the time.

Now, ideally, we want to see 100% out-performing, but the reality is, if we compare TAP to other large-scale reforms out there, we know that we are doing a little bit better. RAND did a study of comprehensive school reforms, and they found that only 50% of the schools out-perform their controls, which is basically a coin toss. These were programs that have been in place for significantly longer than TAP.

Based on state assessments from last year, we also have some early indications that TAP schools are doing well. Again, nearly 70% of all TAP schools across the country have maintained or improved upon their percentage of students performing at or above proficient levels. Clearly, student achievement is our ultimate goal. However, there are also other indicators of success that are really important for us to examine. In particular, we have examined the attitudes and opinions of the teachers in our schools. We collect data through annual teacher surveys, and we see the data as impacting our program in two ways.

First, at a national level we're able to look at trends and patterns among states and among schools. However, equally as important is the school-level impact of these results. When we collect teacher data every year, we return the data to the school, so they're able to look at how their individual teachers are feeling about certain elements. These results help the leadership teams assess where they may need to communicate more clearly on certain issues, where additional training is needed, or where they might need to focus some cluster group time.

Today I'm going to show you very quickly how teachers feel about the key elements of TAP, as well as collegiality and satisfaction. The following charts show teacher support levels for the four elements of TAP (Chart 8.14-8.17).

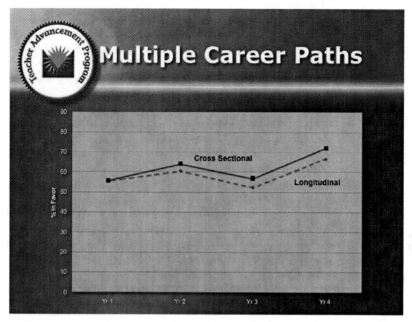

Chart 8.14.

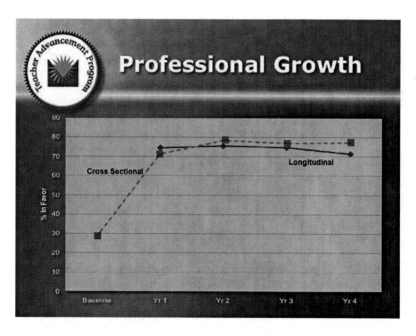

Chart 8.15.

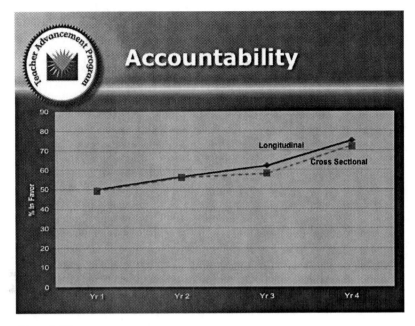

Chart 8.16.

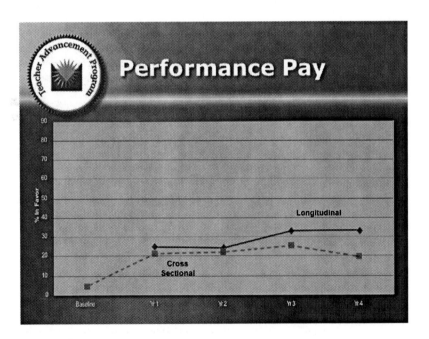

Chart 8.17.

Support for the elements is generally high and increases over time. The level of support for multiple career paths has been strong since the beginning. This factor indicates that teachers have a comfort level with peer evaluations, as well as the quality of the teacher leaders in their classroom and in their school. There's no doubt that professional growth is strongly supported by teachers across all schools, all states, and all years of implementation. The support for the TAP accountability system is also strong and growing.

We knew that performance pay would be the most challenging element to implement because it deviates furthest from the norm of the educational culture. TAP is really at the cutting edge of performance pay. We're the only program in the nation that is linking performance pay to teacher performance, not just school-wide, but to teacher and individual classroom value-added. While we know that it is a difficult cultural shift for teachers, we're optimistic about the gaining support among teachers that we've seen since the start. We also believe that as performance pay becomes more prevalent across the country, the support for this element will increase. It is also important to note that the majority of TAP teachers actually reported feeling average or unsure of the notion of performance pay. It wasn't that 35% were in favor, and 65% were against. Rather, the majority feels either average about or in favor of performance pay.

I've taken up plenty of your time this afternoon, and I hope you have a lot of questions to ask me about the program. But indulge me one more minute to share a greatly paraphrased version of the philosopher Plato's "Allegory of the Cave." The story goes that people were living at the bottom of a cave, in the dark, with little knowledge or access to the world above. They were content, because that was all that they knew. One day, one of the inhabitants ventured to the outside. At first, the light was shocking, and the vast surroundings overwhelming. The person went back into the cave and tried desperately to convince the others to follow to this great, new, bold world above. They were resistant—life was fine in its current form. They knew what to expect. But finally, they agreed to venture above. And just as their leader had experienced, their eyes were overwhelmed by the sunlight and the surroundings. But soon they realized the adjustment was worth the outcome. They could now partake in a world that they never knew. One rich with opportunity and adventure.

So, I encourage all of you to think beyond your comfort zone, to look at change as something exciting and challenging, and consider the journey that teachers and administrators in our TAP schools have taken—one that requires a shift in traditional norms, but has the potential of making great improvements in the learning experiences of our children.

I'm sure that there must be some questions the audience has about TAP.

Audience Question

What kind of information is available about TAP?

Tamara Schiff

We have a comprehensive Web site, www.tapschools.org, and what I'd recommend is that you read a little bit more about the program and look at the work that's on the Web site. Also encourage some of the stakeholders who might be involved to take a look at that and educate themselves.

Audience Question

You mentioned that one part of the program is standardized testing used to track student achievement. I would imagine then that different states use different standards and that concerns me since standardized tests can't always capture the thinking that kids do or the knowledge they can produce.

Tamara Schiff

That's why student achievement gains are a part of the bonus, but not the entire bonus. State standards are what we expect our children to learn, so while it does not capture everything that a child learns, it does capture important elements. We utilize the tests that are given in the state. We work with the states, to use their existing systems.

Audience Question

Can you explain a little bit more about how the leadership teams are developed once a school becomes a TAP school? Also can you elaborate more on how collegiality and competition work out?

Tamara Schiff

The Foundation provides comprehensive training for the leadership teams. During this training, the leadership team learns how to become evaluators, they then take a test and become certified. It is training that continues throughout the process of TAP implementation and even beyond that first year or so. We also go into schools and do program reviews, where we look at how implementation is going in each school. The state director is the primary Foundation representative who is in the schools 80% of his or her time. The director's job is not only to assess how well things are going, but also to provide support for how they might improve or further align the school to the TAP model.

In terms of the collegiality versus competition, I think the system builds such a collaborative environment that it just isn't competitive. What happens is that when master and mentor teachers are providing the level of service and support for teachers in the classroom that they should, and teachers are meeting two times a week or three times a week in those professional dialogues, the mindset of the teachers shifts and they realize that the program is not an evaluation program but a reform program for their school. Once teachers start experiencing the level of support they're giving you, your schools come to have a collegial atmosphere.

The other thing to remember, if you are worried about competition in your school as a result of TAP, is that it's not a mandated program. The level of buy-in and agreement from the teachers helps to ensure that the teachers are going to be onboard with the program and not compete with their colleagues.

Audience Question

Where do you find the master teachers for the school? Do they come from within the school, or do you look outside as well?

Tamara Schiff

They come both from within and without. As Lowell said earlier, human capital is what makes the difference. People make the difference. Some schools enter the program with the capacity to have leaders within their midst. Others do not. So, we encourage a competitive hiring process. We encourage schools to look beyond just their school.

NOTE

1. TAP is now at work in over 100 campuses throughout the nation, impacting more than 45,000 students and 3,100 teachers.

CHAPTER 9

PRESENTATION BY SENATOR MARY LANDRIEU

Mary Landrieu

Introduction by Lewis Solmon

It's my great pleasure to introduce a special guest, Senator Mary Landrieu from Louisiana, who has been referred to as one of the Senate's foremost leaders in education. Now, she's been referred to that way, and I've got a text prepared, but I really have to say that hearing Senator Landrieu talk about education, the understanding she has, and the inspiration that she imparts to other people—I don't think a formal introduction could do justice.

Senator Landrieu has really been a leading light in advancing the ideas of the Teacher Advancement Program (TAP). In terms of early childhood and strengthening families through foster care and adoption, she understands human capital. Her passion in promoting the importance of education—not just for her state, but for the nation—is truly inspiring. We were standing outside as the Senator was addressing the delegation from Louisiana, and I was literally getting chills up my back. Rather than me talk, I'd like to call on Senator Landrieu, who is really one of the great leaders in the Senate today.

The Challenges of School Reform: Implementation, Impact, and Sustainability, 145–149
Copyright © 2006 by Information Age Publishing
All rights of reproduction in any form reserved.

Mary Landrieu

Thank you for that introduction. It really is humbling because I realize I'm in an auditorium of the real experts—those who are on the front lines in the classroom, running school systems, raising money, thinking outside of the box, and doing all the things that help to make this nation a great nation. I am truly humbled. I'm also really honored to be here and was asked just to speak for a few minutes about a couple of things that are in my heart and mind.

I have such an admiration for the Milken Family Foundation and what they're doing to partner with us, helping to create a vibrant, robust, exciting, equitable, education system for our nation, which hopefully will continue to lead the world in so many areas. I was fortunate enough to be able to attend one of the Milken Educator Award notification ceremonies here in D.C., just like the one that all of you experienced when you got your award. Do you remember sitting there, unsuspecting, not knowing it was going to be your name that was called? Well, I was so excited because they had clued me in, and I'll never forget, for as long as I live, the expression on this teacher's face. But the expression on her classroom children was the most amazing thing I've ever seen. This second-grade class lost it. These little second-graders started squealing and making that joyful sound that you could only get out of children who are just totally uninhibited. They ran up to their teacher, and I'm telling you, there was not a dry eye in the place watching this ceremony unfold.

For all of you who received this award, I know that not only your family and your spouses, but your students, are so proud of you because without magnificent and wonderful teachers, our system wouldn't be anywhere. I'll never forget that, and I'd go to every one of these ceremonies if you'd invite me. Though, my voting record would be shot if I left the floor to do this.

I want to make a couple of brief remarks. Sometimes you can't always see the light about where you're headed. You kind of knew why you got started, but then things start happening, and you're no longer sure you're on the right path. I'd like to quote something that I keep on my desk and try to read occasionally when the way gets tough. It's a great quotation:

> We possess all the resources and all the talents necessary, but the fact of the matter is that we have never made the national decisions or marshaled the national resources for such leadership. We have never specified long-range goals on an urgent time schedule or managed our resources and time to ensure their fulfillment. Let us be clear. I'm asking the Congress and the country to accept a firm commitment for a new course of action—a course which will last for many years and carry a very heavy cost. If we are only to

go halfway, or reduce our sights in the face of difficulty, it would be better not to go at all.

You might remember this speech; it was given by President Kennedy when we got ready to launch and put a man on the Moon. But I think the challenge that President Kennedy issued to our nation then is as relevant today for a different issue, one could even argue, is greater. If we cannot launch every child in this nation to a place where they can fulfill their responsibilities and live up to the talents and abilities that God has given them, then our nation fails a little bit every day, and our nation is that much weaker every day.

While I understand that we cannot be perfect in our democratic efforts, that there'll always be imperfections, I like to be a part of this team because I like to try to be as good as I can possibly be. To try to be the best. To reach for excellence. I don't wake up every day to go to the Senate and think, "Well, maybe we can be a halfway country. Maybe we can just sort of get it halfway right." I really hope that you all share this sentiment because you've been given these awards of excellence, but I think I'm speaking to a group of people who believes in trying to go for the stars.

President Kennedy literally reached for the stars in this challenge to our nation, and we made it. A long-term goal included sacrifices that had to be made, rethinking, and recommitment, but we got there. A nation that has championed and won so many great battles in the past, whether they were military battles or economic challenges, most certainly can get this system of educating every child right. We've heard the barriers; we understand that there's inequity of funding. We understand that there's too much micromanagement. We understand that there's an intricate balance between the federal government, the state government, and the local government; but I know that I'm speaking to a group who—in your own way, in your own school, in your own classroom, in your own parish, in your own county, in your own state—have overcome those barriers, despite the obstacles. To follow the adage of one of my great role models and mentors, Paul Vallas, who was on an earlier panel, "Just do it."

I know we could spend all of our time complaining about how No Child Left Behind isn't perfect or that this is not working well, but if we stay the course and understand that the joy and the treasure at the end— a school system where every child can get that kind of quality education— is within our reach, and we push ourselves, then that means we sometimes have to change a little bit of our laws. Sometimes we have to change our direction. Sometimes we must open our eyes to see different things. We can most certainly do it. While I understand and am aware that there are some problems with this new federal effort, let's fix those problems and continue to get to a point where we can say we want to reward excellence.

We want to duplicate it, and we want to replicate it. Let's identify the failures and eliminate them. Reward success and accountability, and believe that we can have a system.

Then let's work on the funding equity issue, which Congressman Chaka Fattah can speak better about than almost anybody in the nation. We should heed what he says about the fact that some of our school districts are trying to do this with two hands tied behind their back because they don't have the resources. Let's not stop trying to be excellent. Let's untie those hands and get more resources to those school districts.

One thing in closing about the Teacher Advancement Program. When I saw this model, I thought that this was something Louisiana needed. We are one of the poorest states in the union, but we've got great leadership. I have to say I know the lieutenant governor very well; he happens to be my brother. And he's doing a great job. Cecil Picard is our state superintendent. We have so many great local superintendents in our state, and the leadership team is there. I agree with the concept of supporting teachers by rewarding them and giving them time to do what they do well, to teach and support them in their teaching by mentorship and master teachers. This is a real component of our education reform efforts in this nation.

To achieve our vision of every child having a quality education, it really must be about teachers. It is about empowering them by giving them the tools and the help they need to minister to the children they have in their classrooms or their schools. When we saw the TAP model and saw that it works, I said to Lowell Milken that we wanted to help to lead this effort, and I helped to orchestrate the first federal commitment to TAP. Our superintendent quickly recognized the value of TAP, that it is something that could really work.

This year, one of our Louisiana TAP school districts is implementing TAP parish-wide; it's not a small school district with only a few schools implementing TAP. There are 27 schools in the Calcasieu Parish school district, which is a fairly good-sized school district. They are going to collapse some of their federal money and basically create a TAP parish. All the teachers, with the support of the Milken Family Foundation and our state, are going to be able to work in a school that really honors them, supports them, and gives them the time they need to do their job.

I'm thrilled for Louisiana to be a leader in this effort. I'm going to continue to work on the appropriations committee to fund TAP and, with guidance from all of you to move this program out nationally, to grow it in a way that assures quality. With the Foundation's support and guidance, we see this as a real possibility for one aspect of our school reform. As President Kennedy said, "If we're not going to go the distance, we just as soon not have started, and just lived with the status quo the way it is, which is catch as catch can."

There is a movement that's been going on now for several decades, despite the barriers and even with the difficulties, and I see a great deal of progress. Let's continue down the path, martial our efforts, keep our vision clear, and work hard for the kids we're trying to serve. Thank you all.

CHAPTER 10

INTERSECTION OF PERFORMANCE PAY AND PROFESSIONAL DEVELOPMENT

Kristan Van Hook, T. Kenneth James, Cecil J. Picard, Alice Seagren, Lewis C. Solmon, and J. Todd White

Kristan Van Hook

We have here some of the leading experts in the country on the issues of professional development and performance pay, and are very much looking forward to hearing from them as they help to explain how some of these issues are playing out at the state level, what some of the challenges are, and what some of their plans are going forward. As schools and districts work to meet the goals of NCLB, what does this mean in the area of professional development, and how can professional development better align with student achievement goals and measures?

At the same time, we've heard quite a bit about performance pay and teacher compensation systems. For those concerned with teacher quality, how can we harness growing support for performance pay and help that to lead to greater compensation for teachers? And then finally, I'm going to leave it up to this group to answer the questions of, "Why are these two con-

The Challenges of School Reform: Implementation, Impact, and Sustainability, 151–169

cepts on the same panel? How do they fit together, and how is it working in the states?" Starting with Ken James from Arkansas, I'll turn it over to you.

Ken James

I want to talk to you very briefly about what we've done in Arkansas with the infusion of new dollars into the educational arena. We have just completed our legislative session, which we've enjoyed because it was a great session. So I'm going to go through some numbers here for you, because we feel very fortunate about what has happened in Arkansas, in terms of money that has been infused into our system.

We are now the only state in the country that has an act on the books (Act 108), which says when revenue gets distributed in our state, K-12 education gets first call on the dollars. That does not make me very popular with some of my fellow agency heads when I go in and out of committee meetings, but it's where the emphasis needs to be. We are very fortunate and very proud to have that in the state of Arkansas.

I want to highlight that in the 2004 special session, significant dollars went into K-12 education in Arkansas. National school lunch money received $148 million. State foundation aid got an additional $281 million. Alternative learning was given $16 million; this is an additional amount that goes for alternative students and bona fide alternative programs. We had $22 million put into professional development after this special session, and the Better Chance program, our early childhood program, received almost $40 million. I'm proud to tell you that we just placed another $20 million into that program.

If we are going to close the proverbial achievement gap, then we have to begin early. We have to start with those students who often do not come on a level playing field. If we're to get them to the point where they need to be by the third or fourth grade, in terms of being able to take our state-wide benchmark examinations or being able to read at the end of grade level, then we're going to have to start early. That's the only way we're going to begin to first narrow the gap before we can get to closing it, because we're not going to easily make that jump.

As we've seen from the statistics, our state is no different. We held a high school summit a couple of weeks ago with about 600 people. The first thing we started talking about was the significant gap that we have across-the-board and the fact that we've got to drill down and begin talking significantly about this issue across the state. We can begin to make sure we get to the point where we can do what we need to do for kids. That's why we're all here.

Most recently, the 85th General Assembly increased the level of funding. National school lunch money—money that goes for high poverty, at-risk students across our state—received an additional $14 million. An additional $12 million was placed in state foundation aid, and alternative learning got another $28 million. This is over a two-year period. Facilities funding was the second leg of Arkansas' lawsuit on equity and adequacy; this time, it was addressed in terms of additional funding for significantly improving facilities across the state, so that your ZIP Code does not determine the quality of your facilities. We all have places in our state where we've had inadequate facilities for students to learn, and Arkansas is taking a first step in changing that. Also, the teacher insurance program in the state was moving toward what was termed to be a "death spiral," and if things were not done to rectify that system, it was predicted to go down in a blazing fashion in a couple of years. So significant dollars—$71 million over the two years—have been placed into shoring up the teacher insurance program in the state of Arkansas.

Let's discuss the topic of professional development. This is a $4 million line-item to the State Department of Education, on top of what is now going out to the school districts; a $50 per student allotment will be used to begin work on our educational television network for online professional development. An evaluation system and things of that nature will also be included. One of the things we've found in Arkansas is that we had the $50 per student allotment going directly to the districts as a result of the special session, but as we worked on the rules and regulations to develop that, we realized we needed much more accountability for those professional development opportunities. Legislators heard from teachers, and it became clear that the level of quality for professional development across the state was not equal. We had some very, very good things going, but we also had some isolated pockets where the money was not being used for quality professional development.

What comes with all these new dollars that are going into education in Arkansas? Each and every one of us knows that it is increased accountability as we move forward. As we go back before the legislature and our constituents as good stewards of resources, we're going to have to make sure that we demonstrate very significantly, how all these new dollars have had an impact on student learning. At the end of the day, if we can't demonstrate that, then we're going to have difficulty legislatively and with our taxpayers.

I was a superintendent for 11 years before getting into the state school chief's position. There are some days I would lie awake at night and want to go back and be a superintendent, because the superintendents in our state right now have more money to work with than they've ever had before. That's a good thing. But, with that goes increased accountability so that each and every one of us is going to have to make sure we're able to demonstrate the good things we've been able to do. Short of that, we're going to have difficulty. We also have a provision for AETN, Arkansas

Educational Television Network, to assist in this process. They're already doing some video streaming and things of that nature with professional development across our state. We need to have more significant development in terms of that particular piece as we move forward.

One other thing that we're very excited about is that we received special language this session, which ties in some assistance. We didn't name TAP, but we stole some of the special language from our colleagues in South Carolina for TAP-like programs that are focused on what TAP stands for. Each and every one of you know those criteria, and you've seen all of those charts. What we're going to do with this additional infusion of money—on top of what we already have as the result of contributions from the Walton Family Foundation and other entities—is target this money toward schools that need improvement. We're going to provide the schools with the TAP model; because, for whatever reason, they've not been able to make significant strides over time in professional development activities in their district. As we continue to have legislative sessions in the future, we hope that we can make this grow. This will be an infusion to make sure that we're putting some dollars into significant projects across our state, to work with school districts and give them a model that has proven to be successful.

We're very excited in Arkansas about what TAP has done. I had the personal privilege of putting TAP into two schools in Little Rock when I was a superintendent there. When I went to Little Rock and told them I wanted to do TAP, they told me it would never happen because we had a strong collective bargaining unit. They told me, "You're crazy. You're insane." Well, we found more than two schools, but we only had resources to start with two schools. We talked to their staffs, and overwhelmingly their staffs voted by over 80% to implement this program. They're still extremely happy with it. I'm hopeful that we can continue to grow with TAP in the Little Rock School District, as well as across the state, because these are significant changes we need to be making in education. TAP provides an outstanding model for us. I know we're not supposed to do public relations announcements or a media blitz, but I want to say to you that we need to be candid about what these things stand for.

The collaboration of these teachers, as they come together to talk about what's going on in the classroom and what they can do to benefit the instruction for those kids, is good, sound practice. Whatever we call it, those are the kinds of things we need to be doing. We need to continue to embellish that and grow that as we move forward. We're proud to be a part of the program, and we're proud of what's going on in Arkansas.

As a result of this last special session, we also had significant changes in our accountability program and significant powers placed upon the state board with potential takeovers and things of that nature. I know "take-over" is a hostile word, a bad word. When you take somebody over, you had better have a good plan about what you're going to do with them. You better have an exit strategy as to what you're going to do at the end of that conversation.

When Ray Simon talked about building technical capacity in state departments, that's something all of us across this country are going to continue to face, because we have more to do. The reality is that most of us have less to do it with than we've had in the past. One last item I've got to plug. This last session, we got probably the most significant piece of legislation passed in the history of the State Department of Education. Representative Dangeau led that effort for us by sponsoring that bill. We had a management audit that had started when I got there. The end result of that management process is that we are now going to get the opportunity to reorganize the State Department and pay significant salaries to be able to compete with school districts out there for high quality people.

I'm going to have the latitude for 25-plus positions, to be able to pay significant salaries for high level, high quality folks to come in and shore up our State Department, so that we can deliver those kinds of services that we need to do for our schools and our state. My agency coworkers and directors told me, "You'll never get this done. This is crazy. They've never let a state agency do this." And as I walked out of that last personnel committee meeting smiling ear-to-ear, I waved to each and every one of them. Now they all want to do it.

We've been given an opportunity and a pilot to move forward, and I'm hopeful that other state agencies will get that same thing. But again, we're going to have to produce. We're going to require results as we move forward. If not, then it will not be something successful for people who follow. But this is a phenomenal opportunity in Arkansas for us right now, as we move forward on educational reform. We're excited to be here today.

Kristan Van Hook

Thank you, Dr. James. Next, we'll hear from Louisiana Superintendent Cecil Picard about the efforts that he's been making in terms of professional development, where those are heading, and if there is any intersection in the compensation area.

Cecil Picard

The title of this panel is most appropriate for our discussion here today. There is truly an intersection where professional development and performance pay meet. Any meaningful discussion of performance pay must take place within the context of professional development. Louisiana's professional development efforts are grounded in the belief that the best professional development is school-based and closely aligned with the needs of both students and teachers.

We have taken a comprehensive approach to provide professional development that is school-based, has a leadership component, focuses on curriculum, is built around learning communities, and contains an evaluation component. In the interests of time, I'll outline a couple of our programs for you. First is our Grade Level Expectations Education Model (GLEEM). This gives teachers what they need to know in order to implement the state's grade-level expectations and the new comprehensive curriculum. It's the first professional development model to roll out with both face-to-face and online activities. It provides online, anytime/anywhere professional development. In addition, it's convenient and there's no lost instructional time.

Another program we have is called Learning Intensive Networking Communities for Success or LINCS. It's a nationally recognized program that establishes professional learning communities where classroom teachers increase content knowledge and develop standards-based lesson plans to incorporate in their daily instruction. It utilizes leadership teams and learning groups. We began with 48 elementary schools in the 2000-2001 school year. We currently have 170 elementary, middle, and high schools and 5,700 teachers currently participating in 1,100 LINCS study groups. Results include increased student test scores, and higher school performance scores.

Another program we have is one you're likely very familiar with, and that's the National Board Certification for Professional Teaching Standards (NBPTS). It's a recognized symbol of teaching excellence. Our state provides a stipend of $5,000 per year for the life of the certificate, which in our case is 10 years. When I became superintendent in 1996, there were five nationally board certified teachers who had become NBPTS on their own. We now have 578, with another 450 in the pipeline, which puts us eighth in the nation in eight short years.

I haven't been prompted to mention this, but I would be remiss if I didn't mention TAP and the difference that it's making in Louisiana. We started with six schools in four parishes. We've had outstanding results, and the teachers and the schools are just enthusiastic. We expect to add 29 schools and two additional districts next year. We have the superintendent of Calcasieu Parish here, who is going to incorporate 27 of his elementary, middle, and high schools into TAP, utilizing and collapsing Title I, Title II, and Comprehensive School Reform (CSR) monies. I was just amazed when Calcasieu came and made the presentation to me. I said, "There's got to be something here. Why would all of these schools, with

75% of the teachers voting in favor, want to become a TAP school?" We figured it out; those schools were LINCS schools. They now see TAP as three notches above LINCS. We're going to continue to expand TAP in Louisiana, as far and as wide as funding will permit, because we believe quality teachers deserve quality pay.

The level of pay for teachers in Louisiana, like many other states, is almost criminal. The average teacher salary in Louisiana is $37,918. The national average is $46,826. We're $3,500 below the Southern Regional Educational Board average and $8,500 below the national average. You simply cannot attract and retain the caliber of teachers that children in schools need and deserve with substandard pay. Participation in programs such as national board certification, LINCS, and TAP shows that teachers, in increasing numbers, are willing to link their performance to their compensation. Louisiana, like many other states, is gradually moving toward performance pay for teachers. Teachers should be recognized and rewarded for outstanding classroom performance that translates to increased student achievement. And states must provide comprehensive professional development that will serve as the underpinning for a performance-based system. I'm excited about that because I truly believe that the single most important indicator of student performance in the classroom is the classroom teacher.

We know that students who are taught three years in a row by an ineffective teacher absolutely never recover, so, in a poor state like Louisiana, it's imperative that we get a highly qualified, certified teacher for every child in every classroom. Thank you.

Kristan Van Hook

Next, we will hear from Minnesota Commissioner of Education, Alice Seagren. Commissioner Seagren has not only a history of having worked on many of these issues, but also a pending proposal in Minnesota that's quite exciting.

Alice Seagren

It's really wonderful to be here with all of you. I love the Milken Family Foundation. I was first exposed to the Foundation in 1999 when I was still a legislator, beginning my journey as the K-12 education finance chair. I have actually been very interested in reform, long before I had the opportunity to be the chair of K-12 education finance. I've also probably been known over the last 20 to 25 years as the thorn in the side of every school board, school district, etc., as a parent.

I have a unique background. I have a daughter who is very gifted and a son born handicapped. Out of those two circumstances began my journey of wanting to have an educational opportunity that was excellent for all children. I would read a lot of research and look at the things that make a difference in a child's life. I ran for the school board and was elected; I then ran for the legislature and was elected. My journey continued, and last July, I was appointed commissioner of education by our governor.

Governor Pawlenty and I really believe strongly that teachers are the key to success for every one of our children in our state. In Minnesota, we all live in Lake Woebegone, where all of our children are above average. Oftentimes, I hear teachers say that the achievement gap is much wider because all of our children are so much more brilliant. However, we have a serious achievement gap in the state of Minnesota, and we've been working very aggressively to close that gap.

Back in 1999, I came to Milken National Education Conference and listened to what at that time was the seed of TAP. They were looking at differentiated staffing, at actually using the existing dollars within a site, and at restructuring the system to provide the kinds of resources to get the job done. I was also looking at research from Dr. Alan Odden, who was also looking at alternative compensation systems—how we can attract and retain the best and brightest into the teaching profession.

As a K-12 committee, we brought in Dr. William Sanders, who was working on a value-added growth model, because you can't legitimately measure the academic impact upon a classroom if you don't have some way of showing that impact. Sanders' research is very, very strong and has been repeated several times during this Conference. If you have a teacher who's ineffective for three years in a row, that teacher's student almost never recovers. So it's extremely important that you have quality teachers.

I decided to put all of this stuff together about five years ago, when we created a pilot program. It was an alternative compensation model that required a demonstration of academic achievement, but also professional development that was aligned to district and site goals that made a difference for your students in your particular situation. It was passed, and we had four rural districts and Minneapolis School District, one of our large urban districts, to participate. Forty percent of the teachers in Minneapolis decided to move into this pilot program.

It was based on a number of things, and I'd be glad to share the initial legislation later on, if you're interested. But from that time on, we kind of spun our wheels. We ran into some financial difficulties in the state of Minnesota. We had a $4.5 billion deficit that we had to take care of, so we stalled for a while. However, we continued the program, and this year, we have decided to take it up to the next level. We are so fortunate because TAP and the federal government combined forces and offered Minnesota an opportunity to get involved in TAP.

We have our Waseca School District participating in TAP, plus three sites in Minneapolis that also were in our original pilot program. They were ready to move up to the next level and incorporate the four elements of TAP—evaluation, professional development, a career ladder, and some monies based on performance. The key component that is most exciting to me is professional development, because that's what teachers have been wanting for years and years; teachers want professional development with their colleagues during the week, where they can get together, look at best practices, strategize, and then go back into the classroom and implement those best practices.

So often, we have teachers who go to an in-service, learn something, then put it on the shelf and never use it. You need to have that reflection, that teamwork, and the strategic time to do it. That is the lynchpin of our Q Comp, or Quality Compensation for Teachers, plus evaluation. In our state, before you are tenured, there is a three-year probationary period. After that probationary period, a teacher is only required to be evaluated once every three years, so you can be teaching for 30 years and only be evaluated 10 times. Now, our teachers, especially our more experienced teachers, have gotten a little bit uncomfortable with being evaluated, saying, "I know how to teach." While the majority of them *do* know how to teach, all of us can learn how to be better teachers. So part of this whole system is a real, meaningful evaluation, not about "getting" teachers, but to help them improve and to be the very best they can be. That's what we want for our kids: to have that best quality teacher in the classroom.

Our governor has proposed $260 per pupil in the formula that will be embedded and ongoing if districts move into our Quality Compensation program. Our old pilot offered $150 per pupil. We've ratcheted it up to the next level, so we're really intensely working on that. The program will be able to fund 50% of our students in the state of Minnesota. It's interesting—when it was first unveiled, the discussion indicated that people didn't really think there would be that many districts interested. Now the discussion is that we don't think there's going to be enough money, so we're extremely excited about it. It's not about laws and legislation, no matter how you implement it in your state; it's about having those four elements. When you have that package of elements together, particularly professional development and the evaluation components, then you can really take teachers to new heights.

Kristan Van Hook

What is it about the four elements together—the career ladder, the professional development, the evaluation, and pay? I know many of you in your own classrooms and your own schools have many of these aspects and elements. Why is it important to have four together? What is it that is so different about this program? I'd like to ask Lewis Solmon to come up and talk about those issues.

Lewis Solmon

I want to reinforce some of the points that were made earlier in this conference. We heard a discussion earlier about non-school factors and what impacts how much students learn. Research shows that 49% of the influence is from the home and family, 43% is teacher qualifications, and 8% is class size. Let's not focus on the 49%; let's focus on the 43% that says teachers are the single most important school-related factor responsible for increasing student achievement. Therefore, improving teacher quality is essential.

Chart 10.1 highlights some initial propositions for improving teacher quality. Most people want to spend money on effective teachers, but the way we spend money today on experience and on postbaccalaureate credits does not correlate with increasing student achievement. We heard this morning that salary was third or fourth on the list of factors, compared to support, stability, safety, and respect.

Maybe it's because I'm an economist, but I think when you pay people at the level that you pay teachers, particularly effective teachers, you're not showing them respect. There's a correlation between showing respect and paying people what they're worth. We keep hearing that money is not important to teachers because they love kids, and they want to make kids learn. Well, doctors love making people healthy, but that doesn't mean they can't earn a living. Lawyers want justice. That doesn't mean they shouldn't earn a living. So I don't see why good intentions preclude earning money.

Also, I think that there's an ethos in teaching that when you do these surveys, it's simply not appropriate for teachers to say that money is important. That's simply the way it is. But they do say it, in several other ways. They say it by leaving. They say it by going into administration, when they'd really rather be in the classroom, or by leaving the profession altogether. College graduates say it when they don't enter the teaching profession at all. When we ask whether money's important, we have got to look at the people who don't come in, rather than the people who do.

Chart 10.2 lists the reason why people don't choose teaching. In what other profession do you start on day one with a job description and a title, have a successful career, then, 30 years later, retire with the same job description and the same title? It's not very appealing to the go-getter college graduate. Further, in what other profession do you go into a room,

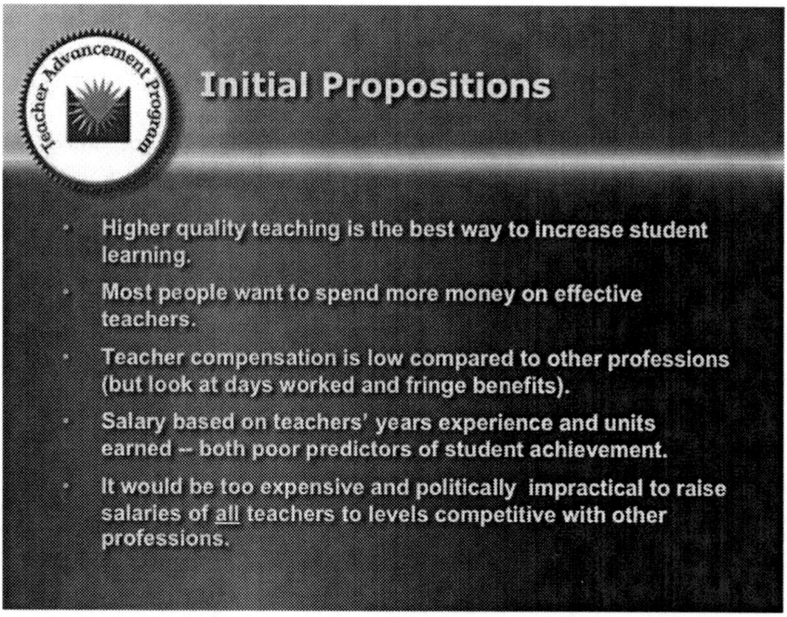

Teacher Advancement Program
Initial Propositions
Higher quality teaching is the best way to increase student learning.
Most people want to spend more money on effective teachers.
Teacher compensation is low compared to other professions (but look at days worked and fringe benefits).
Salary based on teachers' years experience and units earned -- both poor predictors of student achievement.
It would be too expensive and politically impractical to raise salaries of all teachers to levels competitive with other professions.

Chart 10.1.

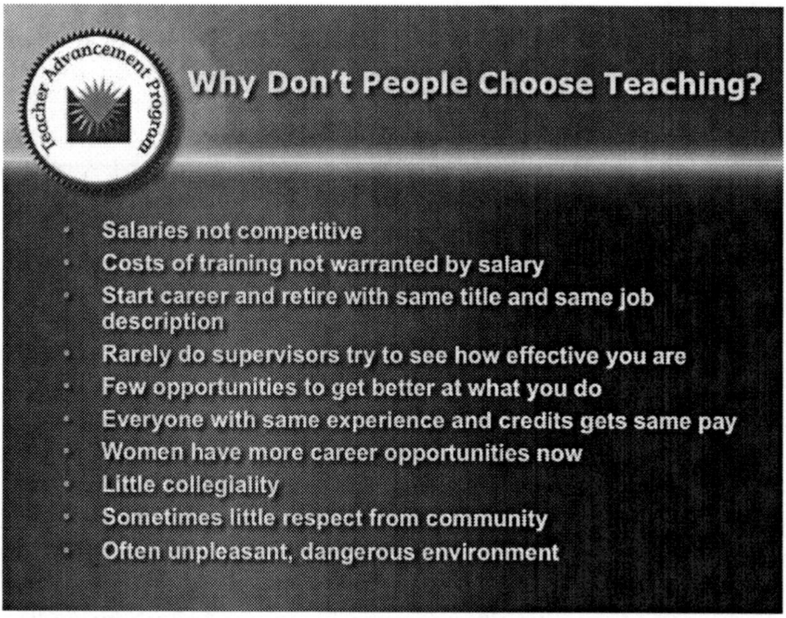

Teacher Advancement Program
Why Don't People Choose Teaching?
Salaries not competitive
Costs of training not warranted by salary
Start career and retire with same title and same job description
Rarely do supervisors try to see how effective you are
Few opportunities to get better at what you do
Everyone with same experience and credits gets same pay
Women have more career opportunities now
Little collegiality
Sometimes little respect from community
Often unpleasant, dangerous environment

Chart 10.2.

close the door, not communicate with other adults during the day, and nobody knows how good you are?

TAP counters many of the traditional drawbacks that plague the teaching profession: low compensation, lack of career advancement, unsupported accountability demands, little collegiality, and ineffective professional development. TAP provides an integrated solution to these challenges—changing the structure of the teaching profession within schools, while maintaining the essence of the profession. It allows us to take a small group of high quality master teachers and implement a program that enhances the talent of *all* teachers at the school. Teachers are held accountable for their instruction and the impact they have on their students' achievement. With that accountability, there are rewards—both in monetary form and in terms of professional development and support. The ultimate goal of TAP is to increase student achievement by maximizing teacher quality.

The most discussed of the four elements of TAP is performance pay. We asked the question, "Why do performance pay plans fail?" There are a lot of reasons why these programs have not worked in the past, and in developing TAP we took those into account. Performance pay plans are usually imposed. We don't impose. We involve teachers from the beginning and explain the program to them. We solicit their input. And only if they want to do it, we do it.

Another criticism we keep hearing is that teachers don't want to be evaluated. They don't want to be held accountable. This is a fallacy. Sometimes teachers are reluctant to be evaluated if they don't think they will be able to perform well on the evaluation. If there is a professional development mechanism whereby teachers, if evaluated poorly at the beginning, can then know that there's a way for them to get better next year, that's acceptable. They just don't want to be in a place where they don't know what to do, they're not going to get compensated, and they have no idea how to ever change the situation.

Then there's the whole issue of being fair. If we have trained, certified evaluators evaluating teachers based on a set of scientifically-based rubrics, with more than one evaluator and multiple evaluations a year, then it's pretty hard to be biased. Also, a lot of these past programs did not set enough money aside to pay for the program. I was talking with people who were considering implementing a performance pay plan, and they were wondering whether it should be $300 or $400 a teacher. Teaching is a lot of work. Three hundred or $400 just is not going to work. The teachers are going to lose interest quickly. We think bonuses should be substantial, not trivial.

There is also a fear that the program might not be sustainable. What we've learned is that, as most of our TAP states are now doing, there has to be shared funding and participation by the schools, the districts, and the state from the beginning. A grant is a wonderful thing. But you've got to make sure that there's a mechanism built-in so that when the grant money runs out, or when the federal money runs out, there's a way to sustain the program. It's also important to get buy-in from all of the leaders in the state, particularly the teachers.

The conclusion is that performance pay alone is not enough. It must be supported by a strong, transparent, and fair evaluation system, professional development, and significant bonuses. What I would say is that there is some cost involved in TAP, as most of you know, but the money can be found. However, as was said in the first chapter of this book, you can't keep layering reform on reform on reform. I hope that one of the messages our Foundation gets out is that when things don't work, stop doing them.

Todd White

I've run into thousands and thousands of teachers across the country, and what I find is that teachers go into the classroom every single day, and do the very best job they know how to do. I've yet to run into a teacher who said, "I think I'm going to be bad today. You know, I'm going to just do the worst I can possibly do."

I want you to think of this system as a scale. We have a system that is heavy on accountability. The problem is that we're real light on the other side of the scale, so we need to bring some balance into it. One of the things that TAP does is try to bring that balance in there. I hear it again and again from people; they want assistance with being better in meeting those standards. Teachers don't mind accountability when they have the support in place to meet it. In TAP, we have a simple process for going through that support piece (Chart 10.3), we call is the TAP Steps for Effective Learning.

In the first Step, we look at student data. The data tells us what the specific needs are with kids, and then we begin to work with it. We also use data from teacher evaluations, because there are very clear and specific things teachers need assistance with. So we marry those two components, and go into Step 2. Again, the assumption in Step 2 is that there needs to be new learning. If there's a deficient area, either in the teachers or the students, then we need to learn something to fill that area and to meet that need. Step 2 uses master and mentor teachers to field-test strategies and prove that these strategies work with the little faces in that building before taking it further. The master and mentor teachers then lead that

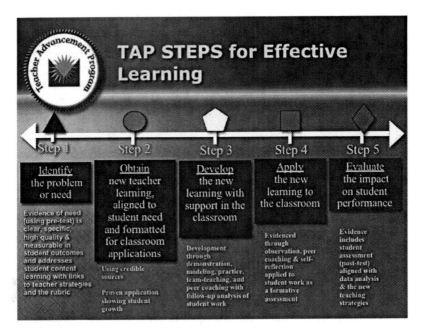

Chart 10.3.

learning of new proven strategies, one on one. They also lead it in professional groups that take place two to three times a week.

We know that in professional development, if somebody tells you to do something, you can't magically go back to the classroom and do it perfectly. We're like kids—a skill takes development time. That's what Step 3 is all about. With the assistance of master and mentor teachers, new learning goes back into the classroom and is supported. There are teachers who need to see it, so master and/or mentor teachers demonstrate it. There are teachers who need to walk through it with someone, so they team teach the strategies together, to work on perfecting those skills. There's a lot of observation and feedback, again on the area of student and teacher need. As we move into Step 4, it's the application in the classroom that increases expertise. As you get better and better with the skill, you're able to take that skill and transfer it to different areas. That's what Step 4 is all about.

Again, you see the observation, peer coaching, and reflection that goes on with TAP. One of the things I have not mentioned is that in Steps 2, 3, and 4, student work is used to teach, to develop, and to apply. We're constantly looking at what's happening, in terms of every single kid, with the strategies and things we're trying. Master and mentor teachers are work-

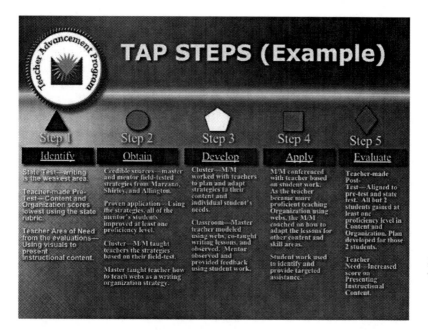

Chart 10.4.

ing with career teachers to teach them how to do that. They work on what patterns to look for, and then what interventions to plan for in Steps 3 and 4. Finally, if we've identified a problem and implemented a strategy to deal with it, Step 5 addresses what we need to see happen. We look at that in terms of both students and teachers.

Chart 10.4 brings the STEPS to life with a real example. I was in a school in Louisiana, and I decided—what better thing to do than to take something that a real teacher had presented? In Step 1, they presented and the work that they had done, showed that writing was the area of need. But it wasn't good enough to say that writing's the problem. The master teacher and career teacher worked together to do a writing prompt to further narrow down the specific problems in writing that kids were having.

They found from the pretest that content and organization is where the kids were really falling short. They also looked at the teacher evaluation data, and for that teacher, they found she was having trouble with presenting instructional content. In particular, she was grappling with the use of visuals in presenting content to kids to help them understand. In Step 2, the master and mentor teacher field-tested a couple of different strategies using real research and showed that it did work with kids in that building.

They sat down and worked with the teacher, both in professional development cluster group meetings and individually, on what those strategies were. Then they began the work in the classroom; they started to take it from their cluster groups back into the classroom. The master/mentor teacher looked at the students in that classroom and worked with the career teacher to adapt those strategies to meet the needs of every kid in the classroom. They also went in and modeled a series of lessons using webs to get kids to understand the prewriting process and how to take that and turn it into a paragraph.

The master/mentor teacher modeled, demonstrated, and observed. The career teacher talked about the support she felt and how she walked through her understanding of how to help kids become better writers. They had conferences constantly, and that's one of the things they talked about. The teachers pulled out student work, and they were saying, "Here's what we see in this kid's work, and here's how we adjusted for this kid. Here's what we see happening for this kid over here, and here's what we're doing there."

As the teacher became more and more proficient in the strategy, he or she talked about how to adapt that writing strategy into science and social studies. How do you take that strategy and then teach kids how to use that information to write a better essay answer in science and social studies? Again, student work was examined, and found that they had some kids who needed some double teaching. The students needed a double dose of writing instruction, and the teachers made plans and adjustments for that.

Finally, when they looked at the results, they found that, unlike the rest of the class, two of the students did not achieve a level of proficiency or above on this work. The teachers said, "We're not stopping with those two kids." And they worked together to develop a plan of what to do next to bring those kids up.

Again, last week, I was in Louisiana, and I had the good fortune to hear TAP teacher after TAP teacher talk about the kids who weren't quite there and the extra work they did to help the children—how they targeted exactly what the kids needed, and the kids got there. It was success story after success story in school after school.

The last piece is the teacher need. In this example, in presenting instructional content (which, on the TAP evaluation rubric, is where you would see the use of visuals), this teacher also saw an increase in her evaluation score. Teachers and teacher professional development should support teachers' growth and be connected to performance in two ways, and it is in TAP. The first way is increasing evaluation. We know the rubric is tied to good teaching practice, so an increase in evaluation scores would result in an increase in payout. Teachers see that as a positive. The second thing is that on the value-added model, if the kids are better writers in our example before, then they're making that growth. Again, the teacher is rewarded for the growth that kids are making in that area. It is not just where professional development and performance pay intersect, it's where they collide and really come together.

Kristan Van Hook

Thank you. I think in the interest of time, instead of the whole list of questions that I've got here, why don't we just take two questions from the audience.

Audience Question

I taught in the literacy program at Millikan High School in Long Beach, California, about four years ago. Our students came to me in ninth grade reading at the third-to-fifth grade level. By the end of the year, along with the team of teachers I was working with, we were able to raise them three years, three grade levels, and 83 API points, which was a huge gain for our campus. However, students were still reading below grade level. So, according to the state standards, I was failing.

According to the value-added model, we were a tremendous success. What I'm trying to figure out is: how is TAP going to affect state testing? Because the bottom line is, this is fantastic—teachers getting rewarded for doing a good job. When kids come in reading at the third-grade level, what am I supposed to do? I did what I could, and the kids rose. However, according to the state, I'm still not doing my job. So, where do we reconcile the two? How do we blend the two together?

Alice Seagren

In the state of Minnesota, we got legislation this year to actually develop our value-added model, and we're going to be doing that in spite of No Child Left Behind. Certainly, I think the TAP model that we're implementing is going to recognize value-added for the purposes that you described. If you have made this tremendous gain, you should be rewarded for that. It also serves as a control in the fairness issue, between teachers who may have easy-to-teach children versus teachers who might have hard-to-teach kids.

It's demonstrating that growth over time. When you ask what will happen with the state assessment, I think what we're really talking about is what will happen with No Child Left Behind. I would think these would be two separate issues. We would not be judging teachers based on the AYP and rewarding them on that; we would be basing the reward on value-added and what's going on in their school districts and their site. So, we see them as different things.

We will still have to meet the requirements of No Child Left Behind. We certainly will still be measuring that, but we're hoping to kind of blend those. Eventually, the feds will hopefully let us do that, so that we actually will have a safe harbor provision. Before we get that flexibility, we will not be linking those two necessarily to reward performance.

Ken James

Just the same thing in my state—we have recent legislation with value-added and also longitudinal tracking, which kicks in later on in the cycle. What we're seeing is this disconnect in terms of this growth model that you're talking about. That's something that we are going to be talking to the federal government about, to make sure that we bring these into sequence and that we're working together on this.

We heard this morning about the kids that grew from below basic to basic, and that's a significant jump for some of these youngsters. If you're at the bottom end of that band and below basic, and you move to basic, then you've made significant growth. Since right now there's no recognition of that, we have a real disconnect with this entire process that we've got to continue to dialogue around, to hopefully bring other people along with us.

Audience Question

This isn't really a question; it's just kind of a story. Five years ago, I turned in my resignation to my principal to get out of teaching, and he asked why I was doing this. It was because of money. As much as I loved teaching and the kids, I loved my family more. My wife stays home, and we have three kids now; I just knew I needed to do something different that would pay me more money, but I had no clue what that was.

So my principal said, "I'm not going to let go of you yet. Take a couple weeks; evaluate this. Think about it and come back." He suggested we write down some goals, which I never do, but I actually focused my attention and wrote down some goals. I went back to the master's program at college. The stinky part was that I had to put it all on my credit card. So, I was going in debt more to try to catch up, which it makes no sense. I still wasn't catching up, and I knew I was never going to catch up.

Then I realized it's not about the money. And we all know it's not about the money. I think our hearts are in the right place. I started to tell people that teachers had started to complain to me about money. I said, "Well then, quit and just get out. We don't want you here, because it's not about the money." Two weeks later, I got this sweet Milken thing, so I guess I have a point: My point is that I think performance pay is a rocking sweet deal. I think that the teachers who would get into it are the kind of teachers you would want. I love that whole cyclical thing. You know, as the teachers get better, then the kids get better. And we pay the teachers, and then it all cycles in. I think the teachers who will do this are the teachers who would get on the committees, anyway. I mean, it's those teachers that are always on the committees, so to reward them is just awesome.

PANEL CONTRIBUTIONS

CHAPTER 11

ENCOURAGING TEACHERS TO INVEST PAYING OFF FOR LOUISIANA

Remarks by Louisiana State Superintendent Cecil J. Picard

Budgets are tight in Louisiana. And educational budgets across the nation are similarly slim. So when faced with the challenge of rewarding teachers for a job well done, Louisiana has struggled to provide teacher pay raises in our poverty stricken state. However, tough times sometimes provide an opportunity to discover unique solutions, and Louisiana may have done just that.

When Louisiana was unable to reach the southern regional average for teacher pay and continued to lag far below the national average, we did not lower our heads in defeat. We instead began to encourage our teachers to invest in themselves. And the more they did, the more benefits they, and our state, began to reap. This strategy was quickly dubbed "the tripod" because it involved three programs that recognized and supported outstanding teachers who chose to use professional development as a means to improve student achievement, and at the same time, provide themselves a well-deserved monetary supplement.

The three legs of "the tripod" include: The Teacher Advancement Program (TAP), the Milken Educator Award and the National Board Certifi-

The Challenges of School Reform: Implementation, Impact, and Sustainability, 173–174
Copyright © 2006 by Information Age Publishing
173

cation Program. All three of these programs provide a way for teachers to gain meaningful and relevant professional development opportunities while also networking with their fellow educators both locally and nationally. And the bottom line is, these programs pay.

TAP is a program where professional development and performance pay intersect in a very direct way because incentives are strictly tied to student achievement. However, programs like the Milken Educator Award, which provides $25,000 to teachers chosen for their outstanding work and National Board Certification, which provides $5,000 per year for the lifetime of the certificate also offer teachers the chance to demonstrate their effectiveness in the classroom and share those experiences with their peers.

As Louisiana has encouraged our teachers to invest in themselves, our state has also experienced significant academic achievement and national recognition. In 2005, 75% of Louisiana's schools improved, *Education Week* Magazine ranked our efforts to improve teacher quality first in the nation, and we continue to see a narrowing of the achievement gap on both state and national assessments. Can all of these accolades be directly tied to teachers investing in themselves? Probably not, but it can be attributed to Louisiana's effort to attain systemic reform which included a sharp focus on teacher quality.

So while states across the nation struggle to provide meaningful teacher pay raises during tight budget times, there is an opportunity to combine high quality professional development with supplemental pay for those teachers willing to invest in themselves. And at the same time, districts, schools, and students can reap the benefits of improved academic achievement. A win-win situation for everyone.

CHAPTER 12

SHOULD WE PAY AND TRAIN TEACHERS DIFFERENTLY?

Alice Seagren and Ken Wolf

Minnesota K-12 schools face the daunting challenge of filling more than 24,000 teaching positions by the year 2004, vacancies created largely due to retirements. Many school districts are even now struggling to attract and retain new teachers, many of whom are instead opting for jobs outside the classroom.

Is the teacher shortage a crisis? Yes, but it's also an opportunity. This fall, a House K-12 Education Subcommittee on Oversight and Efficiency held hearings on this issue. From a varied group of stakeholders—teachers, administrators, principals and education policy experts—there was a clear consensus that good teachers were critical to student achievement. And there was general agreement that schools are experiencing troublesome turnover among beginning teachers and that this turnover can be linked to at least two conditions: starting salaries are often uncompetitive with the private sector and current staff development programs are often inadequate in supporting new teachers.

The Challenges of School Reform: Implementation, Impact, and Sustainability, 175–177
Copyright © 2006 by Information Age Publishing
All rights of reproduction in any form reserved.

Starting Salaries

We often hear that schools seem to be underfunded. We constantly hear about teacher layoffs, program reductions and larger class sizes. But how could this be? The state provides funding increases each year, including a billion dollar increase in 1999. Where did all that new money go? Not surprisingly, the bulk of new funding is used for teacher salaries, the largest item in any school budget. That is appropriate.

However, many school districts settle teacher contracts at dollar amounts greater than the additional funding provided by the state. Therefore, increased expenses exceed increased revenues no matter how much the state increases funding. In addition, using the traditional step & lane negotiating methods, the new money is distributed in a way that rewards teachers on the basis of years spent teaching (steps) and the time a teacher spends acquiring continuing education credits (lanes). As a result, funds are not available to provide the starting salaries necessary to attract talented college graduates to high-demand beginning teaching positions.

There is public and bipartisan legislative support to fund schools generously and pay good teachers commensurately. But we believe that today's rigid steps and lanes salary schedule is unsustainable and will not be able to respond to the economic realities of today's marketplace.

We believe the public and many teachers would embrace alternative compensation systems that reward schools that demonstrate improved student learning and that pay teachers based not just on educational degrees and years of experience in the classroom, but also on their skill as classroom teachers. At the subcommittee hearings we saw many school districts and teachers experimenting with such alternative compensation models. The Marshall school district is looking at group performance incentives in its contract. Minneapolis has a bonus program for some of its schools which can demonstrate student achievement measured by an internal testing program which tracks student progress.

No one wants to replace the current collective bargaining process. It's important that teachers have professional representation in labor negotiations. But the legislature should encourage and support local collaborations between teachers and school districts which are willing to try new methods to compensate staff that are more closely linked to student performance and public expectations. We shouldn't be afraid of acknowledging and rewarding excellence.

Training and Staff Development

Good teachers matter in student achievement. But do teachers receive the training and support they need to succeed and which results in student improvement? While our state's colleges of education are beginning to respond to the teacher training needs of our K-12 schools, on-going staff development is often haphazard, especially for beginning teachers. As the subcommittee learned, staff development and mentoring are critical if new teachers are to succeed. Too often, however, new teachers can be set up to fail. Not only do they receive low starting salaries, they are often given the hardest-to-teach classes.

It's important to identify the skills teachers need in their particular school and focus professional development on those skills. Such on-going staff development should include on-going assessments for content and teaching skills as well as evaluations by peers, parents and students. St. Paul Superintendent Pat Harvey said that if we have standards for kids, there must also be standards for the teacher who teaches to those students.

We all support individual teacher efforts to improve professionally earning a master's degree, obtaining board certification, etc. But such development should not just be another way to earn more money on the salary schedule. Additional professional development and education should result in increased student performance. Too often, additional education has not been linked to enhancing one's specific skill deficiencies.

We believe the legislature can play a supportive role in advancing alternative teacher pay and training models. In the weeks ahead, we will consider a number of ideas, from loan forgiveness programs to lengthening the teacher contract year. But as the subcommittee learned, it isn't easy to change our current school culture. We all want better teachers and an educational system that allows them to advance professionally and financially. The question is, does our current system attract the best and the brightest? If it doesn't, are we prepared to change it to ensure student academic success?

CHAPTER 13

TEACHER QUALITY KEY FOR SCHOOL REFORM

Lowell Milken and Lewis C. Solmon

Editor's Note: The following op-ed was published in the *St. Paul Pioneer Press* on August 30, 2005.

The entire nation should closely monitor the path-breaking $86 million K-12 school reform called Quality Compensation for Teachers, or Q Comp, that recently was signed into law in Minnesota.

Govenor Tim Pawlenty's rigorous, systemic program is modeled in part after the Teacher Advancement Program, a powerful system to attract, develop, motivate, and retain high-quality people for the teaching profession.

Research shows that high-quality teachers are the most important school-related factor influencing student achievement. Q Comp focuses new education funding on making teachers more effective.

By combining performance pay with opportunities for school-based professional development aligned to actual school and student needs, instructionally based accountability for all teachers, and opportunities for career advancement, Q Comp supports and rewards teachers in improving their knowledge and professional skills. It encourages highly qualified

The Challenges of School Reform: Implementation, Impact, and Sustainability, 179–181
Copyright © 2006 by Information Age Publishing
All rights of reproduction in any form reserved.

teachers to undertake challenging assignments and helps districts recruit and retain highly qualified teachers. Teachers will be challenged but they will also be given every opportunity to acquire the skills and behaviors that lead to student learning.

And if properly executed, Q Comp will yield a host of benefits. The most important of these will be improved student achievement.

This has been our experience with the Teacher Advancement Program. Since its launch in 1999, TAP is already at work in 12 states, including Minnesota.

Debate about what makes a great teacher still exists, but we know from research that teachers' course credits and experience beyond the first few years are not related to how well students learn. With the current system, we cannot hope to attract and keep talented professionals in the classroom, especially in schools with the highest need. Q Comp has been designed to change this dynamic.

How then do we keep talented teachers in the classroom and entice large numbers of talented people to become teachers? Teachers often say they are not motivated by money. But when we speak with college graduates who rejected teaching as a career, the most frequent reason they give for their decision not to go into teaching are low salaries and the lack of reward for accomplishment. It is only professional, respectful and fair to provide additional opportunities for compensation for those teachers who are able to realize improvement in student learning.

Because fairness is key to any discussion of performance pay, both Q Comp and TAP have been designed with a sensitivity to this issue.

It is not fair to hold teachers accountable for student learning gains when they have not been prepared to meet the requirements of their evaluators. That is why the professional-development component of Q Comp is so important. It is not fair to restrict opportunities to earn additional pay to a limited group of teachers. That is why all teachers who meet performance and student achievement standards should be rewarded accordingly. It is not fair for already overburdened principals to have the sole responsibility for evaluating teachers. That is why multiple evaluations by more than one trained and certified evaluator, using a clear set of scientifically validated performance rubrics, are needed. Finally, it is not fair to pay teachers based on what levels their students achieve at the end of the year because some kids from more disadvantaged circumstances start the year at lower levels of achievement. That is why teachers should be judged by how much their students improve rather than by where they end up.

But it also is not fair to pay a highly effective young teacher much less than a 30-year colleague who has not kept up and whose students consequently do not make learning gains. It is not fair to pay more to a teacher for having taken graduate courses if they are unrelated to the instructional needs. To pay the same salaries to teachers with different skills and abilities, who take on different responsibilities, and who get different results for their students is not fair at all. Q Comp has been designed to change these dynamics.

Minnesota is embarking on a new path to meet the challenges facing public education. Q Comp is a comprehensive approach to attract, develop, retain and reward talented people in the teaching profession.

To succeed it must involve teachers every step of the way. By forming partnerships among educators and their unions, administrators and board members, business and community leaders, and parents, it can achieve its intended goals.

Schools and districts now have the opportunity to study, discuss, prepare and implement Q Comp in the true spirit in which it was developed. Doing so will propel Minnesota schools to the highest levels of student achievement by giving children what they most deserve: a rigorous educational experience led by a high-quality teacher in every classroom every year.

Milken is chairman of the Milken Family Foundation and chairman and founder of the Teacher Advancement Program Foundation. Solmon is president of the Teacher Advancement Program Foundation. TAP is being implemented in three schools in Minneapolis and four in Waseca, MN.

PART IV

**FRAMING THE FUTURE:
PRE-K THROUGH HIGHER EDUCATION**

CHAPTER 14

EARLY CHILDHOOD

The Proper Path for the Future

**Stephen Goldsmith, Libby Doggett, Ron Haskins,
Sharon Lynn Kagan, Dennis Vicars, and Elanna Yalow**

Stephen Goldsmith

Good afternoon and welcome to this panel on early childhood education. Let me first introduce the panel and then tell you what we hope to accomplish.

I am joined by Libby Doggett, who is the executive director of Pre-K Now and was previously at the National Head Start Association, where she worked on the Head's Up reading program. She has done much work on early childcare, particularly looking at issues with the Americans with Disabilities Act. Libby, like almost everyone on the panel, has a Ph.D. When I asked Libby what her most important credential was, she said, not surprisingly, "I'm a teacher."

Next is Lynn Kagan, the Virginia and Leonard Marks professor of early childhood and family policy and associate dean for policy and research at Teachers College of Columbia University. Lynn has also been at Columbia and Yale, is the author of many books, and the past president of the National Association for Education of Young Children.

The Challenges of School Reform: Implementation, Impact, and Sustainability, 185–216
Copyright © 2006 by Information Age Publishing

Then is Elanna Yalow, who is the president and chief operating officer of the Knowledge Learning Corporation, a large private supplier of early childhood education. She is an author, as well. She, too, is overly educated, having an MBA and Ph.D. from Stanford. She is an expert on the design and evaluation of educational programs for children.

Next is Dennis Vicars, who has advised numerous governors on how to set up programs on early childcare education. He's currently executive director of the Professional Association for Childhood Education and Alternative Payment Program in California. He has more than 25 years of experience in early childhood education.

Finally, we have Ron Haskins. Ron was at the House Ways and Means Committee and was one of the most influential people in Washington, D.C., in developing legislation for children. He now works at the Brookings Institution, which is an organization that conducts independent research and works to find innovative policy solutions. In addition, he too has a Ph.D., in developmental psychology.

The purpose of the panel is not to spend 90 minutes with everybody agreeing that early childhood education is important. We probably have something of a consensus on that, but we also recognize that this is a difficult time in many states—Medicaid budgets are placing stress on state legislatures and in turn are making the K-12 funding issues more difficult.

The K-12 system faces substantial challenges. Any elected official who decides he wants to do something important in education must ask where best to inject new spending. In a stressed system, the questions are: Should we invest those dollars in early childhood education? And if we do, in what manner should we? And what should we expect? What are we trying to accomplish? I want to call on Libby first.

Libby Doggett

Thank you. I'm delighted to be with such esteemed teachers and would like to offer my congratulations to each of you for your amazing award. I know what you do; I have children who went through the public school system. I went through the public school system, and now I have a new granddaughter who will soon be a public school student. Currently, I run an organization called Pre-K Now; we're funded by the Pew Charitable Trusts and a number of other foundations to secure high quality Pre-K for all kids.

I think the teachers in this audience really know why we're dedicated to this cause—and that is because it isn't just for *some* kids. Quality Pre-K education is important for *all* kids. Every child needs Pre-K, and I would like to call up a couple of charts to show you why Pre-K is so important for

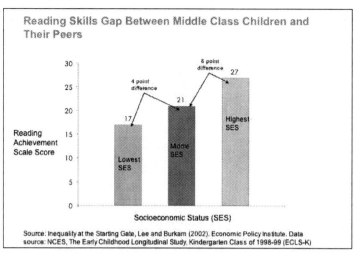

pre[k]now

Reading Skills Gap Between Middle Class Children and Their Peers

Source: Inequality at the Starting Gate, Lee and Burkam (2002). Economic Policy Institute. Data source: NCES, The Early Childhood Longitudinal Study, Kindergarten Class of 1998-99 (ECLS-K)

27 April 2006   www.preknow.org

Chart 14.1.

all children, because I think that there will be controversy on this panel about where middle-income children fit into the early childhood education debate.

Chart 14.1 shows the reading gap between upper-income, middle-income, and lower-income children. What this chart does not show is that because low-income children are getting Head Start, it's the middle-income children that get left behind in many cases. In addition to Head Start, low-income families often get childcare vouchers. Although the quality of care is not great, it allows for the parents of these families to go to work. As for the families of upper-income children, parents are able to buy the best childcare available, or in other cases they can afford to have one parent stay at home with the children. As you can see then, it's the middle-income children who are losing out.

Chart 14.2 shows that as children enter kindergarten many of them are unprepared. We have one third of middle-income children who don't know their alphabet. And that's with Sesame Street and all the environmental print in our world today!

This chart also shows that one quarter of upper-income children don't know their alphabet. Clearly, there is the need to get high quality Pre-K, not just for poor kids, but for every child in this country. There are, of course, a number of issues that arise with this goal. First, the Pre-K education has to be good quality. And the best way to do that is to have certified

pre[k]now

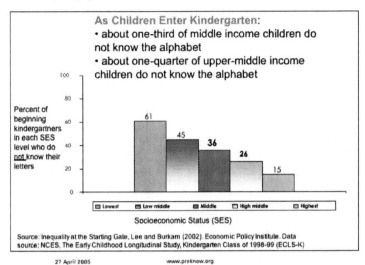

As Children Enter Kindergarten:
• about one-third of middle income children do not know the alphabet
• about one-quarter of upper-middle income children do not know the alphabet

Percent of beginning kindergartners in each SES level who do **not** know their letters

Socioeconomic Status (SES)

☒ Lowest   ☒ Low middle   ☒ Middle   ☐ High middle   ☒ Highest

Source: Inequality at the Starting Gate, Lee and Burkam (2002). Economic Policy Institute. Data source: NCES, The Early Childhood Longitudinal Study, Kindergarten Class of 1998-99 (ECLS-K)

27 April 2005   www.preknow.org

Chart 14.2.

teachers. What you're doing in the classroom for the older children needs to be done in classrooms for younger kids.

Stephen Goldsmith

Lynn, let's try to keep narrowing the discussion a little bit. Please talk to us about evaluation. You're an expert on it. What works? Let's challenge Libby's statement here a little bit about the middle-class kids. Tell us what we know works, and also talk about middle-class children as contrasted to disadvantaged children. Are we trying to close the opportunity gap? Are we trying to help everybody?

Lynn Kagan

There is a big debate in the field of early childhood education about where the priority emphasis should be for services, particularly when they are not required or are not an entitlement, as K-12 education is in our country. If you look at the numbers of children below the age of five (the age of formal school entry) who are receiving services, you will see that either the very rich or the very poor have the greatest access to these services. So, if you're talking about an access question, Libby is absolutely right.

If you're talking about a gains question, I think the gains are really questionable. Indeed, one of the legitimate reasons why we have so much emphasis on early childhood education is related to the fact that, in terms of the investment, when children are in a high quality Pre-K program, poor children benefit more than middle- and upper-class children. Every study that I know of shows this.

There is no uniform agreement about what ages should be included in early childhood education. Some people think that early childhood encompasses children from birth to age eight. Some people think it is birth to age five. And some people think it really is only three- and four-year-old children. But essentially, when you are talking birth to age five, you are dealing with a highly informal system of education, characterized by over 70 federal programs, hundreds of state programs, and thousands of individual programs, many of which function in the private sector. Indeed, early childhood education has been characterized by economists as a series of micro-enterprises and by early childhood educators as a confused non-system of diverse services.

Historically, the vast majority of programs for preschool-aged children have been in the private sector. As the publicly funded pre-kindergarten has grown, the public sector role has expanded dramatically. Simultaneously, we are expanding services to more children and converting what has been primarily a private sector endeavor to one that is growing in the public sector. So, we are challenging a lot of the fundamental beliefs and orientations about what this movement is. Helping to professionalize early childhood education is one of the movement's greatest contributions, because attendant to this movement is a commitment to standards, to accountability, and to the professionalization of the teacher workforce. Thus there are many, many benefits. However, I think if we are honest with ourselves, we will realize that there are a lot of people who are a little concerned about the vastness and the speed with which the Pre-K movement is accelerating. I will just share a couple of reasons why they feel this way.

The first is that we can't just define early childhood as pre-kindergarten or center-based services for children who are three and four years old. Most early childhood educators would say that a quality system of early childhood education certainly embraces that definition, but it also includes family support programs. Further, it includes family childcare, which is the largest form of childcare in our country, and it includes all of the supports that are necessary.

Second, early childhood education is not only about services for four-year old children; it is about a continuum of services for children from birth to the age of school entry.

Third, there is concern about the degree to which policy tends to focus on increasing the quantity of direct services for children, and the lack of attention to the development of an infrastructure, or the things that make those services high quality. Remember, every shred of data regarding children's successful outcomes and costs saved is predicated on high quality programs. We don't see those same kinds of gains when the quality of the program is very, very low. And yet, if you look at the vast majority of public policy, the emphasis on quality and the emphasis on the infrastructure is very limited. We have 4% of funding set aside in one of our major federal programs, and 8% in another.

The bottom line, though, is that if you really look at preschool education, it is lacking the very infrastructure that K-12 is blessed with. The major difference between Pre-K and K-12 is that there is not a consistent system of preparing teachers. Early childhood does not have a consistent system of governance; it does not have a consistent system of regulation; and it doesn't have a consistent system of accountability. Given these realities, I receive the Pre-K movement with joy, because it has the potential to enrich the way we're thinking about services for young children. And indeed, it is enriching the policies. However, this could be an opportunity misused if we don't focus on supporting the infrastructure, the quality as well as the quantity of the services, and the policies that are being funded.

Ron Haskins

I want to make sure we don't get away from Lynn's point about the budget before we make a point here about the universal focus. Everybody here lives in a state, and state budgets have recently been through a crisis. They have had a crisis pending for years and probably decades into the future because of the cost of health care. The federal government is also hugely in debt, and this debt will increase grandly over the next three or four decades. In short, there is a huge financial squeeze in this country.

Anybody here from California avoids this squeeze by having a popular vote on it and then taxing the wealthy, or taxing cigarettes, and then devoting that money exclusively to a certain purpose. But very few places have systems like California. When we talk about whether early childhood education should be universal or focused on low-income children, I think that, especially at the federal level, the responsibility is primarily to the low-income children.

The goal of preschool programs is not to stamp out individual differences. It's to bring truly disadvantaged kids up to a minimum line of achievement and to send them to the schools performing at a proficient level. Even after 40 years of preschool, we are nowhere near this. Therefore the financial decision is a huge issue here. Again, I think we should focus the resources on low-income kids.

Stephen Goldsmith

Let's be careful because we have several different questions that we're actually talking about as if they're the same question. One question is: "Who is Pre-K? Who does Pre-K help, generally?" The second is: "Which children should be funded by government?" And the third is: "Who should provide the services with whatever funding is available?"

Ron, you happen to be a welfare expert. Can you speak about how the billions of dollars that come from the federal government are being spent? What is the effect of spending on Pre-K funding and results?

Ron Haskins

I think between the federal and the state government, we're spending something like $25 billion now, with probably a little bit more on childcare. The main federal instrument is the Child Care and Development Block Grant, which has entitlement funds that will not go away. While these are really quite safe, they *are* appropriated funds and any year these could go away.

We need to have high quality education for low-income kids. I personally believe very much in quality, but let's not forget that the second vital function of the market is to provide inexpensive childcare so that low-income mothers can work. We have millions of low-income mothers in this country, many of whom work more now than in the past. However, if these mothers have to spend $8,000 in childcare, they would not be able to work at the same rate. So, we have to preserve that part of the market.

The government spends something like $7 billion on Head Start, and the states spend upwards of maybe $3 billion on state preschool programs. It's grown quite a bit in the last decade. Some states actually supplement Head Start, and we currently have 40 states with money in state preschool programs. All states supplement the day-care money that comes through the Child Care and Development Block Grant.

Not only that, but a great surprise that nobody predicted was when we passed welfare reform in 1996, we gave the states a block grant of $16.5

billion for welfare, and told them they could spend it how they chose on a whole range of services. This caused the welfare rolls to fall by 60% in the average state, and the states now use about $3.5 to $4 billion of that savings from welfare to purchase childcare, much of which unfortunately is not high quality preschool. That's how we spend the money—about $25 billion.

Lynn Kagan

Don't forget No Child Left Behind money. Title I money goes into it as well.

Ron Haskins

I think there's something like $800 million in Title I money. There are also other smaller pots; there's Individuals with Disabilities Education Act (IDEA) money, for example.

Stephen Goldsmith

I want to come back to quality, but let me first introduce Elanna to talk about the last point. What happens when you furnish services to kids of various ages? What happens with the tension between childcare and early childhood education? What happens if the four-year-olds come out of your system and go to public Pre-K as it relates to the full-time working mother/affordable day care issue? There is this issue regarding a mother's need to go to work and also to have affordable day care. How would you address that tension?

Elanna Yalow

There are a few issues I would like to address that are related to this issue. First, just to refocus, we certainly agree that we live in a time of limited funding available to support early childhood education services. There is an infrastructure, although it is somewhat fragmented, that does provide care. Our company alone provides care to about 150,000 children every day, as shown on Chart 14.3. The research is pretty clear that children from disadvantaged backgrounds benefit from quality early child-

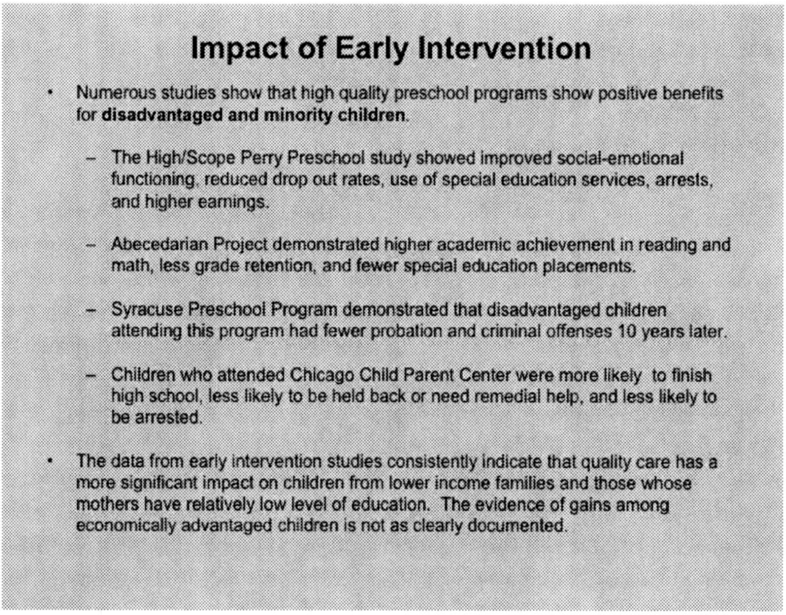

Impact of Early Intervention

- Numerous studies show that high quality preschool programs show positive benefits for **disadvantaged and minority children**.

  - The High/Scope Perry Preschool study showed improved social-emotional functioning, reduced drop out rates, use of special education services, arrests, and higher earnings.

  - Abecedarian Project demonstrated higher academic achievement in reading and math, less grade retention, and fewer special education placements.

  - Syracuse Preschool Program demonstrated that disadvantaged children attending this program had fewer probation and criminal offenses 10 years later.

  - Children who attended Chicago Child Parent Center were more likely to finish high school, less likely to be held back or need remedial help, and less likely to be arrested.

- The data from early intervention studies consistently indicate that quality care has a more significant impact on children from lower income families and those whose mothers have relatively low level of education. The evidence of gains among economically advantaged children is not as clearly documented.

Chart 14.3.

hood experiences. The research is much less clear as to the impact on children who come from more advantaged backgrounds.

The critical discussion for me isn't so much about universal preschool, but about our obligation as early childhood educators to support school readiness. What is it going to take to prepare children to be successful in school and later in life? We've heard many times today that school readiness begins with infants and toddlers, and we should understand that children's relationships with their parents and other caregivers impacts a child's lifelong social and emotional development. We know that vocabulary development begins with language experiences that start during the infant and toddler years. By the time children are three, intervention often cannot make up for any gaps that the children have already experienced.

The problem is that universal preschool programs or Pre-K programs that ignore the impact on the service delivery system for children between zero and three threaten the entire early childhood education experience. They risk negatively impacting the service delivery system that provides the foundational skills necessary for preschool success. They can disrupt our ability to bring qualified teachers in to support the development of children between zero and three years of age. And we can't evaluate any one program, absent its impact on the entire system that currently exists to service early childhood education and school readiness.

Libby Doggett

I think that we're all actually talking about a mixed delivery system. For those of you who don't know what that is, we are actually advocating a system that uses public schools, childcare, faith-based initiatives, or any other program that meets the high standards we advocate and that the state puts in place. Any of those programs can participate because we really do want to increase the quality of care for all kids.

I've gone to a number of programs, particularly in Oklahoma, where they have a Pre-K program in the First United Methodist Church. In that four-year-old program, you have a certified teacher who uses a wonderful curriculum. All the teachers in that center are able to participate in school-sponsored professional development. So now, there's a linkage between childcare and the school-based system. What we actually have seen is that while we want a system for all children ages zero to eight, that is not practical right now, and it's better to focus on building up the early childhood system through improving the quality for three and four-year-olds. This leads to improvements in quality for everyone.

Stephen Goldsmith

Let's try to distinguish the issues. I would like to come back to "What does quality mean?" for a second, and also discuss "How do you measure quality and hold people accountable?" But right now we're in the middle of talking about the delivery system. Even if there is a private delivery system, it has to be accountable to somebody if it is using public dollars. Who sets the standards for you? And how would they be enforced upon your private delivery system?

Dennis Vicars

I think the standards are a collaborative effort. I see the beauty of this whole preschool movement right now, and it's an opportunity like we've never had before. All of you are here as public school teachers or administrators, and there are many, many, many positive things to say about public schools. I went through the public schools, and I was a public school teacher. I was even teacher of the year, one year. But, I left public schools for a lot of different reasons.

What you have is the situation where we all want to be honest. There are things, such as what we don't like in public schools which we will quietly talk about among colleagues. If you look at the public school system in the last hundred years, we can talk about this movement. It truly hasn't changed a lot. The system boils down to one thing: the commitment and dedication of a teacher. Put curriculums aside, put whoever is in charge aside—the coach that got promoted to superintendent who's clueless. Sorry, just a little side note, but all those types of things have happened in our process. What this offers us in early childhood is the opportunity to truly come together and to really create something special.

If you look at the beauty of early childhood education, you have a lot of different delivery systems. You have the Montessorians. You have the faith-based systems. You have the developmentally appropriate (which I find really shocking because good education is developmentally appropriate anyhow). We've got this beautiful situation in front of us, and at the same time, I see what my greatest fears are: the interest groups that come in, the unions who come in, the textbook sellers who come in, and the playground salesmen who come in. We get these interesting, different lobbyists trying to change something but have children as the last thing on the agenda. I hope that this governance model will integrate this very collaborative spirit into creating something new and unique.

Lastly, the reason I left public education is this: when you try to change something, and you ask, "How come we're doing it this way?" The answer is usually, "Because we've always done it this way." That answer is not acceptable anymore. For example, the reason we had three months off in the summer was because kids worked on farms, but today we're still doing that stupid model from a hundred years ago. Here's a great opportunity to bring the fabric of different delivery systems together with high-quality standards.

The great thing the private sector offers, that early childhood development can also take advantage of, is that we can get parents involved. I never had this opportunity in the public sector. Every time I tried to get parents involved, whenever I had a teacher's night, the only parents who came were the ones who didn't need to. I was preaching to the choir. Fortunately, when a parent has a three-year-old or a four-year-old, he or she does not drop them off at the bus stop. These parents drive their children to school and come inside. Teachers have to interact with the parents. When you can engage that parent, and when you can have that parent involved, something special is going to happen.

There's another great thing about this collaborative effort. Parents at the preschool level vote with their pocketbook. I've never had a four-year-old walk up to the counter and sign a check for me, so I had better be doing those things that make that parent want to be involved. I had better offer quality, and I had better offer cleanliness, because the pocketbook does the walking and, sooner or later, it walks away from the situation that isn't good. So, when we can take this collaborative effort and bring parents and teachers together, the governance situation will work.

Stephen Goldsmith

Let's get Libby, Lynn and Ron to argue for a minute about what's a reasonable basis for accountability. First, let's assume that these are professionals who care about the education of children—so the better educated children are, when they arrive at the kindergarten or first grade door, the better off they are.

What are the accountability tools? If we're going to set up a system and have accountability, we want the objective to be that kids come to kindergarten ready to learn.

How do we measure that? How do we ensure accountability? Can you assess kids? Help me distinguish quality, contrasting the credentialing of the teachers from the outcomes of the kids.

Libby Doggett

We all want quality, and we know from research that quality means a highly qualified teacher. Further, it means low teacher-to-student ratios. We're advocating no more than 20 children per teacher/teacher aide, and that means with a certified teacher and an aide in the room. We want group size to be low, and we also want a strong curriculum. In addition, we need screening to determine the specific needs of children so that we are able to refer them and get them the supports they need. Obviously the parent is critical, so we want strong family engagement, not just with mothers and fathers but with siblings and grandparents, as well. I think those standards of quality are pretty well agreed upon, and states are moving toward achieving this level of quality.

I think the problem with measurement and assessment is that we're trying to measure things way too early. We can't look at a first-year system and expect it to be perfect. Instead, it is important to measure a system that's more mature. Further, you can't use just one form of measurement with four- and five-year-olds, because some days a child of this age is just not going to answer a question. And you know they know the answer, but you need multiple forms of assessment to get to that answer. We all want a system that is accountable because we know that with high quality and with accountability you're going to get good outcomes. I contend that, not just for poor kids, but for all kids.

Stephen Goldsmith

These sound a lot like input qualifications, in contrast to output qualifications and even better outcomes. They may be reasonable requirements, or they may not, but can't we do a little bit better in terms of accountability and assessment tools?

Lynn Kagan

If we were to design an ideal accountability system for early childhood, it would begin with a set of early learning standards that specify what children should know and be able to do. It should also have a set of measurements that captures all the domains of development that are encompassed in the early learning standards. It should have a data collection and reporting capacity, and there should be thresholds established for poor-performing programs with supports for their improvement in the short term and operational consequences for lack of improvement over the long haul. In addition, we should have an aligned delivery system where the early learning standards, the curriculum, and the assessments are all aligned

Where are we with these standards? In America, 47 states have developed early learning standards for children at the preschool level—three- and four-year-olds—and some states are developing standards for children far younger. The notion that the early years are a time for milling around is outdated; we should not, however, confuse a commitment to the specification of standards with a commitment to more didactic approaches to pedagogy, or to teaching. To the contrary, quality early childhood must still be child-centered, giving children lots of time and space to explore, invent, and be curious.

Early learning standards are not the only kinds of standards that are important to kid. A second kind of standard, though not prevalent in America, is parenting standards. We will never have state parenting standards that specify what parents should do to promote their children's development (because of America's commitment to the privacy and primacy of the family), but lots of nations are moving in the direction of using parenting standards as the basis for parenting education and family support programs—Ghana, the Philippines, Jordan, and the Stans.

A third kind of standard is program standards. Program standards include dimensions of the programs (e.g., indoor and outdoor space; sufficient numbers of teachers and staff). A fourth kind of standards are teacher standards or statements of what teachers should know and be able to do. Ideally, early learning, teacher and program standards would all be aligned with each other.

One is a clear specification of what we want children to know and be able to do—it's the end point—while the other is a specification of the end point. It is feasible to have very high expectations for all children in early childhood, and I actually believe that our states are moving in that direction without controlling the way teachers teach. We are allowing teachers to teach in developmentally appropriate ways that imbue classroom instruction with intentionality and with purpose.

I want to say one other word about assessment. If you take a look at the history of psychological measurement in this country, there is an understanding that people learn in a very linear way. And as we become adults, indeed that is true. For those who study and work with young children, among some there is an understanding that children learn in steps. First, they learn a little bit, and then they plateau for a while. Then they learn a little bit more, and again they plateau for a while. The reality is that children, young children, learn like this. They learn in big cycles and then they go back. So, they learn something, they forget it, they relearn it. It's why little children love to have stories repeated over and over. A three-or a four-year-old asks, "Tell it to me again, Mommy," while an eight-year-old says, "Forget it, I've already heard that."

The bottom line is: when we are considering how to achieve some kind of accountability in early childhood education, we need to have good standards and good assessments. These assessments need to respect the unique needs of young children who can't read, who are highly distractible, and who fear strange people and places. It means we need to construct assessments that are given by people who know children in a friendly surrounding, and we need to be sure to have authentic assessments that assess all domains—not just language and numeracy—of development. We have to administer these assessments often. Young kids need standards, and they also need a specific system of assessment.

Ron Haskins

I want to answer your first question about accountability and measurement. I think there are three crucial elements. We've talked about two, but we left out what I think is the most important one, and that's parent choice. I think parents ought to have control, even if it's public dollars;

they should have a substantial say on where their kids go to school. The parent takes his or her child to school, and this means that the parent sees the teachers on a regular basis. Again, I think it's crucial to have a parent mechanism here. You've got to have a marketlike mechanism and not have the whole thing controlled by professionals.

That being said, I think we do need to have regulations. But I have to tell you, I don't think the research on regulations is overly impressive. The one thing that should be emphasized is class size, in terms of teacher-student ratios. Teacher quality is the one thing that consistently shows up to be important, and especially teachers who have experience and/or training in early childhood. I would say that's important, but at the same time, I am really worried about tying down a market with a whole slew of regulations that tell you how clean the bathroom has to be, and the square feet of space needed in a room, and so forth. I would leave that up to the states and localities, as we do now.

There have been several big attempts to have federal standards, but they have all been defeated. We have very broad federal standards, so it is up to states and localities. I think that's the way it should be. Then, on actual assessment, *testing* is the word I want to use; we ought to have testing not so much for individual kids, though if they can use it that way, that's fine. We need to know how these entities are functioning, and we need to know the scores those kids are making. Let's be clear here: the public dollars are invested in this primarily so that low-income kids can get ready for school. That has been an objective of federal policy since 1965. It's still the right objective, and we need to know whether we're doing it.

Stephen Goldsmith

Earlier in this book, Lowell Milken refers to a chart showing that the longer American students were in the public school system, the further they fell behind on international standards. Let's say you design this high quality program and you force the folks in the room, who are already pretty challenged with K-12, to say what they think about the dissipation of those results over time in the K-12 system.

Ron Haskins

I would not have the public schools play an overly important role in this. I mean, I think they should play some role; they can compete like anybody else. But we should not create a system, like the one they're thinking about in California, where they're going to basically give control to the public schools.

Stephen Goldsmith

Elanna, you represent the private sector here. How do you ensure for your 150,000 kids that, particularly for the four-year-olds, their reading and math readiness is sufficient?

Elanna Yalow

Again, I don't want to just focus on the four-year-olds, because I think our total curriculum and quality model really does start with our infants. Obviously, the curriculum is very different at the various stages and ages of children. But we have a proprietary curriculum that includes both developmental and educational objectives, and even for our youngest children, we have developmental milestones against which we assess our children so that we can communicate with our parents about their children's progress towards critical milestones. We have standardized lesson plans and standardized activities that we expect our teachers to engage in with their children. When you talk about early childhood education, and you talk about a lesson plan, you're talking about just a piece of what happens in a classroom on any given day. However, having that lesson plan does set some standards for what we expect our teachers to provide our children.

Then we have child portfolios. We previously discussed the importance of looking at children's growth and progress at multiple points in time because they will advance, and then they will show some prior skills or lack of skills that you thought they had developed, and then move on from them. Ongoing portfolio assessments allow for numerous assessments that take a child's developmental pattern into account.

We have standardized assessments at three points in time across the year. So again, we have a broad base for communicating to our parents about how their children are progressing, as well as a good way for measuring our own confidence in our program in supporting children's development.

In many ways, the free marketplace is a wonderful thing. Obviously, we care foremost about our children. We also must respond to what the research tells us about child development. We have an obligation to our parents to distinguish ourselves as quality providers from the many other providers that are out there. And, in this course of conversation, I don't want to overlook the point that we do have limited funding sources. While it might be nice to provide the same level of care for all children, it really is critical to look at the children who will benefit from it the most. Unfortunately, however, a deflection of resources away from those children who need it most is currently happening due to the limitations in the state budgets. We're seeing significant cutbacks in quality incentives that were designed for us to provide enhanced care for our subsidized children.

Limited resources are really placing us in a terrible situation, where we may not be able to service those children because we feel like we can't hold true to our own standards. So the concept of limited resources is nothing to put aside. It is also important to have a wish list about what we would like if there were truly enough money to do everything we want to do for early children education.

Libby Doggett

Elanna, how much does a family pay for care in one of your high quality centers?

Elanna Yalow

It varies dramatically by marketplace, but our average is probably about $8,000 to $10,000 per year. In many states, we are getting reimbursed at 65% of that for our subsidized families. Over the past few years, as the states have had less money, we've seen a significant cutback on that reimbursement (which is also tied with a loss of quality incentives); whereas before, when we were accredited by national accreditation agencies, we might actually see an enhancement of reimbursement rates. In response to some of the financial challenges states are having, in more cases than not, we're seeing reimbursements taken away.

Libby Doggett

Are your teachers certified or do they have their associate degree? Do they have the child development associate credential?

Elanna Yalow

Again, it varies by market, and there are great challenges in terms of our ability to attract qualified teachers to the industry. We put a tremendous amount of resources into our own education and professional development opportunities, both in terms of encouraging our staff to take advantage of opportunities available through colleges and through outside programs. We also know that training and development is our job, because not all teachers come to us equally skilled, qualified, or with the same level of education.

Our first commitment to our children and our programs is to make sure that we take on the burden of providing enhanced professional development for all of our staff, which again takes additional resources. This is because it's not just the development of the quality materials; it's also staff training time.

Stephen Goldsmith

As the state budgets have gotten tighter, two-thirds of the states have either reduced the income levels for which people are eligible for childcare, increased the copays, or frozen the payments over time. Then, often because they want to do good deeds, the states increase the mandates, right? So, what Elanna is speaking to is that the dollars available for the children who need the help the most have essentially come down, especially when you deal with inflation-adjusted dollars. In addition, the mandates often go up. The gap is significant, particularly if you're trying to pay attention to the disadvantaged kids. Having said that, Dr. Haskins says that parents should have choice. So, Dennis, how do you keep parents from choosing badly? Or do you think they should have the right to choose badly?

Dennis Vicars

I think it's a lot more complicated than that. I think that the standards have to be such that they are across the board to where there are benchmarks of what we're all going to accept, and what we're all going to agree upon. Twenty years ago, I was involved in Arizona when infant rooms were at an eight-to-one ratio. Now, how in the world can you look at yourself in the mirror and say this is a good thing for kids? It was due to education, parent focus groups, and a collaborative approach that we changed those regulations. We made it right, but one of the things that I think we're talking about, which concerns me about this conversation and so many other conversations, is that we start to be piecemeal. In New Zealand and Australia, they look at early childhood as zero to eight, and in the U.S. we're looking at four-year-olds, and most of the programs that we're looking at last for three hours a day, 180 days a year. What concerns me is that we put all of our energy into that type of program, yet we're forgetting the other two sides of what that is. If you talk to the people out here, kindergarten teachers and first-grade teachers, they have to play reaction instead of proaction. When we can get these programs earlier, and we can look at the early child who is in that zero-to-eight frame, there's an articulation between what's happening up until then. We keep talking about quality improvement, quality improvement, quality improvement. You people get beat to death by the newspapers, the pundits, and everyone else. You're doing a horrible, terrible job, they say. We are not going to change the results of early child education in a three-hour, half-day program with four-year-olds. It's going to start much earlier. I think we need to broaden that conversation. We need to make a decision in this country, are we going to move forward with that agenda, as opposed to a piecemeal one?

Stephen Goldsmith

Libby, can you please comment on the issue of how many hours a day, how many days a year, even without the idea of having to support mom who goes to work? This leads us to more expansive work, just in terms of educational quality, and making sure the child is ready when he arrives in kindergarten. What does that program have to look like, in terms of duration? We talked about quality, but let's deal with the duration issue that Dennis talks about.

Libby Doggett

I'm happy to talk about duration, but I have to comment on two other things first. One is, you keep talking about state budgets. I think there's no doubt that this country has a difficult financial situation and that states are going through some rough times. But I want to ask, how long are our youngest kids going to have to wait? Every single state is making choices every single day. In Washington, D.C., we're probably going to build a big, new baseball stadium, yet Art Rolnick at the Federal Reserve will tell you that that is not really going to bring about economic development.

If you put that money in early childhood, you would have a better return on the dollar, and I think we've waited too long. So, priorities are being set and money is being spent in other ways. Our young children keep getting pushed aside, and then the whole system is pushed aside. I think in early childhood—and Lynn will agree with this—we've been working for a whole system for a long time. We want parental leave, and we want better quality, particularly better quality for our infants and toddlers. We have a whole array of issues.

We have lined this out, and we've talked about governance. But you know what? We've gotten nowhere because we have been unwilling to prioritize. I think if you look at what the Bush administration and some other really savvy Republican politicians have done, they have been very targeted and forceful about doing one thing and doing it well, and that's not where we're going to stop. We're going to start where they have, and then we're going to continue. I think everybody who's working on Pre-K is looking at the whole system, and they're saying that we have an opportunity, let's go do this. And then we'll take the next step.

In terms of time, I want high quality. I'd love to have full-day, year-round. But I'd rather have a high quality part-day than I would a poor quality full-day.

Stephen Goldsmith

Say that you're going to have to make funding choices and you're dealing with public dollars. Would you rather have six or seven hours a day for the most disadvantaged kids or three hours a day for everybody?

Libby Doggett

I am actually promoting in states that we focus on underperforming schools. Let's look at the whole school and the whole area, and go in and provide Pre-K for all the kids in that area. Let's not just say, "If your income is this level, you get it, and if your income is this level, you don't."

Stephen Goldsmith

Disproportionately, those end up being Title I schools.

Libby Doggett

Right, they will.

Lynn Kagan

Targeted approach.

Libby Doggett

Let's start there, but let's not stop there.

Stephen Goldsmith

I didn't take that as a concession, that's just as a priority.

Lynn Kagan

I'm a former Head Start teacher and director, and I have a passionate commitment to seeing that this nation does something to serve its low-income children first. While I support the Pre-K movement very strongly—because I do think it's an avenue that is able to generate a lot of constituent support from both sides of the aisle—my grave concern is that in doing this, we are potentially minimizing the expansion of services for the children in our nation who absolutely need them the most.

I have two other points. Number one, I would rather see low-income children receive two years of service as three- and four-year-olds because the data definitely indicate that two years of intervention are superior to one year of intervention. And my second point is that I am very concerned about what's happening with full day kindergarten in this country. We are spending a lot of time focusing on Pre-K, and we're not spending enough time focusing on full day kindergarten. This country has very sporadic provision of full-day kindergarten, and indeed the data are very clear not only from the voices of teachers who want longer kindergarten days so that they can have sufficient time to elaborate on the curriculum, but also from the working parents.

I am concerned that all the emphasis clogged in one domain strips us both from the zero-to-three focus and also from the kindergarten focus. So, while I support the Pre-K movement, I also think we've got to have broader vision as we are designing the long-term, public support strategy for it.

Elanna Yalow

I want to challenge the concept that you could have the same level of quality with part-time/part-year care. When we look at early childhood education, one of the most important things we look for is consistency, in terms of the child's experience and the family's experience. We are all so appalled about the excessive turnover rates among early childhood educators, because we understand that for a child to go through multiple teachers in a short period of time, it can be difficult and disruptive to their educational experience.

If you have a three-hours-a-day program that's 40 weeks a year, with breaks at holiday time and at the end of the year, then a summer break; instead of a comprehensive system that provides care for the child during that entire year, you have a program that fails to provide consistency and continuity for many families who need it. This is further complicated for families who may have multiple children and have dramatic transportation problems getting their child from a three-hour program into another service delivery system. I question whether that could be as high a quality early childhood experience as it can be if we're providing consistency and continuity for the children in our care.

Stephen Goldsmith

I'm sure you and Dennis would agree that the state regulator should set some qualifications for schools that take children with public dollars. But there must not be some set of qualifications that are so onerous that they're counterproductive, right? Given this, what do you see as a model that accommodates a kind of floor where the public dollar's involved, but without so much intrusion that the costs outweigh the benefits?

Elanna Yalow

I actually think we have the bottom part of the system in place already; it's the top part we're missing. We already have, through state regulations, sort of a floor of minimal quality standards. It certainly varies dramatically across states. There are some states where the minimal standards are consistent with what many of us would consider quality care; then there are other states where that floor is a little bit questionable. But what we don't have consistently are the incentives at the upper end.

There has been some progress towards a consistent floor, but independent of the floor, we can readily service our more affluent parents because they can afford to pay for the enhanced quality delivery. We are challenged because, for the children who need it most—our disadvantaged children who are dependent on government reimbursement to take advantage of the quality services that we provide—the reimbursement levels are not consistent with enhanced quality. There certainly have been times, and there are certain states, where we do get enhanced reimbursement rates for providing enhanced quality. Those are some systems that allow us to make sure we are providing the enhanced quality and the reimbursements; yet in certain circumstances, the floor remains.

Stephen Goldsmith

Do you or Lynn know if, in those states that have a tiered reimbursement rate—let's call it five stars—the fourth and fifth stars are related to reading readiness and math preparation? Or are they related more to credentialing or cleanliness, etc.?

Elanna Yalow

Much more the input variables.

Lynn Kagan

I would say it's totally input variables, and the states vary dramatically. The Quality Rating System movement, next to Pre-K, is the largest single movement in the country This is to the good because for too long, we have focused simply on increasing the number of slots for children, without too much regard for their quality. What's important to remember is that although states have regulations, they are the baseline (or should I say the basement?) of quality. Moreover, the systems for checking on the degree to which those regulations are met, and the criteria for whom they apply, also vary greatly.

Roughly 50% of the childcare programs in this country are legally exempt and do not have to adhere to those regulations, even in high quality states like Connecticut. It is questionable to say we have a floor of regulations because "to whom does that floor apply?" is really the subsidiary question that we need to look at.

Dennis Vicars

I wanted to add that we're all already dealing with standards, usually safety and health, which are probably not even high enough anywhere. The thing that concerns me is that as we start to write educational standards, we get in a situation where the best interests come forward. The quality research from Lynn and others comes forward. And then all of a sudden, the interest groups come in—and educational policy is written by interest groups, instead of by true, quality educational standards.

I'm seeing it happen right now in California with the Reiner initiative. It started off with great intentions, great ideas, great research, and now all of a sudden, the California Teacher's Association is going to decide what the standards are for their own self-serving means.

Stephen Goldsmith

Ron, can you describe what you think the perfect state intervention would be? One of the things I've studied around the country is this kind of government procurement issue. And really, what we're discussing is whether government should make or buy Pre-K. That's inherent in this delivery system issue. My only observation is, not so much just in Pre-K, but in government services in general: if the government entity in charge of buying the service is also making the service, and if the school superintendent is in the business and allowing and determining who his competitors should be, no matter how well-intentioned and how professional that entity or superintendent is, the inclination is to lead the troops. It's very difficult to say "I'm in the business, and I'm going to have a completely open mind. I'm going to fire my own teachers and hire this guy."

We'll first let Ron describe what he things is the perfect system. Let's assume that we all agree that Pre-K is very important to get children ready for school. And to the extent that we do that well, and universally, that's even better. But let's just talk from your perspective. You have some state dollars you want to inject; how would you inject those dollars, and what would that system look like from your perspective?

Ron Haskins

I would do pretty much what I already described. I would make sure that the parents have a strong voice in the selection of care. I would have state regulations, and I'd make sure that low-income parents either have enough for a complete payment, or at least a substantial part of it. I would also have very clear evaluation and testing system, so I could know at the program level how programs are doing. But I would also have regulators who had the power to shut places down if they're not good. I am concerned about really rotten facilities. I don't think we have zillions of them, but we have some and disproportionately, they service low-income kids. Starting 30 years ago, when we started to get state regulations, I think it would have been smart to focus on closing down these poor facilities. You know, it's much more important to have a floor than it is to have a ceiling. Let the market take care of the ceiling, but close down the floor. At least that's what I would do.

Lynn Kagan

And there's federal money going to subsidize these poor quality programs?

Ron Haskins

I would not have the feds touch this problem. Why get the feds involved in marriage and foster care and so forth? No, no, we want the state and local folks to figure that out. The main function of federal government should be to help fund it, especially for low-income kids. Further, the federal government should play a role in providing funds for evaluation and research.

Stephen Goldsmith

Ron, let me just say, I thought you were the person singularly most responsible for the childcare development block grant dollars going out as vouchers. I think I just heard you say a number of those vouchers are ending up in really bad places. So, what did you do wrong?

Ron Haskins

I think this is a failure of state policy, because the states and localities should be responsible for it. However, I also would put some responsibility on child advocates because they focus too much on higher standards and not enough on a floor. If you talk to advocates about their concerns, they usually want low student-teacher ratios and other similar issues. Instead, we ought to focus way more on the bottom than on the top.

Stephen Goldsmith

Lynn, I saw you and Libby react, not violently, but politely negatively. Why don't you pick the points you disagreed with, and we'll come back to Libby, and then kind of move down the line.

Lynn Kagan

I used to ask the same question about education dollars. How can we take that money, give it to a school system, and expect that the school system to then farm it out to other community-based providers of early childhood education? It wouldn't be in their self interest, and they're unlikely to want to do it. The reality is, we have experienced it in many states in the country.

I'll give you an example. New York state has a commitment to universal Pre-K programming, but they do not have enough funds to do it. They have targeted low-income communities as a way to embark upon the journey toward universal Pre-K, and they have given the money to the public schools. The public schools, in turn, can decide if they want to keep the dollars and run the programs through government entities or outsource and buy them. And indeed, what has happened in New York state is that they have done about an equal amount of both. In communities where they feel there are good, high quality programs in the communities, they outsource.

Furthermore, when schools don't have room and when they feel very burdened by No Child Left Behind, they don't want to take on one more responsibility; so outsourcing is actually very common. This is where we use the education system to generate and funnel revenue, and where I distinguish between education as a financing mechanism versus education as a delivery system. Education may be a funder of the services, but it is not a deliverer.

Libby Doggett

I think Lynn has described what we consider one of the ideal systems, where you're really funneling some money in, and you're having some accountability because you have the schools involved. You're linking the system together by linking the early childhood system that's out there to the schools. Further, you're teaching principals. When these kids arrive at age five, they come from somewhere else, and it might be really smart to figure out where they're coming from so that you can establish those connections and help improve that system. I think that's what is happening across this country.

Elanna Yalow

I would go like to go back to the question you asked before, which is, "What does a quality service delivery system look like?" There are a lot of ways to define one, but I think some of the characteristics are: first, it should be targeted to those most likely to benefit from it; then to the extent that there are reimbursement systems, it should be at the level consistent with providing quality care. I think we absolutely have to honor the primary role of parents in their child's life, whether that is through direct vouchers to the parents—to give them maximum choice in terms of making a selection about where they put their child, maximum flexibility to meet the needs of the variety of families or parents that present themselves—or support for parenting skills and prenatal training for families. We want to make sure that there is consistency. As early childhood educators, we definitely are committed, or should be committed, to strengthening program standards consistently across the board. We need to make sure that there are resources to support professional training and development. Then, finally, I think we all could agree that we want to have a system that is accountable, both in terms of the program outcomes and the child outcomes. So, we really do want to look at whether our programs are having the impact we hope they do for our children.

Libby Doggett

The only thing I think you left out is adequate pay for the teachers. For those of us who have been working in early childhood, we will say that a teacher's salary looks really wonderful. We know that teachers don't get paid what they should be paid for their hard work. For people in early childhood care, Head Start and other settings, they're getting paid about half of what a teacher would get paid.

Elanna Yalow

You can't have quality education without quality teachers and appropriate reimbursement.

Stephen Goldsmith

OK, but in this model, which is a cost-sensitive model, would you combine a highly qualified teacher with a teacher assistant? You must have some childcare people, who are really loving folks, working in the centers, who may not have four-year degrees. How do you handle that?

Elanna Yalow

There are lots of ways to define quality. Certainly, educational experience is a critical part of the experience needed to provide care. If you have children for a full day, they need a qualified teacher with them the whole day. We shouldn't think, "OK, this is the educational component, so for these number of hours, they have a qualified teacher. And then the rest of the time, they just need somebody to watch them play with their toys."

The appropriateness of having one lead teacher who is more qualified, with the support of an assistant, frankly depends a lot on the strength of that team. So, while there are a lot of ways to think about a team teaching model, we can't shut off the exposure to a well qualified teacher at some point in the day—because for early childhood education, the entire day is their educational experience, not just the core hours that we think of in a traditional school model.

Stephen Goldsmith

Lynn, help us. We've just spent a little over an hour, and we've designed the perfect system, right? We almost had consensus, momentarily. Let's think for a second. If we assume that Libby gets her way, and we have high quality Pre-K for everyone then how do we deal with the Title I children? How do we transition that child into that K-8 system in such a way that the gains are cumulative and not dissipated? As a Head Start expert, are there any strategies you've seen? What do we see in terms of this kind of transitional linkage that would make sense?

Lynn Kagan

With thanks to the nation's Head Start program—which most people don't recognize is a program that delivers direct services to children and families, yet has supported the richest, most durable research agenda that we have in this nation—we know a lot about how to create transitions that are effective. However, I am concerned that we have been too limited in how we have conceptualized this notion of transition. Mostly, it is viewed as set of one-time activities, such as the transfer of children's records or kindergarten meetings with pre-kindergarten teachers. What this approach misses is that to really foster transition, we need alignment among the standards, curriculum, and expectations for children in Pre-K and in kindergarten, and ideally into first and second grade.

Far too little discourse is happening around the alignment issue. Largely, this happens because in this country because Pre-K is such a fragmented, nonsystem of services. If they want to align with Pre-K's in their communities, schools don't know where to look. Do I align with what's going on with the Head Start standards? Do I align with what the Mom-

and-Pop nursery school is using as its standards? There is very limited consistency, so I would say that we're in a bind about how to architect this transition. Although, there is growing recognition that, indeed, we have been focusing far too superficially. We have to get into the innards of pedagogy and curriculum, and we haven't addressed that successfully yet.

Elanna Yalow

From the provider side, I would argue that it's also our responsibility as providers of early childhood education to align ourselves with the needs of the school districts that our children will ultimately be part of. We have to look outside of our walls to understand what educational expectations are being laid out in the school districts of the markets we serve.

Stephen Goldsmith

We have five minutes left in this panel discussion. Let's use one minute and 20 seconds each for summary thoughts on what you think the best model is in the country. Hopefully, folks will get motivated to follow.

Libby Doggett

I believe that the teacher is the heart of the Pre-K program and that we have been relying upon a system where we've been paying those teachers minimum wage, or slightly more. We put together some pretty good training; we put together some pretty good systems. You have heard about Elanna's wonderful centers all over the country, but those people are still not getting paid a living wage. And when you talk about transition, there's a difficulty, because you have a teacher who doesn't have even an associate's degree, who is a little bit intimidated to go talk to the kindergarten teacher and go over to the school to do the transition. Until we have certified teachers who are paid the same as other teachers, who are respected the way other teachers are, who are given awards by the Milken Family Foundation, we're not going to have a system that really works the way we have talked about it today.

Lynn Kagan

I think it behooves us to try to understand that early childhood education has a lot to contribute pedagogically, as well as structurally, to K-12 education—and that has not been discussed here. I'd like to remind

214 S. GOLDSMITH et al.

everyone that choice really does exist in Pre-K and in higher education. If you take a look at the educational continuum, choice actually exists least frequently in K-12 education. I would suggest that there are some marked issues that K-12 could learn by looking at Pre-K and by looking at higher education, which we have only begun to examine. That's point one.

Point two: while there are many problems, I think that early childhood education in this country has two things to contribute. One has been mentioned—the incredible commitment to working effectively with parents. We know how to do it. We do it every single day. We're trained to do it. To the degree that parent engagement can enhance public elementary and secondary education in this country, people really ought to be looking at early childhood. This is one of the potential spin-off benefits of the universal Pre-K movement.

The other issue that we haven't talked about very much—we've been very polite here—is the issue of ethnic, racial, and linguistic diversity, and these are issues that early childhood education has grappled with for a very, very long time. Not to say that K-12 hasn't, but indeed, we wrote the very first anti-bias and diversity curriculum that existed in the entire education sphere. We understand what it is to be open and honest as we are educating young children about racial and ethnic differences. We need to do more, in terms of education, on linguistic diversity. We are squandering the early years by not teaching children two languages, as every other place on the planet is. It's criminal. Chinese children, at age three, are learning English. In any case, my prayer would be that as early childhood is looking at K-12, K-12 would also look at early childhood.

We know a whole lot about the natural assessment of young children. Every early childhood educator worth his or her salt was trained to wear smocks. You probably all think that it's because we wanted to keep the paint off our clothes, but the reality is, smocks have big pockets. We are the masters of informal assessment because we were trained how to observe and diagnose children's learning needs, so we've done individual assessments for a hundred years. My goal and my hope for the ideal system is that we will affect some real synergy for the first time in our national history across the entire continuum—P-20.

This is why I am so proud of what the Education Commission for the States is doing, because it, along with several other organizations, is really beginning to conceptualize whole education within our country.

Elanna Yalow

In this morning's presentation on the challenges of K-12 education, I was struck with how many of the arguments applied equally well to early childhood education. I think one of the exciting parts of the focus on Pre-

K education, universal Pre-K, and universal preschool is the opportunity that allows us to talk about what children need to be successful in school and later in life, and not compartmentalize it into what children need in a particular age group. That's one reason that I really do want to continue to re-emphasize that critical focus on considering what we can do to support children's needs in the earliest years.

Unfortunately, it seems that there is something of a disrespect for the professional standards that can be brought to infant and toddler care. I think that there are those who believe that really is just Mom's work in the home, and not something that can be enhanced by professional standards and professional expectations. I think we have an obligation, with whatever constituent we are arguing for or about, that we really consider school readiness. We should think about what it's going to take for children to be successful—and not to become advocates for any one program, but advocates for children.

Dennis Vicars

I see it as such a great opportunity. It's not a matter of if, but it's a matter of when. It's not what, but how. It's not one source, but many. And this is such a tremendous opportunity. As a past teacher I know that 80% of the problems you have are because someone between zero and five wasn't on it, and children were neglected or weren't given the opportunities to engender that love of learning and that care and ability.

So much of our job educationally in this country would be taken care of if we can get our heads together on how to do this and not let interest groups and others somehow hijack a situation for kids that is right there before us. Everything that was just said, I agree with totally. We need to really take charge and not only make sure it happens with policymakers, but make sure they do it with the best interest of kids in mind. We should not let the interest groups somehow wiggle their way in and take over so that we end up with a compromised program that none of us really envisioned or thought would be there.

With that being said, I think it's an opportunity. Please, let's not lose that opportunity. Another discussion I hope we have someday is about leadership. We never talk about leadership. We talk about the teachers, and we talk about program. But I'll tell you what—show me who's running your school and I'll tell you if it's any good or not. That goes right on down to the young children, too. We need to work at that end of leadership, as well.

Stephen Goldsmith

Thank you very much to all our panelists.

CHAPTER 15

SHAPING K-12 EDUCATION

Presentation by Governor Tim Pawlenty

Tim Pawlenty

Introduction by Lowell Milken

It's a great pleasure to introduce Minnesota Governor Tim Pawlenty, a man who has made improving educational achievement the highest goal of his administration. He sums up his vision by pledging, "We will establish clear standards, measure performance, and increase opportunities for all of our children." In fact, since the Governor took office in 2002, he's gained a well-deserved national reputation, and that reputation has come in the area of education reform—not the reforms we spoke about and surveyed earlier in this book, not 35 years of reforms that have done little to close the achievement gap. Rather, the Governor has earned this well-deserved reputation for reform that's well designed and implemented to ensure impact and sustainability.

He fought for and passed a dramatic overhaul of Minnesota's education standards, and his excellence and accountability initiative boldly links aspects of teacher compensation to performance. It received support in the form of a 7.8 million dollar grant from the U.S. Department of

The Challenges of School Reform: Implementation, Impact, and Sustainability, 217–226
Copyright © 2006 by Information Age Publishing
217

Education in 2003, and that was to introduce a professional compensation program for Minnesota's teachers, which included the Teacher Advancement Program (TAP).

Recently, Governor Pawlenty further strengthened his commitment to reform and professionalize the teaching profession with his Q Comp legislation. Q Comp, which stands for Quality Compensation for Quality Teachers, is modeled in a significant way after the elements of TAP. Governor, a rose by any other name would smell as sweet. Whether you call Minnesota's program TAP or Q Comp, what is important is the end goal of having a talented teacher in every classroom, in every school, every year. That is a goal we all share.

Please join me in welcoming a man with vision, knowledge, and commitment to make a profound difference, not only for the people in Minnesota, but for all of the citizens across our nation, Governor Tim Pawlenty.

Tim Pawlenty

It is an honor and a pleasure to be here with you. I'd like to tell you a true story about Michael Jordan, who of course was the best basketball player to ever play in the NBA. In the peak of his career, he had some extraordinary games. During one particular game, he scored 56 points by himself! With a minute or so left in the game, the coach decided to pull Michael Jordan out because the game was well in hand, and this way he could walk off the court with the crowd still in attendance and receive an ovation.

To be expected, as Jordan walked off the court, the crowd appropriately gave him a standing ovation. With seconds left in the game, a rookie is substituted in Michael Jordan's place. With seconds to go in the game, this rookie gets the ball. He's about to shoot, but he gets fouled. He doesn't make the basket, but he goes to the foul line, where he shoots one for two, scoring one point. The buzzer goes off, the game ends, and they all go into the locker room.

The reporters understandably hover around the great Michael Jordan and start asking him about his performance. But one enterprising reporter drifts over to the rookie, and says, "You know, this was your first NBA experience. What did you think? What does it mean?" The rookie looks up with kind of a smile on his face and says, "Well, I think tonight should be forever remembered as the night that Michael Jordan and I together scored 57 points." That is a great story about teamwork.

I want to thank Lowell Milken and the people at the Milken Family Foundation for being the lighthouse that sends beacons across this nation about where we've been and where we're headed, in a supportive, constructive, and positive manner, for education reform and improvement. Our hats are off to you.

Whether you're Lowell, Governor Pawlenty, or some other governor or policymaker, we shouldn't forget who the Michael Jordans in education are in this country: They are the teachers, and we are really grateful to have an assembly of some of the best teachers in this nation in this room, talking about and sharing your insights, practices, and recommendations for education reform in this nation. It is one of the most important topics facing this country, and I want to preface my remarks today by sharing with you a little bit of context—because I think the context in which this debate takes place is critically important to understanding the magnitude and the urgency of the issue.

There is a famous Minnesotan who you have heard about, Thomas Friedman. He now writes for *The New York Times*. He's become a big deal, and he's speaking in Saint Paul, Minnesota, tonight about his new book, *The World Is Flat*. I'll save you the time of going to his speech and the $25 you would spend on the book. What it basically says is what we all know—that the barriers between us and the rest of the world, the walls of separation between us and the rest of the world, have melted away to the point where the events around the world now come at us at a quick speed and pace and provide competitive pressures in a way that really has not been recognized or addressed by America as a matter of policy or our economy.

Let me give you a couple of examples. I'm told that the cost of shipping a ton of product from China to the port of San Francisco is $17 per ton. Seventeen dollars per ton! So, if you have a product of any value, the marginal cost of overcoming that geographic distance via shipping is inconsequential to the transaction. Twenty, 30 years ago, that geographic separation was a big deal. Shipping something across the world as an increment of the transaction was a big deal.

Do you remember 20, 30 years ago? I'm old enough to remember this: if you made a long-distance phone call from Minnesota all the way to Kansas, much less California, it was expensive, and that was a significant part of the discussion. You couldn't be on the phone too long because that would run up a pretty high bill. Well, guess what, now if you have the right phone plan, there's no roaming charges, no long distance charges, and it doesn't matter much where you call. The relative cost of calling Kansas, California, or some other place around the world, for that matter, to transmit voice is almost inconsequential to the interaction.

The same is true with massive exchanges of data through large internet pipes. The relative cost is inconsequential. It used to be that if you were at the University of Minnesota, or some other place where you had a new invention, application or concept, you could have relative advantage for a while because it took awhile for the news to spread. You could keep it in the upper Midwest, and by the time it reached some other land, country, or culture, it could be years, sometimes decades, before they could get a hold of it, understand it, deploy it, and apply it. Well, now, if you have an idea, a mouse click sends it around the world instantly.

So, the point of all of this is that the differences between us and the rest of the world as measured by distance, time, and cost, have melted away. That results in what we now understand to be a hyper-competitive global economy that is putting very significant pressure on our country and other developed countries, and forcing change.

As humans, we don't like change. We're people of habit; we're people of routine. We get up at about the same time every morning, and then we eat about the same things for breakfast. We hang out with about the same people. We drive about the same route to work. We eat at about the same restaurants. A lot of times we even order the same items off the same menu at the same restaurant. And so, when somebody or some external force says that things need to change, it's a little unsettling.

It is not an option to stand still in a rapidly changing world. We can't be what we were. Nostalgia is fun, but it's not a strategic plan for the future. And so—like everything else—public institutions and educational institutions need to change.

One thing that is putting another sense of urgency all over the United States is the fact that places like Minnesota aren't going to be the world's cheapest-screw turners anymore. One generation ago, if you grew up in my home town of South St. Paul—which is a first-ring suburb with a proud tradition of being a blue-collar, meat-packing town—you didn't have to do so well in school. In fact, even if you dropped out of high school, you could go get what they called a strong-back job down at the local stock-yards. You could cut meat. You could drive a forklift. You could load and unload freight or something like that. You couldn't get wealthy, necessarily, but you could make an OK living for yourself and maybe even for your family.

Well, guess what, those jobs are essentially gone. Now, if you don't have a skill or an education that is related to the economy of today, you are in deep trouble. Education is now more important than ever. It is imperative that we have more children who are more prepared than in the past. We really can and should be proud of our educational system. Our educational system and our educators have a heart for children, a heart for learning, and a motive that recognizes that you know you're not going to get wealthy doing this (although you want to get paid professionally and paid fairly), but you do it for the tremendous sense of service and meaning. That is tremendously important, so we want to say thank you and that we're grateful for you. We don't ever, ever teacher bash; we teacher celebrate. We thank teachers, and we express gratitude toward teachers.

However, there are some things in education that, as in any constructive partnership, we want to try to improve and change, because there are some pretty bright warning lights flashing on the dashboard at the results in American education. I want to talk to you about a couple of them today. One relates to our teaching profession, while the other relates to the American high school. Finally, I'll close with a few general thoughts.

Do you all remember Conrad Hilton? He was the founder of the Hilton Hotel chain and a very successful businessperson, across the nation and the world, who had done a lot in his life. At the end of his career, he was on *The Tonight Show Starring Johnny Carson.* Johnny, who was a skilled interviewer, said, "Conrad, you're this tremendously successful person. You've traveled the world, you've had enormous business success, you've met people from every culture, every walk of life. You've been a tremendous philanthropist you've been involved in civic activities. If you had to sum it all up and just look into the camera, and tell the American people one thing that it all boils down to that you'd want them to know, what would it be? Turn to the camera and tell them that." Conrad thinks for a minute, he turns to the camera and says, "Well, I guess what I'd tell the American people is this, 'Please put the shower curtain inside the tub.'"

Sometimes we spend so much time talking about the complex, the esoteric, and the academic, that we lose sight of the practical and the here and now. There are some basic things to remind ourselves of. The first is this: even though as public policymakers we can't legislate this, we can encourage it, celebrate it, and foster it. The number one determining factor of how kids are going to do in schools is their parents, so we want to celebrate and encourage parental involvement however we can. I always like to start education discussions with that, because it matters. It matters big time. Now, as you all know, we have some parents who are disadvantaged, who are unable, who are unwilling, who are unprepared, who can't, or who won't. So we need to step into the breach and help in the various ways we can. Looking at the positive side of the ledger, we shouldn't lose sight of things we can do to encourage and promote parental involvement. You all know that from your experience. It's just common sense; there's a strong correlation between parental involvement and educational success.

The second most important factor in determining the likely success of a student is that student's teachers—the quality, competence, and effectiveness of teachers. I've spent some time, as I'm sure you have, following and being involved in the work of the Teaching Commission. They have sent out a warning, and it basically says that 46% of the teachers who enter the profession leave within their first five years. Forty-six percent.

We have teachers who are the most promising and highest quality teachers, who are less and less likely to go to the most challenged sites. This is where we have some of the most disadvantaged students, who have the highest need for the highest quality teachers, so there's a misalignment between availability of the highest quality teachers and the highest needs in some of our schools. We are not preparing teachers like we used to. Many of our college programs in education are not as rigorous or as relevant as they could or should be to today's economy and educational system. Then it lends to the issue of whether teacher pay is appropriately modern and professional.

I don't think teachers make too much money. I think they should make more money. I just think we don't pay you very well, both in terms of the monetary amount and in treating you as modern professionals, which is just as important. I go around and give speeches all the time to noneducators, and now, almost everywhere I go I ask if I could see a show of hands for those who get compensated just for seniority. Then I ask the people who are in government to suppress their hands, and no hands are ever left up.

The world has moved and changed. That doesn't mean seniority can't be a factor, but it shouldn't be the only or dominating factor. So, whether it's TAP or our Q Comp program, we want to encourage, promote, and incentivize a more professional pay system, hopefully related to things that are more relevant to better outcomes in the classroom.

As you know, educators are collaborative. They are not sharp elbow people. We don't want teachers elbowing each other in the chops for an extra $50. It's a team sport, and it's an integrated sport. Thus, we have to do this in a way that says to teachers, the team can win. It's team oriented; it's collaborative. Those are some things to think about.

Our program, which I'll just tell you frankly is a direct rip-off of TAP. Lowell said it was OK, so we're taking some liberties with it. It includes elements that you've been talking about and issues you know about because you've been involved in these kinds of discussions. It recognizes that one of the frustrations of new teachers is getting help. If you need help or if you need mentoring, it's a little awkward to go to your principal and say, "Hey Mr./Ms. Supervisor, I'm deficient. Even though you're the person who writes my evaluations and controls my future, I just want to lay it out there for you. I'm deficient."

It's more comfortable to go to a colleague who's seasoned, who's trained, and who has some insights. We like to designate them as master and mentor teachers, who have the skill, ability, training, and time to pull up alongside and say, "I'll be your mentor teacher." School districts are doing this kind of ad hoc already, but we want to systemize it. We want to recognize and reward it in a way that's fair and appropriate.

We also want to have improvements in staff development. It's really important. Our wonderful Minnesota teachers would say that we all have staff development, but the traditional model is not sustained. It's not continuous; it's kind of episodic. You don't always get the time to fully discuss and implement it. It's not as relevant to the classroom as it could be, so we want that to be in the mix as well.

They would also like to have student performance be part of it. It doesn't have to be the overwhelming part of it, but it should be included. It needs to be done in a fair way. There are ways to do that, and that needs to be part of the program.

Peer review is another part of criteria that's involved. We try to evaluate in three or four different ways that we think are more professional, more appropriate, and more results-oriented.

We're moving ahead with this type of voluntary program in Minnesota. We're offering incentive money to school districts who can qualify for additional money if they join our program. We have the spirit of invention and of innovation, and we should try stuff. If some of it fails, let's just say it failed. But at the same time, let's at least applaud the people who are willing to try something new. I'll be the first one to stand here and commit to you that if some districts try TAP, and it doesn't make a big enough difference, or any difference, or a negative difference, then Lowell and I will come back and we'll say to get rid of it. Let's at least try it, because what we're doing now isn't exactly setting the world on fire in a lot of districts.

The second topic I wanted to talk to you a little bit about is the American high school, which I'm sure you've all heard a lot about in the last six or eight months. It really was an awakening moment for me to be at a conference like this a couple months ago in Washington, D.C., where Bill Gates, the founder of Microsoft, was the guest speaker. He stood up and said that the American high school is obsolete. It is obsolete. This is coming from Bill Gates. He said, "We are preparing students for the economy and citizenship of 40 years ago." Forty years ago. Now that is a stinging indictment, coming from one of our pioneer leaders in this country.

What he means by that are a couple of things: one is that if you have high achieving students, in many cases they get their credits by 11th grade, and then they coast to the finish line. They check out. It's called senioritis. Many of you are familiar with it. I have an eighth-grader who already has it at home. While this is fun for them, it's not so good for us.

There's another phenomenon that we need to understand, which is that many of the school districts across the country have advanced placement and international baccalaureate programs. In Minnesota, we have a program called Post Secondary Enrollment Options, where kids can detach from the school and go to the local college to get some of their credits. But they've got to leave the school site. They're wonderful programs, but the reality of it is that on average there are about 20% of the students who are on that kind of track. As I said earlier, we don't have to have everybody going to college, but you've got to have at least some preparation for a post-high school experience that's educationally relevant or from a skill standpoint. We don't have anywhere near a high enough percentage of children with that kind of rigor and track in high school.

While the existing programs are good, they don't reach enough students. When you have a nation saying that if you don't have a skill or an education that's relevant to the economy, post-high school, you're in deep trouble—and by the way, we have only 20% or 30% of the kids on that kind of track in high school—that's a problem. So we're trying to bring more of that experience—we call it "getting ready" or "getting credit"— into the high school so that we can do things, not just for those top-performing kids who happen to qualify for advanced placement courses, but for a much broader section of students. We can say, "Look, if you want to take some college preparatory classes without leaving the school, your friends, and your extra curricular activities, then we want you to be challenged."

We want to raise the bar and make that experience available to you. You take the class; we'll pay for the test. You pass it; you get college credit. It raises the bar for more kids and provides more opportunity for more kids. They get a running start at college; they'll hopefully finish college quicker. They will make better use of the public resources while they're in high school, and they'll save Mom and Dad tuition money. I mean, this is a win-win situation.

Candidly, the only push-back, is that we have got some of our public colleges saying, "Wait a minute, you're going to take some of our money away by not giving us the full run at the college credits." We have to politely say to them that we've got to do what's in the best interest of the children, not what's in the best interest of our higher education institutions. We want to be sensitive to that, but we can't have that be the deciding factor. There's an opportunity to partner with them in a way that's revenue mitigating.

So, we want to get about the business of redesigning the American high school. The teachers are there; the classrooms are there. The lights are on, and the heat is on. We just need to make sure the curriculum gets converted to something that's more rigorous, more relevant, and more relationship-oriented to the economy of today.

Let me give you a few quick thoughts. One of the biggest challenges facing our country is funding, and one of the biggest challenges within funding is that we have a section of the national and state budgets that's growing so fast that it's squeezing out our ability to pay for other things, in relative terms. That section of the budget is the healthcare budgets of families, individuals, governments, and businesses. We don't have time to discuss that today, nor is that within the scope of my remarks, but I just want to flag this point for you. Part of the public policy debate about funding for education is to make sure that it's a relative priority to the other pressure points in the public policy arena. I encourage you to think about joining the concerns about how we can have a better healthcare system in this country, because it is at least indirectly correlated to how we're going to fund education in the future, as demographics change.

The demographics, by the way, are not getting younger. In Minnesota, for the first time in modern history, we have an actual decline in the number of children in our school system, and we fund our schools per pupil. If we give you an increase per pupil, but you're losing pupils, it's not a good scenario.

Last, we have a real challenge with focusing on the averages. We have disadvantaged children in our country who now, for almost a generation, are not doing well, and the statistics aren't substantially changing. As you look at school districts that have disproportionate challenges, while progress has been made at the margins, it hasn't been made fundamentally. There is no school district with a disproportionately challenged population that to scale has turned it around. There are sites where you have a particularly gifted principal. There are sites where you have some particularly interesting pilot projects. But there really isn't a district that is substantially disadvantaged and that has turned its academic fortunes around.

That's a situation that hasn't changed substantially in a decade. Again, it's beyond the scope of my remarks here today because I was asked to talk about a few other things. But we need to have a very substantial debate and resolution of this issue, because it's becoming an intergenerational statistical failure. I don't want to be part of a policy era where we condemn another generation of disadvantaged students to academic failure, knowing that means failure in today's economy. We have to find some more particular, more aggressive reforms to apply to our most disadvantaged school districts, because what we're doing now isn't working so well, even though in many of these districts we're spending a lot of money. I want to challenge you with that.

I'll close with a quote from Franklin Delano Roosevelt. He said this: "The country needs and, unless I miss its temper, the country demands bold, persistent experimentation. It is common sense to take a method and try it. If it fails, admit it frankly and try another. But above all, try something." Now, I don't think that sentiment can be expressed any better than that. I want to just applaud you for your commitment to excellence, your willingness to try new things, and we are really grateful for what you do.

Martin Luther King said that everybody can be great, because everybody can serve. You are serving at a really high level, doing something that is really important. He also said that the measure of a person is not where they stand in times of comfort and privilege, but where they stand in times of challenge and controversy. And our nation is in challenging times. We have just been through a recession. The economy is recovering in a modest way. We're a nation at war. We've got a lot of polarization in the country. We've got coastal states, heartland states, blue states, and red states, and people yell at each other and call each other names. The discourse needs to be civil, particularly when it comes to education. In challenging and controversial times, you stand for some really important things, and the future of this country is in your hands. I'm old enough to say that it's not going to be too long before the baton of leadership is going to get passed.

This stuff doesn't get embedded into kids automatically. It has to be taught; it has to be role-modeled. It has to be shown, and it has to be given. As a society, as a community, as teachers, as parents, we have to teach them. I want to just say thank you for it. I think we want to join hands with you and say, "Let's try to do it even better."

CHAPTER 16

REAUTHORIZATION OF THE HIGHER EDUCATION ACT

**J. Ted Sanders, Guilbert C. Hentschke, Sally L. Stroup,
Ben Wildavsky, and Susan Tave Zelman**

Introduction by Jane Foley

It is a pleasure to introduce the moderator of our panel, Ted Sand-ers. He has been the chief state school officer in three states: Nevada, Illinois, and Ohio. He has been a university president at Southern Illi-nois University. He has been the president of the Education Commis-sion of the States (ECS). He has been the deputy secretary of the U.S. Department of Education. He has been the acting secretary at the U.S. Department of Education. And yes, he has been a classroom teacher, too.

He is a frequent presenter at our national education conference, but here is something that you may not know about him. He not only attends and presents at our conference, but you will see Ted Sanders sitting in the audience at all the sessions throughout our conference each year. It's obvi-ous to me that he's not only a lifelong leader, he is a lifelong learner. He's going to be introducing us to the panel, but first I would like all of you to welcome our moderator, Ted Sanders.

The Challenges of School Reform: Implementation, Impact, and Sustainability, 227–250
Copyright © 2006 by Information Age Publishing

Ted Sanders

These past two days, we've seen a lot of data that closely examines the issues of teacher supply, demand, and quality. The story these data tell is provocative because they're the most important issues that we face in schools today. As we started, Lowell made this same point as emphatically as it can be made, and he has reinforced it throughout this conference. The message is clear: if we're serious about school reform, if we're serious about closing the achievement gap, if we're serious about improvement of our schools, then we have to look at the human capital in our schools. We need to look at the teachers who labor every day, in every classroom in America.

Chart 16.1 illustrates the variance in student performance by looking at the correlations to home and family conditions, class size, and teacher qualification. Chart 16.2 however, tells the story in an even more powerful way. Looking at the differences in the performance of low-achieving students after one year in an effective teacher's classroom versus a less effective teacher's classroom, the message that you and your colleagues make a difference is clear.

The second important point is that the teaching force in America is declining. We need to add teachers for three reasons: because of the graying of the teaching force, because we're unable to retain a good number of beginner teachers, and because of our commitments to reduce class size. If you look at Chart 16.3, you see that by the end of this decade, we're going to need another three and a half million teachers in the classrooms of America to keep up with student demand.

Looking at Chart 16.4, you see that we have a leaky pipeline or, as the National Commission on Teaching and America's Future (NCTAF) described it, a "leaky bucket." Either way you want to phrase it, we have a difficult time retaining teachers who are entering our classrooms. Beginning teachers are leaving at greater numbers than those teachers who must be replaced due to retirement.

I learned during my tenure at Southern Illinois University that we actually prepare more teachers in our schools of education than will ever find their way into the classrooms. In fact, for every 100 or so teachers we prepare, only 60 of them will actually go into the classroom after they complete a teacher preparation program. Unfortunately, we know very little about the remaining 40%—whether they're selling insurance, raising a family, or contributing to the workforce in another manner.

Today, we know a great deal more about what happens to teachers in those first five years of teaching. Chart 16.5 shows the tremendous loss of teachers across the first five years of teaching. We not only have a problem with our ability to retain teachers, we have a particular problem with our

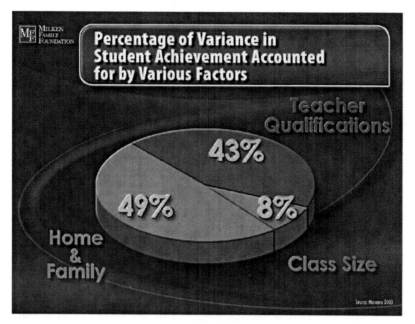

Chart 16.1.

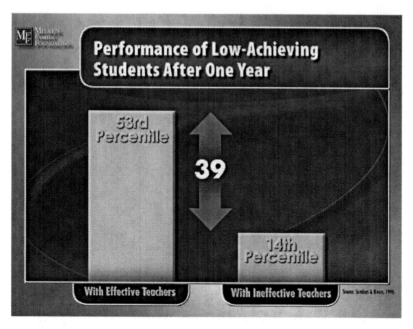

Chart 16.2.

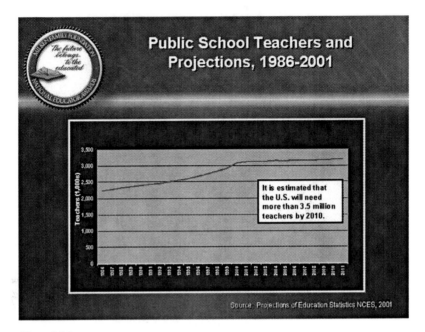

Chart 16.3.

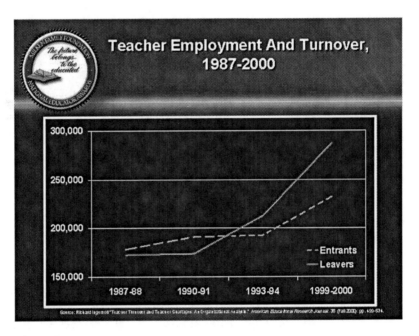

Chart 16.4.

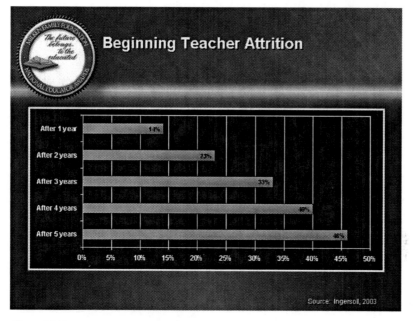

Chart 16.5.

ability to retain highly qualified teachers. Now, most of us would expect that these individuals are capable of becoming high caliber teachers just like all of you in the audience. However, for some reason, we're not retaining the teaching force and thereby allowing time for teachers to become quality educators. We have a several-pronged challenge to overcome in order to correct this trend: we've got to raise the quality of the teaching force, and we've got to increase supply.

The most significant of those problems, as Chart 16.6 shows, is that the teacher turnover rate is significantly higher in low-income schools than it is in high-income schools. And it seems that this is because those teachers who are leaving the poor schools are doing so to work in wealthier districts.

I started teaching in Mountain Home, Idaho, went back to graduate school, and then spent a year teaching second grade on the Navajo reservation to non-English speakers. Afterward, I went to Albuquerque, New Mexico, to teach. The pattern I followed in entering the Albuquerque public schools was very, very different from the other people entering the teaching profession that year. Math teachers who had not previously taught typically started out in one of the poor barrios down along the Rio Grande River in Albuquerque. If they were successful after a few years,

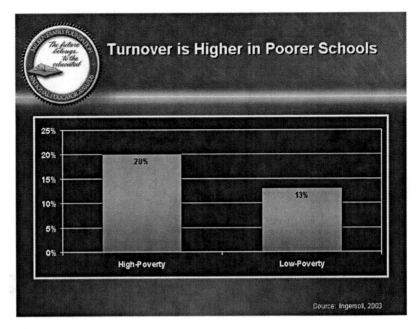

Chart 16.6.

then they would start a migration up the side of Sandia Mountain to the more affluent schools.

This is the same pattern in America today. Teachers tend to leave low-income districts for those that are wealthier. Thus, the most qualified teachers are far less likely to be teaching in the schools that need them the most, where the children could benefit most. If we are really serious about closing the achievement gap, then we have to be concerned about how the talented human capital is distributed in our schools.

Let me introduce our panel to you very briefly. Sally Stroup is the assistant secretary for Post-Secondary Education at the U.S. Department of Education. From my perspective, she has the toughest job at the Department. Sally has a very diverse career. She has been a senior leader at the Apollo Group; that's the University of Phoenix. She was a professional staff member at the U.S. House of Representatives Committee on Education and the Workforce, and prior to that, she worked in the Pennsylvania Higher Education Assistance Agency.

Next we have Ben Wildalvsky. Ben is an education writer for the *U.S. News and World Report*. He supervises education coverage for the weekly magazine and serves as an editor of *America's Best Colleges* and also *America's Best Graduate Schools*. Previously, he was deputy education and culture editor. He helped conceive and edit the award-winning cover stories on the Black and White achievement gap, as well as the new SAT. Ben was also the national education correspondent for three years, as well as the lead author of *U.S. News'* "Ultimate Guide to Becoming a Teacher."

Then we have Gib Hentschke. Gib is the Richard T. and Mary Catherine Cooper Chair in Public School Administration at the University of Southern California (USC). Previously, he also served as the dean of the School of Education at USC. Further, Gib directs programs in business education, including the Galaxy Institute for Education and the school business management program. He's authored numerous books and articles focusing heavily on charter schools and the business of education.

Next is Susan Zelman. Susan is the superintendent of Public Instruction for the great state of Ohio. She's been in that position since 1999 and previously worked in two other state education agencies. Ohio has been recognized for a number of Susan's initiatives, including receiving an A grade for their standards and accountability system in *Education Week's* "Quality Counts" this year. Two years ago, *Gannett Newspapers* named her as one of the 10 most powerful and influential women in the state of Ohio.

Our conversation today is supposed to be about the reauthorization of the Higher Education Act (HEA). We are all familiar with that act because of Pell Grants, Stafford Loans, and helping kids have access to college, but the HEA also has titles that focus on the very issues we've been talking about. Where are we with reauthorization, and what kind of successes have we had under Title II? What's still being debated, and what are you looking to try to accomplish around these issues as the HEA gets reauthorized? Sally, we will start with you.

Sally Stroup

I'm a lawyer by trade, but I got involved in teacher education because I worked on Capitol Hill in 1998, when the Higher Education amendments were passed. This was really the first time that Congress took a serious look at teacher preparation. There had been programs about teacher education, but this was the first time you had members like George Miller from California and Senator Ted Kennedy from Massachusetts saying they were not happy with our nation's schools, and that we need to do a better job.

The problem was, however, that we didn't have good data to see where our strengths and weaknesses were. That is really what led to the 1998 amendments, where Congress did two important things. First, Congress created an accountability system that forced states and schools to give the government information about what is going on with teacher preparation programs. Although there is currently debate about whether this is good data, it has really caused people to look at their state systems and to make assessments of their teacher education programs at a state level.

The second thing Congress did was create the Title II Program on Partnerships and state grants for teacher preparation programs. One of the frustrations that I hear from members of Congress is that there are often college presidents, deans, and faculty in the office complaining about "those people" at the local school district not doing what they should. Of course, you also have the superintendents and the principals saying that "those people" in the college administration don't cooperate either. It was a consistent theme, and we ended up with a partnership program that says to schools of education and schools of arts and sciences, "Get together with a local school district, and we'll give you money to do a lot of good things that you probably are already thinking about doing but maybe just haven't gotten together to do." It's really why we ended up with a partnership program.

The partnership program really was designed to bring people together to try to reform problems in schools of education. A lot of you are teachers, and you really need to speak up about this issue. You are the experts. You went to a school of education, and you have an education degree. Did your education teach you what you needed to know to be a good teacher? It is important to hear your opinion because quite frankly, I don't think we know the answer to that at the government level. We hear people talk about how the government doesn't set curriculum and that we don't tell people what to do. Therefore, the teachers really need to come forward and tell us, "I didn't get what I needed, and here's what would have made it better for me going into a classroom." If you bring that message to the table, it will be more feasible for us to help you.

For those of you in the audience who have partnership grants, I encourage you to get involved in this discussion. Lots of places have partnership grants already, and they are allowing for more communication. I told Susan Zelman that Ohio is interesting to us at the Department because normally colleges are the lead grantee, and they run what gets done. Sometimes I think that the K-12 side of the partnership doesn't feel like they have an equal voice in what goes on. Just this year Ohio won a partnership grant where the lead grantee is actually the local school district. They drive what goes on as they work, and it's totally novel. We're watching this one closely to see how it works out because it is a different dynamic. Right now, however, we believe it is strengthening the K-12 in a teacher preparation program at a college campus.

I held a conference not too long ago on this Title II program, and I asked people what was going on. I said, "One thing Congress has debated is whether college faculty should be forced to go back and teach in class-rooms so they know what you all are dealing with." This idea was hugely controversial when it got to the Hill, and people were very upset about it. I raised this issue again at another recent meeting, and one college faculty woman stood up and said, "I used to teach. Now I'm on the college faculty, and I've been here for three years. It would be a really good thing if you made me go back into the classroom because I already feel disconnected from what's going on."

These are the kinds of things that Congress will look at when they reauthorize the partnership grants and the state grants. Who's doing things that are outside the box? Who is saying, "We're going to do a partnership, and we're going to have our faculty go back to the classroom and teach for a year. We're going to reverse roles and do things differently"?

We will be looking for colleges to be engaged at the presidential level on teacher preparation. Colleges are great about big research issues and big research projects, but sometimes college presidents are not all that engaged in what's going on in teacher preparation. I called some of them and asked if they knew they had Title II grants at their institutions. Of course, the answer was no. Upon hearing this response, I told them that the whole college needs to be involved. We do have some great partnerships. We have people recruiting education students the same way they recruit athletes, treating them the same way, making them feel the same kind of affection for coming to an institution, to attract the best and the brightest students into teaching. We need to get back to doing those kinds of things so that people realize teaching is a great profession, and teaching is what they want to do.

When I looked back through our grants at the state and partnership levels, the biggest expenditures and most of the focus is on recruitment. Everybody is looking for ways to do a better job of recruiting students. People are using our grant money for those kinds of purposes; however, you'll see that when Congress makes their priority list of grant activities, performance pay will be at the top of that list. In fact, Minnesota received one of the grants from the Department of Education, with a primary focus on pay for performance.

We are the incentive machine trying to incentivize people to try some of these things. They may not all work, and they may not be the perfect answer or solve all the problems; however, if it's something outside the box, if it makes a difference in the way teacher preparation is done, then that's going to help the people who end up in the classroom. That's what we're looking for when we look at what happens in teacher partnership and teacher state grants. I do believe that's what you'll see from the government when Congress finally does a higher education bill.

Ted Sanders

That's exactly where I wanted us to start this conversation today. Sally set the stage nicely. I'd like to turn to Susan now and ask, "What are the conditions in Ohio today, and are these partnership grants working?"

Susan Tave Zelman

Ohio is very much committed to No Child Left Behind (NCLB) and to standards-based reform. I think there are really two issues here. One is that as part of NCLB or standards-based reform, we raise the question, "What do we want our students to know and be able to do?" We have a theory of change, which is aligning what we expect from our students, with respect to how we teach, assess, and hold each other accountable. When we have this system in place, I think we then have to raise the next policy question: What do we want our educators to know and be able to do in order to teach in the standards-based system?

I want to look again at Chart 16.1, which relates to the role of the university and the role of presidents. We have to think about teacher education systems in terms of a subsystem of the whole university. When you look at this chart, you see that 49% of the variance is really attributed to home and family.

I would say part of the mission of a university and of our K-12 system is to see both components as a whole. I know we'll be successful when the math faculty of a higher education institution sees themselves as part of the same profession as the high school mathematics teacher or the elementary school faculty. In some sense, we have to think about this as an alliance and look at the need for interdependency. This gets back to the role of the university, in terms of home and family. The university must see itself as part of the economic development of the community in which it resides and believe that teacher education and schools of education are parts of the university that really can work in partnership with the schools.

We also need to think more broadly about this, in terms of what role law school plays in giving legal services to those families. What is the role of the school of public health or medical school in making sure that our kids come to school ready to learn? Again, I see these partnerships in a much broader context, where we're really talking about the quality of life. Education, of course, is key to the quality of life and is integrated into the economic and community development of that particular area.

Ted Sanders

What would you actually do to create this single system solution that you're talking about?

Susan Tave Zelman

I would form a partnership with my local school districts and business community. I would get the deans of each of the different schools around the table, and I would say to Columbus, for example, that we're grateful Columbus has an economic development plan to increase its valuable economy. Karen Holbrook, the president of Ohio State University, and I are working very hard on this partnership to make sure that Ohio State is an integral part of the economic life and vitality of the City of Columbus.

This means partnerships with Columbus State, our two year community college, the Columbus school system, and our neighboring districts in Franklin County, but it really has to be a true partnership. We have to listen to and learn from one another, and we have to learn to understand economic data and workforce policy development. We have to understand how we can work with county government and what kinds of partnerships we could afford in linking health and human services to our schools.

Look at what we've learned from our experiences with the Teacher Advancement Program (TAP) and also at what we've learned from our Ohio Schools of Promise. These are 102 schools in our state that are classified as high poverty, but these schools are also exceeding the state average in their performance. One of the things we know from our research and from our Schools of Promise is that they are in fact doing what NCLB calls for. They are doing standards-based reform. One of the things we understand from research is the importance of embedded professional development. What we actually would love to do is to infuse TAP into some of our Schools of Promise, because we think it would make it stronger. I think the more crucial issue for our schools of education is, "What are we doing to prepare our teachers to teach in the standards-based system? How are we assuring that they have academic content knowledge?" Thus far, our efforts in answering these questions are not enough.

NCLB has made a good stab at this, but just knowing your subject matter is not going to make you a great teacher, nor will it get us the mathematicians or scientists we want for our current and future generations. There is a difference between a chemist and a chemistry teacher. A chemistry teacher knows how to teach chemistry to middle-school or secondary school students, and there's a body of knowledge there that needs to be conveyed through the school of education. Also, what we're finding is that our teachers really need to learn how to work in a professional community. They have to learn how to talk to one another, and they need to see good models of teaching. They have to understand how to use and disaggregate the data, and how to then differentiate instruction.

Those are some of the things we're doing in Ohio. We are rethinking what educators need to know and what they should be able to do in the standards-based system.

Ted Sanders

Gib, you've been a professor and a dean at a very prominent institution that sits right in the second largest and most challenged school district in America. In these roles, you must have thought about these issues. Tell us a little bit about how you have looked at them and also what your experience might teach us today.

Guilbert Hentschke

I think back 40 years to when I started teaching in San Jose and Santa Clara, and I'm recalling how things haven't changed even since then. We heard Lowell allude to all the things we've tried to do to help education that haven't worked, so I'm wondering then what has changed? What is different? This may speak to the conversation we've been having. We've heard versions of this from a number of the speakers, but over that same 40-year period, the returns to schooling are more important than ever. Going to college matters to each of us, and the differences between going and not going are much greater now.

Secondly, we all talked about kids not achieving well, and we talked about low-income children. But we haven't talked about the distance between the poor and the not so poor that is growing worldwide. We continuously talk about the 2% of the world's kids who are in the United States and going to school, but there's still another 98% in the rest of world who are, on average, actually a lot poorer.

Some things have actually changed over that 40-year period. I work at the typical university, ranked somewhere on the list of the top 160 universities in the nation. Today, universities in an average year are conducting about $4 billion worth of research. In an average year, they are moving into the marketplace to commercialize intellectual property at about $400 million a year. That's a huge change from 40 years ago.

You are all likely familiar with United Way giving and how their process of collecting money works. We pass the hat and give the money to United

Way. You might also recall that when the head of United Way got into a little trouble, we took it upon ourselves to collect the money, and then we spent the money as an ongoing grant program for schools in our neighborhood.

Independent of whether somebody comes and goes, we have a process in place whereby schools have a way to find a partner anywhere in the university. It can be the head of parking, someone in the school of education or in the school of engineering, and so on. They think up a project, then there's a whole process that works every year in neighborhood schools. Now, this isn't a hard-nosed curricular conversation, but it has brought a terrific familiarity both onto our campus and out into the schools. Again, the projects are not all fantastic, but I want to emphasize that this type of structural change is sustainable.

In some schools of education, the higher the status of the institution, the less the status of the school of education, and the harder it is to get things done on that campus, with regard to the school of education. This may or may not be a reality for everybody, but it's what I've experienced. It's not that leading universities don't care about K-12 schools; in fact, they care about them a lot. But the incentive drives are not to improve teacher education. Therefore, what can we do if we happen to find ourselves at these kinds of institutions? We've had this conversation with K-12 schools involving regular schools and these newer charter schools, and there's a similar story going on in postsecondary education. There are some newer K-12 providers doing things very, very differently. They're things that we want to at least look at and understand, because they might possibly have some relevance for our long-term relationships.

In this audience today, we have a school superintendent, whose name I will not mention. I recently asked him about the institutions from which his teachers are currently coming. He said, "There's one technical college that is actually right on—practice-based, solid stuff. There is also the research university with well-respected professors, but it's not on target. Then there's a matchbook university, where you actually don't have to spend much time. These three kinds of solutions are what my educators are flowing through." Then I asked him about TAP. He loves it and thinks it is absolutely first rate, so I asked him, "If this were the way the educational administration program in your local university was set up, what would you say?" He replied that it would be fantastic.

Ted Sanders

Ben, you look at these issues through the lens of a journalist, particularly a journalist who's been seriously looking at measures and metrics to try to determine quality. There's been a good bit of effort in Congress to try to think about how to actually measure what's going on in schools of education, so I'm interested in hearing your thoughts. What would you recommend in regards to how we might set metrics that would tell us something about the quality of our schools of education?

Ben Wildavsky

Just as there's been an accountability revolution in K-12 over the last couple of decades leading up to and including NCLB, I think there is also a real yearning for accountability measures in higher education. As journalists, we've catered to that on the consumer end by trying to provide prospective students and parents with a lot of information. It's not always something that college presidents are happy about, but we're not really trying to serve college presidents. We're trying to serve the public. I think that in our way of thinking about these kinds of things, the accountability piece that Sally mentioned in the reauthorization is what I'm most intrigued by.

To some extent I wear a couple of hats at *U.S. News and World Report*. We're always looking at new teacher quality initiatives as weekly stories for the magazine, and last year I wrote a whole book on teaching and becoming a teacher, which includes some case studies about education schools and some policy material regarding the problems facing teaching. Most of it is comprised of listings of education schools, graduate-level education schools, and factual information.

We included pass rates on certification exams, because the last HEA reauthorization required schools of education to report this information. We found in most states that the pass rates are awfully high. The range tends to be between 94% and 100%. There isn't a whole lot of difference between the top schools and the bottom schools. Part of this, which Sally alluded to, is there was a certain amount of gamesmanship that occurred. We're certainly familiar with perceptions of gamesmanship with the *U.S. News* college rankings. Having been told they had to report certification pass rates, a lot of education schools essentially redefined what it meant to be an education school graduate, such as only counting someone as a graduate if they have finished all their course work and passed the state certification test. Thus, by definition, you have 100% pass rate. While that makes you look wonderful, it's in fact meaningless.

This issue was brought up in the House of Representatives a couple of years ago during the earlier stages of the reauthorization act. They tried to close this loophole, and I anticipate that it will happen. There are currently requirements for reporting passage rates on certification tests, such as the Praxis, one of the commonly used tests. But could you imagine having more finely tuned reporting requirements where you say, "We know that they are widely varying cutoffs on the Praxis from state to state, and we're not just simply interested in education school graduation rates. We're not just simply interested in whether or not they pass certification tests. We're interested in where the rubber hits the road—if their graduates demonstrably improve student learning"? One thing you can imagine the Department doing is providing some kind of incentive grants for pilot projects that try to do this.

My sense from having worked on this book about becoming a teacher and on teacher training is that, even at education schools at the highest levels, by and large, there's still resistance to accountability. I think there is a sense in which the establishment is still uneasy about this new era as represented by NCLB, but I think you're finding more friendliness and openness to the idea.

When I talked to Art Levine, who is doing his own series on the problems of education schools, he said, "We're missing an essential piece. What effect do the teachers we produce have on student achievement?" This is the way education schools are going to prove their worth. If you're looking at what the federal government can do or at the kinds of things people can do in an exploratory way, it seems to me on the accountability end to be one of the most intriguing areas.

Susan Tave Zelman

Sometimes we authorize acts, and we don't understand the connections between them. So right now, within the Department of Education's budget, there is money set aside for states to put together data systems. I suggest giving more preference to states that would be willing to link their student testing databases with their teacher preparation databases and allow them to communicate with one another.

In the state of Ohio, we're going to experiment with value-added measures, because we want to do something that is fair and credible. We would be interested in trying to get a more robust data system that would allow the state of Ohio to experiment with that.

The reality is that we can sit here and be critical about teacher preparation programs, but we, as a profession, have never really researched different types of models and looked at their effects on student achievement. If we had those databases and were able to think outside of the box and create a variety of different models—particularly with what the research is saying about professional education, whether it be in a business school or a teacher education school—then we would have a much better empirical sense of how we can improve teacher education for the future.

Ben Wildavsky

One more thing to put on the table is alternative certification. The premise has been that the vast majority of teachers come through conventional schools of education. However, there are exciting alternative program options, like Teach for America, and even some that are university-based, like UTeach at University of Texas, Austin, or the New Teacher Project.

To link it back to reauthorization, can the federal government provide any kind of incentive loans or funds to use the kind of data systems that we're talking about and extend the question to people who've come up through nontraditional means?

Susan Tave Zelman

I think that's a very good idea and really quite important. I want to comment on the term certification. I think it would be awful if we had just one set of standards for people to enter the profession one way and another set of standards to enter another way. In Ohio, we are developing a set of standards based upon what we think education needs to look like for the future. The real issue is how to accelerate the closing of the achievement gap.

With a set of standards we could have a variety of different routes to those standards. We can have a different way of training those people who enter the profession midlife or through the traditional undergraduate route. We can also think about customizing programs to meet specific needs of the district, with a true partnership between the district and perhaps another entity to do that type of training. Regardless, they should be based upon a common set of standards to really drive student achievement.

We're very grateful to Congressmen Boehner and Regula for allowing us to experiment with charter colleges of education. Charter colleges of education were really designed to change the whole notion of who the customer is and to provide some competition to our traditional programs within schools of education. We have about 50 teacher preparation programs in Ohio, and we wrote a Request for Proposal (RFP) asking for out-of-the-box thinking to really address some of our shortages in Ohio—special education, math, science, bilingual education. In some sense, the customer was the state or the school district. We got 17 responses, and we funded three of those. We were hoping that everybody would use this as an opportunity to have conversations with liberal arts, science faculty, and other parts of the university, to stimulate a discussion about how we would rethink teacher education. Instead, many of the proposals we got were really quite traditional.

One of the programs we funded was our educational service center. This is an intermediate district that gives services to schools that work with a college, university, or some school districts, which we're looking at, and they train special-needs teachers that work with severely disabled children. This kind of collaboration is interesting because the small liberal arts college is working with the Cincinnati school district, in terms of training and special education. Unfortunately, in Ohio we have a very high over-representation of African Americans in special education. What was so interesting in this particular design is that they took an area study with an international perspective about teaching pluralism, cultural issues, and attracting mid-career professionals in doing a lot of that training in collaboration with the Cincinnati public schools' central office.

Ted Sanders

Amazing things are going on in this country right now, and I've seen some evidence that there is significant growth in the number of mid-career professionals who would like to pursue some other career path. There are a lot of people my age who don't want to retire, even though they technically could. Others can't afford to retire, but they would like to do something different than what they've done in the past. It's interesting how many of them would like to do something that has a socially redeeming value, and teaching comes up pretty high. We need to have very different ways of allowing these people into the classroom, because traditional methods are keeping them out of the classroom.

Ben Wildavsky

Traditionally, education schools have been a cash cow for universities, so what are the incentives for college presidents to buy into the notion that teacher preparation should be a vital part of their mission? I think one answer may be having external accountability measures that they are responsible for meeting.

I think there really is an economic question of whether the demand is there. I talked to a man who was a U.S. Airways executive, making several hundred thousand dollars a year. He retired early and became a middle-school teacher in the Washington area, taking an 80%-90% salary cut. He had to go through a long series of education school classes, which was a hurdle he had to jump through, and he wasn't thrilled about it. But what is the incentive for that university to say, "We don't need you to be here for a year and a half or two with student teaching. We're going to come up with a six-month streamlined program"? Economically, this does not make sense for the school. Now, maybe if you can persuade them that there's a market out there that they're not serving, and that they could have a lot more students enrolled if they offered those kinds of alternatives, then maybe they would be convinced.

Sally Stroup

I want all of you in the audience to know that you can apply for a grant from the government to implement alternative certification programs, and we'll give you money to be creative. Currently, the reality of the situation is that almost nobody applies for these grants, and the number of people who are submitting applications at the state level and the partnership level to do new things on alternative certification programs is very small.

Susan Tave Zelman

We've thought a lot about this, because one of our issues is figuring out how we can stimulate out-of-the-box thinking. What we're sort of beginning to learn from our charter colleges of education is that we have to do more professional development for people within the universities and get them to think about a new concept of what schools really need to look like in the twenty-first century.

We also need to educate them about the new technologies out there. When you visit a school of education, you'll see that some of our K-12 schools have more educational technology in them than our traditional schools of education. I think we need to do a better job with that, and I'd like to see, as part of the funding, maybe getting our higher education community together to think about what they need to know and be able to do in education for the next century.

How do we educate them in terms of what's out there, and what can be out there to help them envision the future? We need to stop fighting about standards-based reform and become partners in understanding the issues of the achievement gap, and we need to try to create a sense of urgency around that. We're losing ground in this country.

Ted Sanders

I'm going to turn now to the audience for questions and comments.

Audience Question

Very early in the discussion, it was brought up that in the schools of education only a few of the professors come down from their ivory tower and into the K-12 classrooms. The reason very few of them will ever bring that experience is because of pay. We pay the people who are preparing our teachers very little.

Ben Wildavsky

One thought about the lack of interaction between education and other professions, which you alluded to, is that some of the education schools are putting forth effort to create more interaction—for example, the practicum experience. The Carnegie Corporation of New York has a major initiative, which is in its relatively early days. They've given something like $65 million in grants to many education schools, and they're really looking at three things. One of their big criteria is creating better connections between the education schools and the K-12 schools. They want to have the schools they're working with create many field experiences. They use the metaphor of doctor residencies. They want teachers going out often, and they want faculty going out often.

The second is that they also want to better integrate the faculty of the education schools with the arts and sciences, which gets back to the point about content knowledge. Thirdly, they're also interested in the results-oriented approach. They are trying to make sure that education schools think in terms of measuring how well their graduates are teaching. One of the strongest incentives for change within a school of education is to change the promotion and tenure policy.

Guilbert Hentschke

We have a two-tier system at USC: a tenure track system and a clinical system, not unlike medical schools. So, what you have is a practice-oriented side of the house and a research side of the house. For better or worse, it's got its own problems and prospects, but at least we're getting more emphasis on the practice side. That's the good news. The bad news is that the clinical faculty sometimes feels like they're second-class citizens.

Audience Question

There's great disrespect to that nonresearch side, and the nonresearch side does not feel like they are a true part of the university because of it.

Susan Tave Zelman

Not only that, but we still have the dichotomy between basic and applied research, and we need a lot more applied research to move the profession.

Audience Question

Sally, you said earlier that teachers should be sure to get to the table and share our opinions. It's not always easy for a teacher to get to the table. And then when you finally get there, you're not even sure if it's the right table. Do you have any suggestions on how teachers can get to the tables of federal and government places? Sometimes it's easier for us to deal on a district level, but even then, that's not always guaranteed.

Sally Stroup

I realize that it's not always easy, and sometimes the issues are local issues where we couldn't do anything to help you, even if we tried. However, there are a couple things you can do. When I think about reauthorizing HEA—if you have suggestions for changing Title II, all you need to do is e-mail those changes to us. We keep a master database of these comments at the Department. We organize the comments, and we have people assigned to look at teacher issues and teacher education issues. That's one way to at least be on record. The other thing I always suggest to everybody, and this comes from working on Capitol Hill for seven years, is get to know your member of Congress, as well as his or her staff. A lot of the time, it is just talking to people.

On the partnership side, I think it's really important to look at what Ohio did and find that college in your community to forge a relationship with, get together to submit a grant, and work together. It has made a big difference, from what we can tell, in any of these programs we run, but it really does take people getting together and having a common mission, cooperating, and deciding to work together to really make the programs effective plans of action.

Guilbert Hentschke

We focused on the supply side of schools of education and universities, which is a good topic. Whenever I talk to people in school districts, who actually have the responsibility of hiring a number of teachers, they have clear opinions as to which programs are good and which ones aren't. If we had a *U.S. News* on the demand side, rather than a *U.S. News* on the supply side, then we'd have a different conversation. Imagine how the rankings would change if school districts were asked to rate the quality of education provided to their employees.

Ben Wildavsky

We are always trying to improve what we do, and we have these ongoing debates. In our graduate school guide, which just came out a month or so ago, we looked at teacher preparation programs, but we focused on the research aspect of the programs. We listed the teacher preparation programs, but we didn't attempt to rank them.

Whereas, with research, you can survey people about the research quality; there has been an absence of good data on achievement. For example, in the case of law schools, we look at measures such as LSAT scores, but we also talk to recruiters. We talk to law firms to get their opinion on how well they are served by the graduates of program X or Y. At least hypothetically, what you're suggesting might be something we could consider, if we're trying to find better quality measures for education schools. One way we're doing that—and again these things are complicated—is that we're going to the big national universe of schools. But if you could find the right people to ask and get a decent response rate, you could then begin to build up some kind of an instrument that would be useful.

Audience Question

I am fortunate enough as an elementary principal to work with the Missouri Partnership for Educational Renewal with the University of Missouri at Columbia. My dean of the college of education is just as concerned about the student achievement of my elementary students as he is about the success of his teacher educators that he's working with.

You mentioned partnering with one of those colleges that want to do that. I don't think that in the crisis of trying to find teachers we can wait for those colleges to be ready for that kind of partnership. How are we going to get all colleges to be ready to really embrace the fact that all students need to achieve, and that colleges of education need to be just as concerned about student achievement from K-12 as we are?

We've got a model that looks at resources differently. Dean Andrews would tell you that it's not about more money; it's about reusing the money in a different way. His college of education faculty now involves so many more people because he has our teachers on board who are part of his faculty.

I have a teacher in my building who's a mentor teacher, which would fit in with the TAP model in a lot of ways. She's paid for by the school district but is a faculty member of the college of education. She's released from her classroom to nurture those new teachers, to nurture bachelor-level students who spend a full year in our school. She works with first-year teachers who are earning their master's, and she works with other new teachers who aren't in the fellowship program. It's working. It's replicable. And it's happening in Missouri. We need to spread the word.

Sally Stroup

Certainly, at the Department of Education's level, at the secretary's level, at my level, and with other people in the department, one thing we try to do is spend a lot of time with college presidents. Sometimes we haul them all into Washington and give them the speech about this. We did it on math and science teacher education last year. We had a whole bunch of people at the table, and we tried to spread that message, basically saying: we will make sure that every public college in the state of Louisiana is accountable for their teachers when they go into the classroom.

We said that we will do assessments and that we will hold people accountable for those kinds of things. It's going to take a massive cooperative effort on a lot of people's parts. We certainly can help do it, because we can fund grant projects that do exactly what you're saying. Make that the priority for the programs.

Audience Question

The flipside of that is that as a school, we are just as invested in the success of the college of education students as they are in our students. It's a true partnership that way, and we've got to do that if we're going to continue the profession to the point that, when we're old and in nursing homes, we can still be proud to say we were teachers.

Ted Sanders

We're nearing the end of this session, so I'd like to give each of the panel members one last opportunity to tell us exactly what it was that they wanted us to learn from them.

Susan Tave Zelman

We must have a policy of coherence so that when we have NCLB and raise the question of what we want our students to know and be able to do, we must also then answer the question of what we want our educators to know and be able to do. I don't think that NCLB alone will get us where we want to be, in terms of closing that achievement gap. We have to work collaboratively as one system to rethink schools for the twenty-first century and to develop new models to close that gap.

Guilbert Hentschke

I think there's a dilemma in my mind, which is, while you are all really good at teaching, you also really know what good teaching would mean in others. As we encourage you to work on that second agenda, I hope it doesn't take you away from the first agenda.

Ben Wildavsky

Not to end on a downbeat note, but I brought with me a recent clipping. The headline is, "Make teacher education a priority, college presidents are told." College presidents should either make teacher education a top priority for their institutions or get out of the business of training teachers.

Sally Stroup

The best thing you can do is get involved with what's going on. I think the connection between the campus, the local school district, and the faculties is the most important thing we can do if we're going to get people to work together.

PANEL CONTRIBUTIONS

CHAPTER 17

CLOSING ACHIEVEMENT GAPS

Ron Haskins and Cecilia Rouse

About the Authors: Ron Haskins is a senior fellow in the Economic Studies program and codirector of the Welfare Reform & Beyond initiative at the Brookings Institution. Cecilia Rouse is a professor of economics and public affairs and the director of the Princeton University Education Research Center. Both are senior editors of The Future of Children.

To read the full report on school readiness, go to www.futureofchildren.org.

By the time Black and Hispanic children reach kindergarten, they are already far behind their more advantaged peers in reading and math readiness. These gaps persist or increase during the school years. Programs for parents and preschool education programs have the potential to close the gap by at least half.

Test score disparities among racial and ethnic groups are a prominent feature of today's educational landscape, with Black and Hispanic children regularly falling far behind White children. Although the achieve-

The Challenges of School Reform: Implementation, Impact, and Sustainability, 253–261
Copyright © 2006 by Information Age Publishing
All rights of reproduction in any form reserved.

From *The Future of Children*, a publication of The Woodrow Wilson School of Public and International Affairs at Princeton University and The Brookings Institution.

ment gaps narrowed somewhat during the 1970s and 1980s, they have proved stubbornly resistant to closing further. If the nation is to achieve the goal of equal education as a "fact and a result," to borrow President Lyndon Johnson's words, we must commit ourselves to overcoming the substantial racial and ethnic differences in educational achievement that remain.

Although the achievement gap is normally seen as a problem affecting school-age children, in fact the gap first opens during the preschool years. The Early Childhood Education Longitudinal Study, Kindergarten Cohort (ECLS-K), a nationally representative sample of nearly 23,000 kindergartners, shows that Black and Hispanic children score substantially (more than half a standard deviation, or the equivalent of 8 points on an IQ test with a standard deviation of 15) below White children at the beginning of kindergarten on math and reading achievement. The Family and Child Experiences Survey (FACES), a test administered to children entering Head Start, shows that the program's children, disproportionately minorities from low-income families, already fall well short (up to a standard deviation, or 15 points on an IQ test) in vocabulary, early reading, letter recognition, and early math by ages three and four. Finally, Christopher Jencks of Harvard and Meredith Phillips of UCLA, using nationally representative data from the National Longitudinal Survey of Youth–Child Data, found that about 85% of Black three- and four-year-olds scored lower on a vocabulary test than did the average White child of the same age.

PRESCHOOL GAPS SIGNAL POOR OUTCOMES LATER IN LIFE

These studies consistently show that poor and minority children have already fallen behind well before they enter the public schools. Such disparities are a serious breach in the nation's commitment to equality of opportunity because children who score poorly on tests of intellectual skills during the preschool years do less well in elementary and high school and are more likely to become teen parents, engage in criminal activities, suffer from unemployment, and become clinically depressed as adults.

The latest issue of *The Future of Children*, a scholarly journal devoted to research on programs and policies related to child well-being, examines the preschool origins of these racial and ethnic achievement gaps. Edited by Cecilia Rouse, Jeanne Brooks-Gunn, and Sara McLanahan, the issue features comprehensive reviews of research on how differences in children's socioeconomic background, parenting, brain development, and health contribute to racial and ethnic disparities in school readiness and also considers strategies for closing the gap. Three strategies hold special promise.

In the long run, research on brain development may prove to be important. Researchers are now making great strides in understanding how the brain develops and what aspects of experience help or hinder development. Educational interventions are already able both to raise children's scores on tests of reading and to increase activity in the brain regions most closely linked with reading. The areas of the brain that are most critical for school readiness may thus prove responsive to therapeutic interventions. Because the field of neuroscience is still in its infancy, however, we think it wise to temper grandiose predictions until large-scale studies confirm the success of brain-related interventions in boosting school readiness.

The two remaining strategies emerge from the consistent finding that poor and minority children as young as three years already perform far below average on tests of school readiness. Unless one believes that this poor performance is due entirely or primarily to genetic factors, it follows that the preschool environments of poor and minority children are deficient in supplying the types of experiences that promote school readiness. And as a careful examination of evidence on behavioral genetics in the journal's current issue, by William Dickens of the Brookings Institution, concludes, "the evidence argues against a significant genetic role in explaining the gap." Thus, the search for ways to alter children's preschool environment to improve school readiness is well justified.

TEACHING BOTH PARENTS AND CHILDREN

Two types of programs seem most promising--those that help parents learn the behaviors that promote child development and school readiness and those that directly teach poor and low-income children school readiness skills, both intellectual and behavioral.

Another article in the issue, by Jeanne Brooks-Gunn of Columbia and Lisa Markman of Princeton, reviews extensive research showing that Black and Hispanic mothers engage less often in important parenting behaviors than do White mothers and that these parenting differences parallel racial and ethnic difference in school readiness. Brooks-Gunn and Markman attribute as much as half the gap in school readiness to differences in parenting. Most strikingly, Black and Hispanic parents have been found to be less likely to talk responsively and to read to their infants and young children, and to have fewer books and other educational materials in their homes—important dimensions of parenting that contribute to child development.

A LONG HISTORY

Interventions to help parents alter their behavior to improve children's development and school readiness have a long history. Many have failed to affect materially either parenting behavior or children's development. But some large-scale and well-designed studies have both changed parental behavior and, through the reshaped behavior, improved children's achievement. A family literacy program designed by Grover Whitehurst, now the federal commissioner of education, taught parents to read with their children, ask probing questions, and initiate discussions that went beyond the reading material itself. Parents receiving the training changed their reading practices, and their children had higher language scores than children in a control group whose parents had no such training. The Infant Health and Development program, an eight-site randomized experiment involving nearly 1,000 families with low birth weight babies, provided parents in the treatment group with both center-based care and home visits from birth through age three. At the end of the study Black children and their mothers showed more learning and less punitive discipline than comparable children in a control group. Similarly, the seventeen-site national evaluation of the Early Head Start Demonstration, another randomized study, found that Black mothers in a home-based and center-based intervention program were more likely than Black mothers in the control group to read to their children, were more emotionally supportive, provided more support for language and learning, and were less likely to spank their children.

Preschool programs, with or without associated parent programs, have also directly improved children's development and school readiness. The Perry Preschool program in Ypsilanti, Michigan, and the Abecedarian program in Chapel Hill, North Carolina, have been arguably the nation's best model programs. Perry included a home visiting program during the preschool years; Abecedarian did not. Both produced long-lasting gains in school performance and a host of other outcomes. Although both featured random assignment, multiple measures of outcomes, and long-term designs (meaning that the children were followed for many years), all marks of high-quality evaluations, most observers agree that their small size calls into question whether large-scale programs could attain similar success.

This problem is overcome to some degree by the Chicago Child-Parent Centers, a long-term study of more than 550 children in the Chicago school system. The children participated in up to six years of intervention, from preschool through grade 3. Participants scored higher in reading achievement through seventh grade and had lower rates of grade retention and special education placement than comparable children who had not received the intervention. The Chicago study is notable because of its large-scale, long-term follow-up and because it was implemented in regular public school classrooms. It was not based on random assignment, raising some concern about the validity of its findings. Even so, this study suggests that big gains are possible in large-scale programs implemented in regular classrooms by teachers with a minimum of special training.

Preschool's Growing Enrollment

The finding that preschool programs can boost development and school readiness has prompted a steady increase both in the number of such programs and in enrollment. In addition to Head Start, which now enrolls almost a million three- and four-year-olds predominantly from poor families, more than 40 states have initiated their own preschool programs. At the same time, steadily increasing pressure from the federal government to move poor mothers off welfare and into jobs and the resulting increase in employment by low-income and never-married single mothers has driven up funding and demand for child care. Child care facilities, however, vary widely in quality. The best reach the moderately high quality of Head Start and the state preschool programs, but many and perhaps most are worse and are, like the home environments of many poor and minority children, inadequate in promoting development and school readiness.

Despite the unevenness of quality, a recent study by Katherine Magnuson of the University of Wisconsin at Madison and her colleagues seems to demonstrate that, taken as a whole for the nation, center-based programs are helping prepare children for school. Using data from the Early Childhood Longitudinal Study and controlling for differences in family background and other factors, Magnuson found that children who had attended a center- or school-based preschool program the year before entering kindergarten scored higher on tests of reading and math skills at kindergarten entry than children who had not attended such programs. The differences remained at the end of kindergarten and first grade. In addition, children who attended a center-based program were less likely to be retained in kindergarten.

Both parenting and preschool programs, then, can contribute to closing the achievement gap. The nation has been gradually moving toward universal enrollment of all low-income and minority children in at least one year of preschool. Although there is widespread agreement that high-quality programs that emphasize school readiness and parent involvement can reduce the achievement gap, expanding most existing programs is by no means certain to close the gap appreciably because their average quality is not high enough to produce lasting gains. Even after completing the Head Start program, for example, the FACES study shows that the average poor child still falls short in reading and math. If Head

Start and other preschool programs could be improved to achieve the quality of the Perry or Abecedarian programs, they could reduce the gap by as much as half. If the quality of the programs were as high as the Chicago Parent-Child Centers, a program that demonstrates that high-quality programs can be implemented on a much broader scale than Perry or Abecedarian, they would also substantially narrow the gap. If the programs were no better than Head Start or the current state preschool programs, however, the impact on the gap would be modest.

INCREASING ENROLLMENT AND QUALITY

In our view, there are two keys to using preschool programs to reduce the achievement gap. The first is to enroll all children from low-income families, which are disproportionately minorities, in a preschool program; the second is to provide high-quality programs, including well-qualified teachers and systematic school readiness activities that develop appropriate reading, math, and social-emotional skills. An article in the current issue of *The Future of Children* by Magnuson and Waldfogel estimates the effects of various combinations of increased enrollment and increased preschool quality on the gap in school readiness for Black and Hispanic children. They estimate that if all low-income children (those with family income below 200% of poverty) were enrolled in high-quality programs, the Black-White gap could narrow by as much as one-quarter; the Hispanic-White gap, by as much as 36%. The effect would be greater for Hispanic children primarily because fewer Hispanic than Black children are now enrolled in center-based programs.

We estimate that a quality preschool program costs around $8,000 per child. We also estimate, based on numbers from the Census Bureau and from the Magnuson and Waldfogel article, that a little more than 800,000 low-income four-year-olds are not now in a center-based program. Thus, it would cost around $6.5 billion a year to provide a high-quality program for all low-income four-year-olds not now in a center-based program. Placing all low-income four-year-olds in a high-quality program would add to the overall cost because many of those now in preschool programs are in lower-quality programs costing less than $8,000 a year. Improving these programs would require additional money.

STEPS TOWARD PROGRESS

Given the federal government's large budget deficit, such funding is unlikely to be forthcoming soon. But it does not follow that no action is possible. We recommend that the federal government sponsor state-wide demonstration programs in several states that agree to enroll all or nearly all low-income four-year-olds or three- and four-year olds in high quality programs. In order to participate, states would have to agree to meet a series of conditions. These include:

- involving the parents to the maximum degree possible,
- coordinating the preschool program with the kindergarten program in the public schools,
- maintaining standards at least as strong as Head Start standards,
- providing professional development to all teachers in the program,
- outlining a plan for coordinating all state and federal resources for providing quality preschool programs, including Head Start, Title I, the Child Care and Development Block grant (at state option), and state spending on preschool programs;
- maintaining at least current state spending on preschool programs;
- participating in a third-party evaluation of program impacts.

Clearly such an expansion and improvement of preschool is expensive. However, a large portion of the money to pay for such high-quality programs could come from the approximately $25 billion that the states and the federal government currently spend on child care and preschool programs. Under current policies, preschool children are in programs that are paid for by separate funding streams and are operated under separate authorities. Some children are in Head Start, some in a state-sponsored preschool program, some in programs paid for by Title I (Elementary and Secondary Education Act), and some children are in facilities paid for by federal or state child care funds, especially funds from the Child Care and Development Block Grant. A first step in building toward expanded and higher quality programs for all low-income four-year-olds would be to use all these funds to create a single coordinated program. The major goal of the state demonstration programs would be to determine whether it is possible to create and implement a state-wide program that effectively increases access and improves quality while efficiently coordinating all sources of funding. Answering the numerous questions encompassed by this goal will require well designed third-party evaluations. There is simply no way to know whether programs work unless they are subjected to carefully designed evaluations that follow children over a period of years after they leave the program. Only quality evaluations will prevent excessive claims about program effects and administrative efficiency and allow policymakers to make wise decisions about future directions.

Congress should provide the secretary with modest additional funding for five years to help participating states implement the demonstrations.

The secretary must also have the authority and the funding to hire third-party evaluators to test the effectiveness of the state programs. In addition, Congress should urge the secretary to negotiate with at least one state to provide two years of preschool to a substantial group of children and to evaluate that program as well. The research literature does not permit the confident conclusion that one year of preschool will sufficiently boost school readiness. A comparison of one-year with two-year programs would therefore be wise.

In participating states, the secretary should also have the authority to provide funding for all Head Start programs directly to state officials. Any state that wants to exercise this option, however, must show that it has negotiated with state Head Start officials. The most important argument against our proposal is that it might damage Head Start without putting a better program in place. For this reason we recommend giving only a few states power over Head Start spending. Before more states can be given the opportunity to coordinate all funds for preschool in their state, it must be demonstrated that coordinated funding improves preschools and boosts the school readiness of children from low-income families. As the FACES data show quite clearly, the current Head Start program is not fully preparing poor and minority children for the rigors of schooling.

MAKING A VISION A REALITY

Justice Sandra Day O'Connor has recently predicted, referring to university-based affirmative action programs, that "25 years from now, the use of racial preferences will no longer be necessary." Although Justice O'Connor did not reveal the evidence or reasoning behind her claim, the implication is that the nation will have achieved equality of educational opportunity within a quarter-century and that affirmative action will no longer be necessary. But such optimism defies the evidence on the pre-school and school-age gaps in achievement. We now know, more than four decades into the nation's vigorous pursuit of President Johnson's goal of equal education as "a fact and as a result," that there is nothing inevitable about achieving that goal. If the United States is truly committed to equal opportunity, its leaders must find ways to coordinate all preschool funding streams, raise the average quality of preschool programs by training effective teachers, create curriculum activities for reading, math, and social-emotional development, and achieve greater coordination between the preschools and schools. Expanding enrollment in and raising the quality of its preschool programs will give the nation the best chance to make Justice O'Connor's—and President Johnson's—vision a reality.

ADDITIONAL READING

Brooks-Gunn, Jeanne, and Lisa Markman. "The Contribution of Parenting to Ethnic and Racial Gaps in School Readiness," *Future of Children* 15, No. 1 (2005): 139-168.

Brooks-Gunn, Jeanne, Pamela Klebanov, and Fong-Ruey Liaw, "The Learning, Physical, and Emotional Environment of the Home in the Context of Poverty: The Infant Health and Development Program," *Children and Youth Services Review* 17, no. 1/2 (1995), 251.

Campbell, Frances A., and others, "Early-Childhood Programs and Success in School: The Abecedarian Study," in *Early Care and Education for Children in Poverty*, edited by W. Steven Barnett and Sarane Spence Boocock (State University of New York, 1998), pp. 145-66.

Campbell, Frances A., and others, "Early Childhood Education: Young Adult Outcomes from the Abecedarian Project," *Applied Developmental Science* 6, no. 1 (2002): 42-57.

Coleman, James, and others, *Equality of Educational Opportunity* (U.S. Government Printing Office, 1966).

Jencks, Christopher, and Meredith Phillips, eds., *The Black-White Test Score Gap* (Brookings, 1998).

Lee, Valerie E., and David T. Burkham, *Inequality at the Starting Gate: Social Background Differences in Achievement as Children Begin Kindergarten* (Washington: Economic Policy Institute, 2002), p. 14.

Magnuson, Katherine A., and Jane Waldfogel, "Early Childhood Care and Education: Effects on Ethnic and Racial Gaps in School Readiness," *Future of Children* 15, no. 1 (2005): 169-196.

Magnuson, Katherine A., and others, "Inequality in Preschool Education and School Readiness," *American Educational Research Journal* 41, no. 1 (2004): 115-57.

Mathematica Policy Research, Inc., "Making a Difference in the Lives of Infants and Toddlers and Their Families: The Impacts of Early Head Start (Executive Summary)" (Washington: U.S. Department of Health and Human Services, 2002).

Reynolds, Arthur J., and Judy A. Temple, "Extended Early Childhood Intervention and School Achievement: Age Thirteen Findings from the Chicago Longitudinal Study, *Child Development* 69, no. 1 (1998): 231-46.

Schweinhart, Lawrence J., and David P. Weikart, *Young Children Grow Up: The Effects of Perry Preschool Program on Youths Through Age 15* (Ypsilanti, Mich.: High/Scope, 1980).

Whitehurst, G.J., and others, "Outcomes of an Emergent Literacy Intervention in Head Start," *Journal of Educational Psychology* 86, no. 4 (1994): 542-55.

CHAPTER 18

OHIO'S APPROACH
TO HIGH QUALITY TEACHING

Susan Tave Zelman

The vision we have for Ohio's educational system is higher achievement for all students, no matter where they live or what their backgrounds might be. Through an educational system that is based on clear, challenging standards with aligned instruction and assessment, we can level the playing field for all students. This means clear and challenging standards for what our children should know and be able to do from preschool through high school and into postsecondary education.

To accomplish this vision, we must have effective teachers in our classrooms. We know that the quality of the teacher in the classroom is the single most important influence on whether our students learn and succeed in school. That's why our vision for Ohio's teachers is that the state, school districts, colleges and universities, and our local communities do everything possible to give educators the support and resources they need to provide the best instruction for every student.

The Challenges of School Reform: Implementation, Impact, and Sustainability, 263–266
Copyright © 2006 by Information Age Publishing
All rights of reproduction in any form reserved.

This article originally appeared in *Quality Teaching*, Volume 14, Issue 1, Fall 2005, published by the National Council for Accreditation of Teacher Education. Visit www.ncate.org.

We have articulated what our students should know and be able to do—and now we are in the process of developing standards for what our educators should know and be able to do. We need clear and challenging standards for educators and these standards must drive a seamless human resource system—from recruitment to initial preparation, through induction and ongoing professional development.

To accomplish this goal, Ohio created an Educator Standards Board and charged it with developing standards for what teachers and principals should know and be able to do, and standards for ongoing professional development. The new teacher standards, in draft form, are aligned with the state academic content standards and include knowledge and skills needed by beginning teachers, experienced teachers and distinguished teachers.

The educator standards are designed to serve as a framework for both teacher preparation programs and continuing professional development. They also will serve as a framework for schools' teacher evaluation systems.

ACCOUNTABILITY FOR TEACHER PREPARATION AND LICENSURE

An important part of developing a quality teaching force is ensuring that teacher education programs prepare teachers who have the knowledge and skills needed to successfully educate all students. Ohio institutions that prepare teachers must demonstrate the alignment of their teacher education programs with Ohio's academic content standards for students, and must meet performance benchmarks.

The first benchmark is an institutional summary pass rate of 80% or greater on the Praxis II examinations. Of the more than 30 states that use Praxis II, a series of tests designed to measure pedagogical and content-area knowledge, Ohio's required scores for passing these tests are among the highest in the nation, ranking in the top three in the pedagogical knowledge tests, and close to the top in the content-area tests.

Ohio's second benchmark, Praxis III, is an in-classroom performance assessment completed during the first year of teaching. Ohio was the first state in the nation to use this assessment, which involves direct observation of classroom practice, a review and analysis of written documentation prepared by the teacher, and semi-structured interviews before and after the observation.

The third benchmark is approval of the teacher education program based on national accreditation standards. Today, there are 22 NCATE accredited institutions of higher education and 10 NCATE candidates or pre-candidates, for a total of 32 out of 50 teacher education institutions in

Ohio. Ohio educators and policymakers are active in NCATE's performance-based system. NCATE's Board of Examiners (on-site team members who evaluate colleges of education according to NCATE standards) includes 27 members from Ohio, as well as 36 program reviewers (specialists in content/developmental areas who review specific programs within colleges of education for NCATE accreditation). These individuals from Ohio review colleges in other states, an NCATE requirement to avoid any potential conflict of interest. In addition to meeting the NCATE standards, Ohio's colleges and universities are required to meet the national professional association standards in each licensure area.

The Ohio Department of Education monitors data on the performance of Ohio institutions in meeting accreditation standards. Recently, we found that of the six NCATE standards, significant improvements could be made in the area of Standard Two, Assessment System and Unit Evaluation. The Department responded to this data by sponsoring a statewide assessment conference for institutions of higher education, focusing on development of assessment systems. The conference included nationally-known experts in assessment, data analysis workshops, and information on evidence-centered design and value-added assessment. Small planning grants were made available to institutions to develop and implement their assessment systems for teacher education.

A second conference on assessment will be held soon, with a focus on continued development of assessment systems and use of data in evaluating programs. In providing such resources, Ohio continues to strive to achieve its goal of implementing a data-driven system of teacher preparation and continuous support to ensure that all students have qualified teachers.

TEACHER INDUCTION

Another critical element in ensuring a quality teaching force is providing support, assistance and continued training during the beginning teacher's entry into the profession. To support its beginning teachers, Ohio has implemented Entry Year Programs designed to provide direct assistance to Ohio's beginning teachers via mentors, who offer the support necessary to help new teachers meet the challenges of the classroom. While pilot Entry Year Programs have operated with state support since 1994, mandated statewide implementation of the Entry Year Program as an integral component of teacher licensure began in 2002. Ohio provides funding for one year of support for new teachers, and several of our largest school districts fund a two-year induction program for new teachers. These programs include both a formal program of support for beginning teachers and assessment of their performance. To qualify for a professional license, all beginning teachers must successfully complete the Entry Year Program and pass the performance assessment.

Once the Entry Year Program is completed and teachers have moved to Professional Licensure, each teacher must complete an Individual Professional Development Plan aligned with the needs of their students and school, and must complete a master's degree within ten years. Many teacher education institutions have developed master's degree programs specifically for teachers who want to stay in the classroom, with a focus on helping them continue to refine and develop their teaching skills.

By the 2007–2008 school year, Ohio's accountability system for schools will include a value-added component. Once such data is available, it will be possible to identify teachers who excel in increasing student achievement—and to study how those teachers were prepared. With this in mind, Ohio has launched the Teacher Quality Partnership, a research collaborative involving the Ohio Department of Education, all 50 teacher education institutions, and the Ohio Board of Regents. Encompassed within the research design are studies of how teachers were prepared and how they fare during their first years in the classroom.

Given the significant impact that teachers have on student achievement, it is imperative that we continue our efforts to constantly improve teacher performance. NCATE plays a critical role in strengthening teacher education programs and in increasing the quality of teachers in our nation's schools.

CONFERENCE PRESENTERS

Lowell Milken

Widely known as an educational pioneer and reformer, Lowell Milken is chairman of the Milken Family Foundation (MFF), which he cofounded in 1982. Under his leadership, MFF has become one of the most innovative private foundations in the United States, creating national programs in K-12 education and medical research. Among his contributions to strengthening K-12 education, Mr. Milken conceived the Milken National Educator Awards in 1985 to recognize the importance of outstanding educators and to encourage talented young people to choose teaching as a career. With a network of nearly 2,000 recipients, the Milken Educator Awards is today the nation's largest teacher recognition program, active in 47 states plus the District of Columbia. Recognizing that sufficient numbers of quality teachers would never result from current education practices, Mr. Milken launched the Teacher Advancement Program (TAP) in 1999 to restructure and thus revitalize the teaching profession. TAP's comprehensive and systemic approach makes the teaching profession more appealing, the job conditions more manageable, and the pay for high quality teachers more generous. TAP schools are currently in nine states, with additional districts and states preparing to implement TAP. Mr. Milken has been recognized for his achievements in education with awards from such organizations as the National Association of State Boards of Education, the Horace Mann League, and the National Association of Secondary School Principals. Named by *Worth* magazine as one of America's most generous philanthropists, Mr. Milken is also an involved businessman who is chairman of London-based Heron International, a worldwide leader in property development, and co-founder of Knowledge Universe, a company focused on meeting the lifelong learning requirements of both individuals and businesses. Lowell Milken is a product of California's public school system, graduating *summa cum laude* and Phi Beta Kappa from the University of California at Berkeley in 1970, where he received the School of Business Administration's Most Outstanding Student Award. He earned his law degree from the University of California, Los Angeles, with the distinctions of Order of the Coif and *UCLA Law Review*. He and his wife of 31 years, Sandy, have four sons.

Kimberly Firetag Agam

As a senior research associate for policy analysis, Ms. Agam's work at the Foundation focuses on local, state, and federal educational policy, specifically emphasizing teacher quality. She helps to secure funding for the teacher advancement program and assists states and the United States Congress in analyzing legislation. Recently, she tracked and analyzed the reauthorization of the Elementary and Secondary Education Act (ESEA) in Congress to determine its policy implications and how funding in the bill can be used to support the Teacher Advancement Program (TAP). In addition Ms. Agam oversees the data collection on and analysis of TAP teacher attitudes and satisfaction. Ms. Agam has authored and edited articles on educational issues including the recently released *Improving Student Achievement: Reforms that Work*. Ms. Agam earned a bachelor's degree in public policy studies from Duke University, as well as a master's degree in public policy from the University of Southern California.

Anthony Amato

As superintendent of New Orleans Public Schools, Anthony Amato oversees approximately 70,000 students, 135 schools and centers, and 10,000 employees. He introduced a new concept in "themed-learning" known as Signature Schools, as well as new district-wide reading programs through the institution of Success For All and Direct Instruction. Most notably, Mr. Amato has heralded the cause of parental involvement through the institution of mandatory citywide parent meetings where he insists on talking to and fielding questions from concerned parents and the community. After his first year in this position, Mr. Amato earned an "A for effort" from popular local media. Prior to joining New Orleans Public Schools, he served as superintendent of Hartford Public Schools. Mr. Amato began his career as a middle/high school math and science teacher. He earned a bachelor's degree in science and education, and a master's degree in bilingual education, administration and supervision from City College of New York. He is presently pursuing a doctorate at Columbia University Teacher's College.

Antonia Cortese

Antonia Cortese is executive vice president of the American Federation of Teachers (AFT). She has served as an officer of the New York State United Teachers (NYSUT), which represents more than 500,000 people in New York's public schools, colleges, universities, and health facilities. Ms. Cortese began her education career as a fourth-grade teacher and school social worker. Among her many professional activities, she served as an appointee of the U.S. Department of Education to the National Assessment Governing Board. She is an AFT representative to the Learning First Alliance, and has served on the New York State Education Department's Task Force on Closing the Performance Gap. She also served on the Governor's Task Force on School Violence. In 1990, Ms. Cortese was honored by Utica College as an alumna of achievement in her field. She was NYSUT's chairperson for "Making Strides Against Breast Cancer" and was cochair of the United Way of Northwestern New York's 2004 campaign. Ms. Cortese earned her bachelor's degree in psychology from Utica College of Syracuse University.

Libby Doggett

As executive director of Pre-K Now, Libby Doggett, Ph.D., directs the organization's efforts to educate state policymakers, the media and the general public about the potential that preschool offers to improve outcomes for young children. Prior to joining Pre-K Now, Dr. Doggett worked for the National Head Start Association, where she directed the HeadsUp! Reading program. She also worked in the U.S. Department of Education, where she served as special assistant to the director of special education (OSEP) and as executive director of the Federal Interagency Coordinating Council. Dr. Doggett co-authored the first book written on childcare and the Americans with Disabilities Act. She has received an appointment to the Texas Commission on Children and Youth, the Governor's Trophy from the Governor's Committee on the Employment of Persons with Disabilities in Texas, and the Friend of Early Childhood Intervention award. She holds a Ph.D. from the University of Texas in Early Childhood Special Education and is an adjunct faculty member at the Georgetown Center for Child and Human Development in the Department of Pediatrics.

David Driscoll

As the 22nd commissioner of education for the Commonwealth of Massachusetts, David P. Driscoll, D. Ed., has overseen the implementation of the Massachusetts Comprehensive Assessment System (MCAS), the school and district accountability system, the educator certification test, special education reform, and the historic high school graduation requirement instituted in 2003. Already at the forefront of education reform nationally under Dr. Driscoll's leadership, Massachusetts was named one of the first five states in the country to have its No Child Left Behind accountability plan approved by the federal government. Dr. Driscoll's career in public education and educational leadership spans 40 years. A former mathematics teacher, he served as assistant superintendent and then superintendent of schools in Melrose before being appointed deputy commissioner of education in Massachusetts under Robert V. Antonucci. Currently, Dr. Driscoll is the 2004-05 president-elect of the Council of Chief State School Officers (CCSSO). He earned his bachelor's degree in mathematics at Boston College, his master's degree in educational administration from Salem State College, and his doctorate in education administration from Boston College.

Chaka Fattah

An experienced lawmaker serving his sixth term in the U.S. House of Representatives, Chaka Fattah represents the Second Congressional District of Pennsylvania. He created the nationally funded GEAR UP (Gaining Early Awareness and Readiness for Undergraduate Programs); the CORE Philly Scholarship, a one-time scholarship grant designed to double the number of high school graduates as well as the number of children attending college; and the College Retention Program, which has provided more than a million students with financial assistance. Mr. Fattah was also an original cosponsor of the Help America Vote Act of 2002. *Time Magazine* named him one of the country's 50 most promising leaders. A lifelong resident of Philadelphia, Congressman Fattah attended city public schools, the Community College of Philadelphia, the University of Pennsylvania's Wharton School and the University of Pennsylvania's Fels School of State and Local Government where he earned a master's degree in government administration.

Stephen Goldsmith

Stephen Goldsmith is the Daniel Paul Professor of Government and the director of the Innovations in American Government Program at Harvard's Kennedy School of Government. He is also the chair of the Corporation for National and Community Service and of the Manhattan Institute's Center for Civic Innovation. Mr. Goldsmith previously served two terms as mayor of Indianapolis, America's 12th largest city. As mayor, he reduced government spending, cut the city's bureaucracy, held the line on taxes, eliminated counterproductive regulations, and identified more than $400 million in savings. He reinvested the savings by leading a transformation of downtown Indianapolis that has been held up as a national model. Mr. Goldsmith was the chief domestic policy advisor to the George W. Bush campaign in 2000 and was district attorney for Marion County, Indiana, from 1979 to 1990.

Ron Haskins

As a senior fellow in the Economic Studies Program at the Brookings Institution and a senior consultant at the Annie E. Casey Foundation in Baltimore, Ron Haskins' areas of expertise include welfare reform, childcare, child support enforcement, and child protection. Prior to joining Brookings and Casey, Dr. Haskins spent 14 years on the staff of the House Ways and Means Human Resources Subcommittee. In 1997, the *National Journal* selected him as one of the 100 most influential people in the federal government. Dr. Haskins has coedited several books, including *Policies for America's Public Schools: Teachers, Equity, and Indicators*, and has written articles and editorials that have appeared in several newspapers and periodicals including the *Washington Post*, *The New York Times*, *Policy Review*, *State Government News* and the *Weekly Standard*. Dr. Haskins holds a bachelor's degree in history, a master's degree in education, and a Ph.D. in developmental psychology from the University of North Carolina, Chapel Hill.

Guilbert C. Hentschke

Guilbert C. Hentschke is the Richard T. Cooper and Mary Catherine Cooper Chair in Public School Administration at the University of Southern California's Rossier School of Education, where he served as dean from 1998 to 2000. He directs programs in the business of education, including the Galaxy Institute for Education and the school business management program. An author of numerous books and articles on education reform, charter schools and the business of education, Dr. Hentschke's most recent publication, co-authored with Terrence Deal, is *Adventures of Charter School Creators: Leading from the Ground Up*. Dr. Hentschke serves on the boards of directors of several education-oriented organizations, including the Aspen Education Group, Century/LIFT, the National Center on Education and the Economy, WestEd Regional Educational Laboratory and several Los Angeles charter schools. He earned his bachelor's degree in history and economics at Princeton University and his masters and doctorate in education and business at Stanford University.

T. Kenneth James

Ken James, Ed.D., was appointed as director of education for the State of Arkansas by Governor Mike Huckabee last year. Prior to this appointment, as superintendent of Fayette County Public Schools, he oversaw programs and education policy implementation in 53 schools serving nearly 33,000 students. Starting his career as a classroom teacher, Dr. James also served as assistant principal, principal, assistant superintendent, and ultimately superintendent of schools in both Little Rock and Van Buren, Arkansas. In 1998, Dr. James was named as the Superintendent of the Year for the State of Arkansas. He presently serves on the University of Arkansas Educational Administration Steering Committee, the State Advisory Board on Reforming Education, and the American Association of School Administrators (AASA) Board of Directors. Dr. James earned a bachelor's degree from Arkansas State University, a master's degree in educational administration from Northern Arizona University and a doctorate in educational administration and supervision from Northern Arizona University and the United States International University in San Diego.

Sharon Lynn Kagan

Sharon Lynn Kagan, Ed.D., is the Virginia and Leonard Marx Professor of Early Childhood and Family Policy, codirector of the National Center for Children and Families, associate dean for policy at Teachers College, Columbia University, and professor adjunct at Yale University's Child Study Center. Author of more than 150 articles and 12 books, Dr. Kagan's research focuses on the institutions and policies that impact child and family life. She consults with numerous international, federal, and state agencies, congress, governors, and legislatures. She is a distinguished senior fellow with the Education Commission of the States, a member of 40 national boards, and past president of the National Association for the Education of Young Children and Family Support America. She has received numerous awards, among them an honorary doctoral degree from Wheelock College, a Distinguished Alumna award from Teachers College, Columbia University, and the 2004 Distinguished Service in American Education Award from the Council of Chief State School Officers (CCSSO).

Mary L. Landrieu

Mary L. Landrieu has been referred to as "one of the Senate's foremost leaders on education" by colleagues, and has become a national voice on the importance of strengthening families through foster care and adoption. She worked across party lines in 2001 to craft the No Child Left Behind Act, and has worked to bring Louisiana the dollars needed to effectively improve its schools. In 2001, Ms. Landrieu led a successful effort to ensure that federal Title I dollars make it to the schools and children that most need help—those schools with high concentrations of poor children. As the Senate Democratic cochair of the Congressional Coalition on Adoption, she believes Congress has the power to assist state and local efforts to improve foster care and promote adoption. Ms. Landrieu's pro-growth, pro-business voting record has earned her the U.S. Chambers of Commerce's Spirit of Enterprise Award, and in 2002, the National Federation of Independent Businesses awarded her the "Guardian of the Small Business Award."

Jennifer Marshall

As director of domestic policy studies at The Heritage Foundation, Jennifer A. Marshall oversees the foundation's research in education, welfare, marriage and the family, and religion and civil society. She has co-authored several publications, including *New Research Brings Good News About Charter Schools* and *Marriage: What Social Science Says and Doesn't Say*. Prior to joining Heritage in 2003, Ms. Marshall worked on cultural policy issues at Empower America. She also served as senior director of family studies at the Family Research Council and taught at the American School of Lyon in France. Ms. Marshall earned a bachelor's degree in French from Wheaton College in 1994, and studied abroad at the Sorbonne in Paris, where she earned her teacher's certification. She lives in Arlington, Virginia.

Tim Pawlenty

Tim Pawlenty was elected Governor of Minnesota in 2002, with the state facing an historic $4.5 billion budget deficit. Just months later, the legislature adopted Governor Pawlenty's plan to eliminate the deficit without raising taxes or cutting funding for K-12 classrooms. In addition to balancing the budget, Mr. Pawlenty fought for and passed a dramatic overhaul of the state's education standards, significant welfare reform, lawsuit reform and a range of new government efficiency initiatives, and passed the largest transportation package in modern history. Mr. Pawlenty has also outlined an aggressive agenda, including a nation-leading effort to make affordable prescription medicine available to citizens. His prior public service career includes being a prosecutor and Eagan City Council member. Pawlenty served 10 years in the Minnesota House of Representatives, including four as House majority leader.

Thomas Payzant

Thomas W. Payzant began serving as superintendent of the Boston Public Schools in 1995. Since then, he has established a blueprint for educational reform in Boston in Focus On Children, a comprehensive plan approved by the Boston School Committee in July 1996. Working closely with leaders of the Boston business community, Dr. Payzant has raised over $30 million to support professional development in every Boston school. As a result, Boston students and schools have demonstrated a consistent pattern of continuous improvement in literacy and mathematics in virtually every grade on a variety of rigorous assessments. Dr. Payzant came to Boston after serving as assistant secretary for elementary and secondary education with the United States Department of Education, and as superintendent in four other communities. Dr. Payzant received his bachelor's degree from Williams College, his master's degree in teaching and his doctorate in education from Harvard. Among numerous other honorary doctorates and awards, Dr. Payzant recently received the Richard R. Green Award for Excellence in Urban Education given by the Council of Great City Schools in 2004.

Cecil J. Picard

As Louisiana State Superintendent of Education, Cecil J. Picard has worked closely with the governor and the legislature to develop and implement a nationally recognized accountability system that enables the state to identify weaknesses in student and school performance and target resources where they are most needed to improve student learning. *Education Week*'s 2005 Quality Counts report ranked Louisiana's accountability system as second in the nation. In 2002, Superintendent Picard's vision of a statewide early childhood education program came to fruition when the LA 4 program was piloted in 11 school districts to serve at-risk four-year-olds. Louisiana has also implemented the Teacher Advancement Program (TAP) in six schools in four districts with plans to expand as funding follows. Before assuming his present position, Superintendent Picard served for more than 20 years in the public schools as a teacher, coach and school principal, and for 20 years as a member of the Louisiana Legislature. Superintendent Picard's leadership has been recognized at the state and national levels.

Citadelle Priagula

As a research assistant, Ms. Priagula provides support in gathering and analyzing literature and information for a wide variety of issues in education, such as teacher quality, the achievement gap and performance-based compensation. She has also provided assistance in publishing a number of Foundation works, specifically Improving Student Achievement: Reforms that Work and Growth of the Teacher Advancement Program. Prior to working for the Foundation, Ms. Priagula assisted in researching structured English immersion curriculum for the Los Angeles Unified School District. She received her B.A. in psychology from the University of California, Los Angeles.

Nina Shokaraii Rees

As assistant deputy secretary for innovation and improvement in the Office of Innovation and Improvement (OII), Nina Rees oversees the administration of approximately 25 competitive grant programs. Working with the Office of Elementary and Secondary Education, she also coordinates implementation of the public school choice and supplemental services provisions of the president's No Child Left Behind Act. Prior to joining the U.S. Department of Education, Ms. Rees was one of four aides to Vice President Cheney, advising him on domestic policy issues, and prior to that, she served as an education adviser to the Bush campaign, helping draft the No Child Left Behind education blueprint for the Bush/Cheney transition team. From 1997 to 2001, Ms. Rees served as chief education analyst for The Heritage Foundation. A frequent media commentator on education issues, Ms. Rees has written articles for national newspapers and magazines, and has appeared on numerous national news television shows. Ms. Rees received her bachelor's degree from Virginia Polytechnic Institute and State University.

Ralph Regula

Ralph Regula has led a distinguished career in public service that spans more than four decades. One of the most senior members of the U.S. House of Representatives, he serves as the vice chairman of the Appropriations Committee and the chairman of its Subcommittee on Labor, Health and Human Services and Education. Prior to his service in the U.S. House of Representatives, Mr. Regula served in the U.S. Navy during World War II, was a teacher and principal in the public school system, a lawyer in his own private practice, a member of the Ohio Board of Education, and a member of the Ohio House and later the Ohio Senate. He earned his bachelor's degree from Mount Union College in Alliance. For his work in Congress, Mr. Regula has been honored by a number of groups, and has received honorary doctorate degrees from the Northeastern Ohio Universities College of Medicine, Mount Union College, the University of Akron, Ashland University, Malone College and Cleveland State University.

Andrew Rotherham

Andrew Rotherham is director of the 21st Century Schools Project at the Progressive Policy Institute and editor of the education blog www.edu-wonk.com. During the Clinton administration, he served at the White House as special assistant to the President for domestic policy and led the White House Domestic Policy Council's education team. Mr. Rotherham is the author of numerous articles and papers about education and is a regular commentator in print, radio and on television. He has testified before committees of the House of Representatives and the U.S. Senate and was recently appointed by Governor Mark Warner to the Virginia State Board of Education. Mr. Rotherham received his bachelor's degree from Virginia Tech and a master's degree in education from the University of Virginia, where he is currently working on a doctorate in political science. Mr. Rotherham lives in Earlysville, Virginia, with his wife Julie, a public high school English teacher.

J. Ted Sanders

Ted Sanders is the executive chairman of the Cardean Learning Group, a prominent online education company, and former president of the Education Commission of the States (ECS), an organization that gathers, analyzes and disseminates information about current and emerging issues, trends and innovations in state education policy. He has wide experience as an educator, including as classroom teacher, chief state school officer in three states, acting U.S. secretary of education and university president. He joined ECS in February 2000 from Southern Illinois University, where he was president since 1995. Dr. Sanders earned his master's degree in teaching mathematics at Washington State University, Pullman, and his Ed.D in educational administration and higher education at the University of Nevada at Reno.

Tamara W. Schiff

Tamara W. Schiff is vice president, education of the Milken Family Foundation and associate director of the Teacher Advancement Program (TAP), a key initiative of the foundation that focuses on improving teacher quality. She is responsible for the planning and administration of the Teacher Advancement Program, and works closely with state and regional TAP directors, as well as district and state education leadership to ensure appropriate implementation of the program. Dr. Schiff has authored and edited numerous monographs and articles on educational issues, including attitudinal results from the TAP program and the recently released *Improving Student Achievement: Reforms that Work*, published by Information Age Publishing. She is active in the Milken Educator Awards program through her participation in the selection process and National Notifications, and her contributions to the Milken National Education Conference. Dr. Schiff serves on the board of trustees for the Milken Community High School where she heads the Education Committee. She also serves on the board of directors for HighTechHigh–Los Angeles, a charter high school in the Los Angeles Unified School District. Prior to coming to the Foundation in 1993, Dr. Schiff received her Ph.D. in education from UCLA.

Alice Seagren

As commissioner of the Minnesota Department of Education (MDE), Alice Seagren is responsible for MDE operations and policymaking for all aspects of K-12 education, implementing the No Child Left Behind Act in Minnesota, early learning, libraries, and adult, career and technical education. Prior to her appointment, Commissioner Seagren served six terms in the Minnesota House of Representatives, during which time she was chair of the House Education Finance Committee and a member of the Education Policy, Education Finance, Ways and Means, and Transportation Policy Committees. Before being elected to the legislature, she served on the Bloomington School Board. She is currently a member of the Normandale Community College Foundation Board and Fraser Community Services, an organization providing services to the disabled. On the national level, Ms. Seagren has served as chair of the Education Committee of the National Conference of State Legislatures' (NCLS) Assembly on State Issues, reflecting her commitment to education and helping people become self-sufficient. Ms. Seagren earned a bachelor of science in marketing from Southeast Missouri State University.

Ray Simon

As assistant secretary of the Office of Elementary and Secondary Education, Ray Simon plays a pivotal role in policy and management issues affecting elementary and secondary education. He directs, coordinates, and recommends policy for programs designed to assist state and local education agencies with such tasks as improving the achievement of elementary and secondary school students. Prior to his appointment by President Bush, Simon was director of the Arkansas Department of Education and served as superintendent of the Conway School District in Arkansas. Simon has been involved in Arkansas education since 1966, when he began his career as a mathematics teacher at North Little Rock High School. He was also an adjunct professor of technology and school finance at a number of universities. Simon earned his bachelor's and master's degrees in mathematics from the University of Central Arkansas. He also holds an educational specialist degree in school administration from the University of Arkansas.

Lewis C. Solmon

Lewis C. Solmon is executive vice president, education, at the Milken Family Foundation, a member of its Board of Trustees, and director of the Teacher Advancement Program (TAP), a major initiative of the foundation focused on improving teacher quality. He has advised several governors and state superintendents in the areas of teacher quality, school technology funding, and school finance, and served on Governor Jeb Bush's education transition team in 2002. From 1991 to 1997, Dr. Solmon was founding president of the Milken Institute, which he built into a nationally recognized economics think tank. He served as dean of UCLA's Graduate School of Education from 1985 to 1991. He received his bachelor's degree from the University of Toronto and his Ph.D. from the University of Chicago, both in economics. Dr. Solmon has served on the faculties of UCLA, CUNY and Purdue, and currently is a professor emeritus at UCLA. He serves on the boards of the Center for Education Reform, the National Council on Teacher Quality and the American Board for Certification of Teacher Excellence.

Margaret Spellings

On January 20, 2005, the United States Senate confirmed Margaret Spellings as the 8th U.S. Secretary of Education. During President George W. Bush's first term, Ms. Spellings served as assistant to the president for domestic policy, helping craft education policies including the No Child Left Behind Act. She was also responsible for the development and implementation of White House policy on health, labor, transportation, justice, housing and other elements of President Bush's domestic agenda. Prior to her White House appointment, Ms. Spellings worked for six years as Governor George W. Bush's senior advisor, responsible for developing and implementing the Governor's education policy. Previously, she served as associate executive director of the Texas Association of School Boards. Ms. Spellings earned her bachelor's degree in political science and journalism from the University of Houston in 1979. She is the first mother of schoolchildren to serve as U.S. Secretary of Education.

Sally L. Stroup

As assistant secretary for postsecondary education for the U.S. Department of Education, Sally L. Stroup serves as the principal advisor to the secretary on all matters related to postsecondary education. She coordinates department programs relating to financial assistance for eligible students enrolled in higher education institutions and recommends policies to recruit and prepare disadvantaged students to enroll in and complete postsecondary educational programs. Before joining the department, Ms. Stroup served as the director of industry and government affairs for the Apollo Group Inc./University of Phoenix. From 1993 to 2001, she was a professional staff member for the U.S. House of Representatives Committee on Education and the Workforce, and prior to that, was with the Pennsylvania Higher Education Assistance Agency, serving first as a staff attorney, then senior staff attorney and then senior vice president of legal services and the chief counsel. Ms. Stroup is a graduate of Indiana University of Pennsylvania and Loyola University School of Law in New Orleans.

Paul G. Vallas

Before coming to Philadelphia as chief executive officer, Paul G. Vallas was chief executive officer of Chicago Public Schools from 1995 to 2001. He was responsible for the development, implementation, supervision and management of numerous reform measures within the city's public schools. His accomplishments in education led to the transformation of the third largest school system in the nation from being branded as "the worst in the country" to becoming "a model for the nation." During his term, Mr. Vallas implemented an unprecedented capital improvement program through which 76 new buildings were built and more than 500 existing buildings were renovated. Mr. Vallas is also credited with ending social promotion, reorganizing Chicago's high schools, and establishing the largest after-school and summer reading programs in the country. Prior to serving as chief executive for Chicago's public schools, Mr. Vallas was budget director and revenue director for the City of Chicago, executive director of the Illinois Economic and Fiscal Commission, and policy advisor to the Illinois State Senate. Mr. Vallas earned his undergraduate and master's degrees from Western Illinois University.

Kristan Van Hook

Vice president of public policy at the Milken Family Foundation, Kristan Van Hook has 15 years of professional experience working in government and public policy. Ms. Van Hook develops and implements strategies to build support for the Foundation's education initiatives, including the Teacher Advancement Program (TAP). She works with policymakers at the national and state levels to promote teacher quality initiatives and education reforms, helping to ensure that every child has a quality teacher. Prior to her work with the Foundation, Ms. Van Hook worked for the U.S. House of Representatives' Energy and Commerce Committee and the U.S. Department of Commerce. She also ran a successful public policy firm representing corporate and nonprofit clients in the fields of telecommunications, media and education. She recently served as executive director of the Partnership for 21st Century Skills, a coalition of business, community and education organizations. Ms. Van Hook graduated from Dartmouth College and the Kennedy School of Government at Harvard.

Dennis Vicars

Executive director for the Professional Association for Childhood Education Alternative Payment Program (PACEAPP), Dennis Vicars has more than 25 years of early care and education experience. He has been a speaker and workshop host for the National Association for the Education of Young Children (NAEYC), the National Child Care Association (NCCA), and the Professional Association for Childhood Education (PACE). Nationally recognized as an expert in early care and education, Mr. Vicars has assisted on numerous advisory boards, including those in Maryland, Virginia, Oregon and Washington. He participated on California's Master Plan for early childhood education as well as on advisory panels for State Senators Alpert, Steinberg, Burton and Runner. More recently, he served as an advisor to Rob Reiner's proposed Preschool for All initiative; chair of Sacramento's Local Planning Commission; board member for the Child Development Policy Institute (CDPI); and legislative committee member for PACE and the California Alternative Payment Program Association (CAPPA).

J. Todd White

J. Todd White, a 2000 South Carolina Milken Educator, is the national training director for the Teacher Advancement Program (TAP). Mr. White accepted this post after serving as executive director of the South Carolina Teacher Advancement Program (SCTAP), overseeing implementation of TAP in six demonstration schools throughout the state. Mr. White spent five years as an elementary school teacher before moving into administration. He has been acknowledged as the First Union Administrator of the Year, the South Carolina PTA Principal of the Year, a National Distinguished Principal, and in 2002, Furman University Outstanding Young Alumni. Mr. White received his bachelor's and master's degrees from Furman University in Greenville, South Carolina.

Ben Wildavsky

As education editor of *U.S. News & World Report*, Ben Wildavsky supervises education coverage for the weekly magazine and serves as editor of *America's Best Colleges* and *America's Best Graduate Schools*. He was previously a deputy education and culture editor, helping conceive and edit award-winning cover stories on the Black-White achievement gap and the new SAT, and was also national education correspondent for three years. He was the lead author of the *U.S. News Ultimate Guide to Becoming a Teacher* (Sourcebooks, 2004), which the Progressive Policy Institute's 21st Century Schools Project calls "must reading" for aspiring teachers. Before coming to the magazine, Wildavsky covered economic policy for *National Journal*, wrote on higher education for *The San Francisco Chronicle*, and was executive editor of *The Public Interest*.

Elanna Yalow

Elanna Yalow is president and chief operating officer of Knowledge Learning Corporation (KLC). She joined KLC in 1989 to initiate the development of its employer-sponsored services division. In her current role, Dr. Yalow supervises corporate operations and oversees several support functions including human resources, marketing, corporate services, and education training. With a background in educational research and development, Dr. Yalow has contributed to numerous statewide and national curriculum development and assessment projects. She has also written extensively on matters related to the education of young children. Dr. Yalow earned her Ph.D. in educational psychology, with an emphasis on the design and evaluation of educational programs for children, at Stanford University's School of Education, and her MBA at the Stanford University Graduate School of Business.

Susan Tave Zelman

Superintendent of public instruction for Ohio since 1999, Susan Tave Zelman, Ed.D., believes that all children can learn and achieve in an educational system that has high expectations and multiple pathways to success. Dr. Zelman is working to raise expectations for all students by setting clear and high academic standards, strengthening schools and school districts with fiscal and human resources, and improving student performance through accountability. Ohio received an "A" grade for its standards and accountability system in *Education Week's* Quality Counts 2005 report, and over the past five years, students' average proficiency test scores increased by almost 13 points. Dr. Zelman holds a doctorate in education from the University of Michigan, an honorary doctoral degree in public education from the University of Rio Grande in Ohio, and an honorary doctoral degree in the humanities from Youngstown State University. In March 2003, Gannett Newspapers named her one of the 10 most powerful and influential women in Ohio state government.

Printed in the United States
53586LVS00004B/39

9 781593 115197